THE TRINITY IN OUR SPIRITUAL LIFE

THE TRINITY IN OUR SPIRITUAL LIFE

*An Anthology of the Writings
of Dom Columba Marmion, O.S.B.*

COMPILED BY
DOM RAYMUND THIBAUT, O.S.B.

THE NEWMAN PRESS
WESTMINSTER, MARYLAND
1953

Nihil obstat: Edward A. Cerny, S.S., D.D.
Censor librorum

Imprimatur: Francis P. Keough, D.D.
Archbishop of Baltimore

November 12, 1953

Library of Congress Catalog Card Number: 53–5593

Copyright, 1953, by

THE NEWMAN PRESS

Printed in the United States of America

Foreword

The period from April, 1899, to September, 1909, was spent by Dom Marmion in the Abbey of Mont-Cesar, Louvain. These years, notable for the development and enrichment of his spirituality, may well be counted the most important in his life. He was, above all, continually favoured with very abundant interior lights followed by insistent calls to union with God. All these illuminations and calls had as their focal point the Person of the Word Incarnate. They invited him to complete self-abandonment in order to live thenceforward in Christ and in Christ only—for the glory of the Father.

The Father's great thought, as Dom Marmion called it— a thought found in St. Paul, his favourite author: namely, "to submit all things to Jesus, the Son of predilection"—became, at that time, a real leitmotif of his interior life.

On January 29, 1906, under the guidance of heavenly inspirations, he penetrated more deeply into the divine secrets and considered the life of the soul in its relationship with each of the Persons of the Blessed Trinity.

These pages written with a single stroke of the pen, rapidly and without corrections, form a sublime doctrinal and ascetical synthesis of the intimate life of God and of the life of the soul in God.

This became for Dom Marmion the starting point for constant new ascensions which ended in an act of consecration to the Blessed Trinity, written nearly three years later, Christmas, 1908. The essence of all his illuminations and of the resulting aspirations fostered in his soul by them are contained in it. This Consecration, the ripe and savoury fruit of a generous and complete fidelity to the inspirations of the Holy Ghost, crowns magnificently a whole period of his interior life. By an intimate union with Christ it plunged his soul, so that he might make it his home, into "the bosom of the Father."

Coming from a theologian's pen and a mystic's heart, the Consecration conceals, behind its brevity, great riches of doctrine and life. We wish to reveal these hidden treasures by means of extracts borrowed from the writings of Dom Marmion; in this way he will be the commentator of his own text.

In undertaking this task, our special concern has been the good of interior souls who are eager to slake their thirst from living and highly beneficial sources. Therefore we have made this collection plentiful and present it to such souls as a series of readings which invite reflection and incite to prayer.

The dogma of the Trinity is the fundamental dogma of Christianity. The Trinity contains everything. It dominates the whole series of Christian dogmas. Hence the reason for its continual mention in the Church's acts of worship. *"Gloria Patri et Filio et Spiritui Sancto"* resounds ceaselessly throughout the Church, the humble expression of its adoration and praise. In heaven, also, the vision of the Blessed Trinity constitutes for the angels and the elect the very source of their eternal happiness.

Nowhere, says St. Augustine, is found more abundant fruit than in the pious contemplation of this mystery. This saying of the great Doctor was fully verified in Dom Marmion, particularly during his stay at Louvain. The Consecration itself was to mark for him the beginning of a new stage in his journey towards saintliness. He confided to one of his followers that "from the time of this act dates a new blossoming of graces in his soul." This is further confirmed by the story of the last years of his life.

May the Most Holy Trinity bless in like manner those who will read these pages written for Their glory. This is our heartfelt wish.

The task of selecting extracts suitable for this book from such a treasure house of riches has proved extremely difficult. We have sought, however, to preserve the outstanding themes which bear the hallmark of Dom Marmion's doctrine.

Most of the extracts are taken from the fundamental trilogy of Marmion's work, *Christ, the Life of the Soul; Christ in His Mysteries;* and *Christ, the Ideal of the Monk.* To these we have added some extracts from his letters of direction which were published under the title *Union with God in Christ,* and from his private notes on his interior life in *A Master of the Spiritual Life,* both of which date from his Louvain days. It will be noticed how life and doctrine were for him closely blended, and how deep a unity connects the work and the man.

We have added here and there a note to explain the choice made by Dom Marmion of a particular scriptural text or to indicate the logical sequence of ideas.

It was Dom Marmion's habit to underline certain words in order to emphasize his thought more clearly or to attract more attention to them. We have adopted this procedure by printing in italics words underlined once by him and in capitals those underlined twice.

Dom Raymund Thibaut, O.S.B.

Abbaye de Maredsous

January 30, 1946

Contents

PART II

The Son

PART III
The Holy Ghost

PART IV
The Mother of the Incarnate Word

Introduction: *The Mystery of the Blessed Trinity*

As an introduction to the commentary on the Consecration, we shall first present a few passages of Dom Marmion's on the Blessed Trinity, together with the text of the Note of January 20, 1906, the importance of which we emphasized in the Foreword.

1. WHAT FAITH REVEALS TO US CONCERNING THIS MYSTERY

Let us penetrate, with the deepest reverence, into the sanctuary of the divinity.

What does faith tell us? That there is in God, the Father, the Son, and the Holy Spirit: three distinct Persons in one and the same unity of nature.

As you know, the Father proceeds from none; He is the Principle without principle, the first Principle of all intimate life in God, the first origin of all the ineffable communications in the Trinity. The Father, knowing Himself, begets by an infinite Word a Son only-begotten and perfect, to Whom He communicates all that He is, except the personal property of being the Father: *Sicut enim Pater habet vitam in semetipso, sic dedit et Filio habere vitam in semetipso.*[1] The Son is equal in all things to the Father; He is the adequate expression, the perfect image of the Father; He possesses with the Father the same divine nature. The Father

[1] Joan. v, 26.

and the Son give Themselves the One to the Other with a perfect love, and it is from this gift of love from the Father to the Son, and from the Son to the Father, that proceeds, in a mysterious manner, the Holy Spirit, the Third Person. The Holy Spirit terminates the cycle of the intimate operations in God, He is the final term of the divine communications in the adorable Trinity.

Between these distinct Persons, as you likewise know, there is neither superiority nor inferiority: it would be a grave error to believe that there is. These Divine Persons are equal in power, wisdom and goodness, because all Three equally possess, in an indivisible manner, one and the same Divine nature with all its infinite perfection. And therefore all our praise is addressed at the same time to the Father, the Son, and the Holy Spirit: *Gloria Patri et Filio et Spiritui Sancto.*

However, if there is among them neither inequality nor dependence, there is an order of nature, of origin, marking these communications themselves. The "procession" of the Son presupposes, without there being, however, inequality of time, the Father, Who is the first principle; the "procession" of the Holy Spirit presupposes the Father and the Son, of Whom He is the mutual gift.

Jesus wills that all His disciples should be baptized "in the name of the Father, and of the Son, and of the Holy Ghost": that is the very language of the Incarnate Word; it contains a divine reality, the intimate comprehension of which baffles our understanding; but because it is the language of Jesus, we must inviolably respect the order between the Persons of the Trinity. And as we must hold intact, in our doctrine and our prayer, the unity of nature, so too we must confess the distinction of Persons, this distinction which is based upon the communications that They have between

Themselves and Their mutual relations. There is, at the same time, equality and order; there is an identical perfection and distinction of properties.

These truths constitute an ineffable mystery concerning which we can but lisp. However Our Lord has revealed to us the existence of this mystery, and He made this revelation in His last discourse with His disciples on the eve of His death, that our "joy may be filled." He Himself tells us that if we are His friends, it is because He has made known to us these secrets of God's innermost life, while we await the enjoyment of them in eternal happiness. And why should He have revealed these secrets to us, if He, Infinite Wisdom, had not judged that this revelation would be profitable to us?

Christ in His Mysteries, Part II, chapter 17, section 1.

Such is the language of Revelation; we could not have attained to a knowledge of these things unless they had been unveiled for us; but Christ Jesus has willed, for the exercise of our faith and the joy of our souls, to give us this knowledge. When in eternity, we shall contemplate God, we shall see that it is essential to infinite life, that it is natural to the Divine Being, to be one in Three Persons. The true God Whom we must know so as to have eternal life, is He of Whom we adore the Trinity of Persons in the Unity of nature.

Come! let us adore this marvellous fellowship in the Unity, this wonderful equality of perfection in the distinction of Persons. O God, Father of incommensurable majesty, *Patrem immensae majestatis,* I adore Thee; I adore Thy Son, for He, like Thee, is worthy of all reverence, being Thy True and Only-begotten Son, God like Thyself: *Venerandum tuum verum et unicum Filium;* O Father, O Son, I adore Your common Spirit, Your eternal bond of love: *Sanctum quoque Paraclitum Spiritum.* Blessed Trinity, I adore Thee! . . .

> *Christ in His Mysteries,* Part I, chapter
> 3, section 1.

2. THE DOCTRINE OF APPROPRIATION

As you know, there is *in God,* only one intelligence, only one will, only one power, because there is only one Divine nature; but also there is distinction of persons. This distinction results from the mysterious *operations* that are accomplished *in the intimate life of God* and from the mutual relations derived from these operations. The Father begets the Son, and the Holy Ghost proceeds from the Father and the Son. "To beget, to be a Father" is the exclusive property of the First Person; "to be Son" is the personal property of the Son, as "to proceed from the Father and the Son by way of love" is the personal property of the Holy Ghost. These personal properties establish the mutual relations between the Father, the Son and the Holy Ghost, from whence the distinction arises. But setting apart these properties and these relations, all is common to the Three Persons and indivisible among them: the same intelligence, the same will, the same power, the same majesty, because the same indivisible Divine nature is common to the Three Persons. That is what we may know of the intimate operations in God.

As to what concerns the "exterior" works, the actions accomplished *outside God,* whether in the material world, as the action of directing every creature towards its end, or in the world of souls, such as the action of producing grace, these are common to the three Divine Persons. Why so? Because the source of these operations, works and actions is the Divine nature and this Divine nature is, for the Three Persons, one and indivisible; the Holy Trinity acts in the world as one and the same Cause. But it is God's will that men should confess and honour not only the Divine Unity but also the Trinity of Persons. That is why the Church, for example in her liturgy, attributes to one or other of the Divine Persons certain actions which are produced in the world and, although common to the Three Persons, have a special relation or an intimate affinity with the place, if I may so speak, which this Person occupies in the Holy Trinity and with the attributes which are particularly and exclusively His own.

Thus, the Father being the source, origin and principle of the two other Persons—without this implying either hierarchical superiority or priority of time—the works produced in the world that especially manifest power or the character of origin are attributed to the Father. For example, the creation by which God drew the universe out of nothing. We sing in the *Credo:* "I believe in God the Father Almighty, Creator of Heaven and earth." Had therefore the Father a greater part, did He manifest more power in this work than the Son and Holy Ghost? No, it would be an error to suppose so; the Son and the Holy Ghost acted in this as much as the Father, for God works eternally by His almighty power, and almighty power is common to the Three Persons. Why then does Holy Church speak after this manner? Because in the Holy Trinity, the Father is the *First* Person, the Principle without principle, whence proceed the two other Persons. This is His exclusive personal property distinguishing Him from the Son and Holy Ghost, and it is in order that we may not forget this property that the "exterior" actions which, by affinity of nature, place it in relief, are attributed to the Father.

It is the same for the Person of the Son. He is, in the Holy Trinity, the Word proceeding from the Father by way of intelligence; He is the Infinite expression of the Divine Thought; He is above all considered as Eternal Wisdom.

That is why those works in which wisdom especially shines forth are attributed to Him.

It is again the same for the Holy Ghost. What is He in the Holy Trinity? He is the ultimate term of the Divine operations, of the life of God in Himself; He closes, so to speak, the cycle of the intimate Divine life: it is His personal property to proceed from both the Father and the Son by way of love. This is why all that is a work of achievement, of perfection, all that is a work of love, of union and consequently of holiness—for our holiness is measured by our degree of union with God—is attributed to the Holy Ghost. Is it because He sanctifies more than the Father and the Son? No, the work of our sanctification is common to the Three Divine Persons; but, once again, as the work of sanctification in the soul is a work of perfecting, of achievement and union, it is attributed to the Holy Ghost because in this way we more easily remember what are His personal properties so as to honour and adore Him in that which distinguishes Him from the Father and the Son.

God wills that we should have it as much at heart to honour His Trinity of Persons as to adore His unity of Nature, and therefore He wills that the Church even in her language, should recall to the minds of her children not only that there is but one God but also that He is in Three Persons.

This is what is called *appropriation*. It is founded on Revelation; it is employed by the Church; [2] it has for its aim to place in relief the attributes proper to each Divine Person. In doing this, it makes these properties known to us and makes us love them more. St. Thomas says it is to help our faith that the Church, following Revelation in this, observes the law of appropriation: *Ad manifestationem fidei*. During

[2] In his Encyclical letter of May 9th, 1897, Leo XIII says how aptly this is done by the Church, *aptissime*.

all eternity, our life, our beatitude will be to contemplate God, to love and enjoy Him, as He truly is, that is to say, in the Unity of His nature and the Trinity of His Persons. What is there astonishing in the fact that God, Who predestines us to this life and prepares this beatitude for us, should will that, even here below, we should remember His Divine perfections, as much those of His nature as the properties that distinguish the Persons? God is infinite and worthy of praise in His Unity, He is equally so in His Trinity; and the Divine Persons are as admirable in the unity of nature which they possess in an indivisible manner, as in the relations they have with each other and on which their distinction is founded.

"Almighty God, Eternal God, Blessed God, I rejoice in Thy Almighty Power, Thy Eternity and Thy Blessedness. When shall I behold Thee, O Principle without principle! When shall I behold Thy Son, equal to Thyself, coming forth from Thy bosom! When shall I behold Thy Holy Spirit proceeding from this union, being the term of Thy fruitfulness and consummating Thy Eternal action!" [3]

> *Christ, the Life of the Soul,* Part I, chapter 6, section 1.

3. HOW TO HONOUR THE BLESSED TRINITY

I have received a strong interior light on the manner of honouring the Blessed Trinity and of acting in such a way that all our life may consist of a perpetual *Gloria Patri.* These reflections provide me with a *framework of meditation.*

The *Father* is the Beginning, the source of all life, *"Fons vitae."* The Word and the Holy Ghost proceed from Him and all creation comes from Him by the Word in the Holy Ghost.

---

[3] Bossuet, *Preparation for Death,* 4th prayer.

We honour His primordial quality of Beginning by laying at His feet our whole being, our plans, our desires, in order to give Him the initiative of everything in us.

In this way we imitate Jesus,

(*a*) Who proceeds *entirely* from the Father;

(*b*) Who thought, desired, acted in *total dependence* on Him: "Amen, Amen, I say unto you: the Son cannot do anything of Himself, but what He seeth the Father doing." "My doctrine is not Mine but His that sent Me." During His whole life He did that which pleased the Father. He remained in obscurity in the workshop at Nazareth for thirty years and did not commence His public mission until the time fixed by His Father. He confined His preaching to the Jews, for He was sent to the flock of the House of Israel only, who were perishing. "All that is written of Me in Moses, in the Prophets and in the Psalms must be accomplished." "One jot or one tittle shall not pass of the law, till all be fulfilled." [4]

I understood that without this absolute dependence on God the most spectacular actions have little value in His eyes, though of themselves they may dazzle men. It is when we leave to our Creator and Father the entire disposal of our persons and of all our activity that we assume our true role of creatures and children of adoption. This is especially true of religious and monks.

The *Son* not only proceeds entirely from the Father and consequently depends absolutely on Him,[5] but being a perfect Son He is the true image of the Father—"image of the invisible God." He is the Wisdom of the Father, Whose whole will, Whose every design He realizes in a *perfect* manner.

[4] Matt. v, 18.

[5] There is no question here of the Father being temporally "anterior" to the Son or of the Son being "subject" to the Father's authority. The Father has a priority of origin only in the divine procession, which is coeternal.

We honour the Son, firstly, by conforming, as He does, to truth and wisdom; secondly, by perfectly fulfilling the Father's entire will, His "expressed" will by executing *all the known wishes of God* with perfect fidelity. These wishes are made known to us by His Commandments, counsels, inspirations and also by the duty of obedience. We conform to His "hidden" will by abandonment. Christ accepted His Father's will in its entirety both on His own behalf and on behalf of His members. Therefore we honour the Son by joining with Him in this acceptance, by asking Him to remove from our hearts all desire or inclination to do the least thing which falls without the orbit of this will. (Inspired by this thought you may meditate on the life of Jesus Christ and this meditation will afford you much peace and union with Him.) "Whatever you do, do all in the name of Our Lord Jesus Christ."

For we only do in His name that which He sees to be the good will of His Father concerning us. The saying "He must increase but I must decrease" [6] is thus fulfilled. Then we become "pleasing to the Father from Whom comes every best gift, every perfect gift." The smallest acts become great because they are "performed in God."

The *Holy Ghost* is the mutual love of the Father and the Son. He returns unto the bosom of the Father and the Son with an infinite love which is Himself.

We honour the Holy Ghost by uniting ourselves humbly through Jesus Christ to that love by which we return to God as our last end. It is this love which gives to our actions all their value. This love proceeding from the Father and the Son carries us towards God in dependence and love. Our whole life in this way comes from the Father in the Son to return to His Bosom in the Holy Ghost.

United thus to Jesus Christ in His Spirit, our life becomes

[6] Joan. III, 30.

a sacrifice of love for God and for souls. "Christ, through the Holy Ghost, offered Himself a spotless oblation to God." If we call on the Holy Ghost with love and confidence He will not fail to fill us with true divine love. Because He is the "Father of the poor." "Hope does not deceive, for hearts are filled with the love of God by the Holy Ghost Who dwells therein."

LOUVAIN, January 20, 1906

Consecration to the Blessed Trinity

ETERNAL FATHER, prostrate in humble adoration at Thy feet, we consecrate our whole being to the glory of Thy Son Jesus, the Word Incarnate. Thou hast established Him King of our souls; submit to Him our souls, our hearts, our bodies, and may nothing within us move without His order, without His inspiration. Grant that united to Him we may be borne to Thy bosom and consumed in the unity of Thy love.

O Jesus, unite us to Thee, in Thy life all holy, entirely consecrated to Thy Father and to souls. Be Thou our justice, our holiness, our redemption, our all. Sanctify us in truth!

O Holy Ghost, love of the Father and the Son, dwell like a burning furnace of love in the centre of our hearts. Bear our thoughts, affections and actions, like ardent flames, continually heavenwards into the bosom of the Father. May our whole life be a *Gloria Patri et Filio et Spiritui Sancto.*

O Mary, Mother of Christ, Mother of holy love, fashion us yourself according to the Heart of your Son.

LOUVAIN, Christmas, 1908

PART 1. *The Father*

According to the order indicated by Christ Himself in the baptismal formula, the act of consecration begins by invoking the Father, the First Person of the Trinity.

The divine perfection which Dom Marmion underlines in the Father is that of "eternity," as the Church does in its solemn liturgy: Te Deum laudamus . . . Te aeternum Patrem . . .

This profession of the divinity of the Father immediately decides the soul's attitude—one of humble adoration.

Dom Marmion then declares the Father's "great thought" so that we may make it the very object of our consecration: to glorify His Son, Who was made flesh for us, Who has been established King of our souls.

By submitting itself entirely to the Son of predilection the soul attains this glorification within itself.

Completely abandoned to Christ and united to Him, the soul will find itself introduced by Him into the sanctuary of the divinity. The final goal of its consecration will thus be achieved.

This invocation, very fruitful in doctrine, contains in a compact abridgement the whole divine plan, from our creation and our adoption by the Father to our return to His bosom through our union with His Son.

Beginning with an act of deep adoration, the invocation ends in a spirit of confidence and love before the splendour of the happiness which awaits God's children in eternity.

1 *O Eternal Father*

1. PATERNITY OF DIVINE ORIGIN

Faith reveals to us this truly astonishing mystery that the power and act of fecundity is one of the divine perfections.

God is the plenitude of being, the shoreless ocean of all perfection and of all life. The images of which we often make use to depict Him, the ideas that we apply to Him by analogy in speaking of what is best in creatures, are powerless to represent Him. We shall never rise to a conception that does not belie God's Infinity by merely extending, even indefinitely, the limits of created being; we must recognise, in the most positive manner, that there are no limits where God is concerned. He is Very Being, the necessary Being, subsisting of Himself, and possessing the plenitude of all perfection.

Revelation teaches us this marvel of God's fecundity; there is in Him an altogether spiritual and ineffable paternity; He is Father, the principle of all the Divine Life in the Trinity.

Being Infinite Intelligence, God perfectly comprehends Himself; in a single act, He sees all that He is, all that is in Him. He comprehends, as it were, in a single glance, the plenitude of His perfections, and, in one thought, in one

5

word that exhausts all His knowledge, He expresses this infinite knowledge to Himself. This thought conceived by the
eternal intelligence, this utterance whereby God expresses
Himself is the Word. Faith tells us that this Word is God:
Et Deus erat Verbum, because the Word has (or rather, He
is) with God one and the same divine nature.

And because the Father communicates to this Word a
nature not only like unto His own, but identical with it,
Holy Scripture tells us that He begets the Word, and it calls
the Word, *the Son.* The inspired books repeat the ineffable
exclamation of God contemplating His Son and proclaiming
the beatitude of His eternal Fatherhood: From the bosom
of My Divinity, before the creation of the light, I communicated life to Thee: *Ex utero, ante luciferum, genui te;*[1]
"Thou art My Son, My beloved Son, in Whom I am well
pleased": *Tu es Filius meus dilectus, in te complacui mihi.*[2]
Because this Son is indeed perfect; He possesses with the
Father all the divine perfections saving the property of "being Father"; so perfect is He that He is the equal of His
Father by the unity of nature. A creature can only give to
another creature a nature *like* to his own: *simile sibi;* but
God begets God and gives to Him His own nature. It is
God's glory to beget the Infinite and to contemplate Him-
self in another Himself, Who is His equal. So equal is the
Son to the Father that He is the Only-begotten, for there is
only one Divine nature and the Son exhausts the eternal fecundity: *Unigenitus Dei Filius;* therefore He is one with His
Father: *Ego et Pater unum sumus.*[3]

Christ in His Mysteries, Part I, chapter
3, section 1.

All the life of the Father in the Holy Trinity is to "utter"

[1] Ps. cix, 3.
[2] Luc. iii, 22; Marc. i, ii.
[3] Joan. x, 30.

His Son, His Word, to beget, by one simple, eternal act, a Son like to Himself, to Whom He communicates the fulness of His being and of His perfections. In this one and eternal Word, infinite like Himself, the Father unceasingly recognises His Son, His own image, "the splendour of His glory." And every word, every outward testimony that God gives us of Christ's divinity, such as that given at the baptism of Jesus: "This is My beloved Son," is only the echo, in the world of the senses, of this testimony the Father renders to Himself in the sanctuary of the Divinity, and that He expresses by a Word in which He places all Himself and which is His intimate life: *Filius meus es tu, ego hodie genui te.*

When therefore we accept this testimony of the Eternal Father, when we say to God: "This little Child lying in the crib is Thy Son, I adore and give myself to Him; this Youth toiling in the workshop of Nazareth, is Thy Son, I adore Him; this Man crucified on Calvary, is Thy Son, I adore Him; these fragments of bread are the appearances under which Thy Son is hidden, I there adore Him"; when we say to Jesus Himself: "Thou art the Christ, the Son of the Living God," and prostrate ourselves before Him, yielding to Him all our energies to serve Him, when all our actions are in accordance with this faith and spring from the charity that makes faith perfect—then our whole life becomes the echo of the life of the Father Who eternally expresses His Son in one infinite word; and this divine action, never ceasing, embracing all time, being an eternal "now," we shall thus associate ourselves in the very life of God. That is what St. John says: "He that believeth that Jesus is the Son of God, hath the testimony of God in himself," that testimony by which the Father "utters" His Son.

Christ, the Life of the Soul, Part II, chapter 1, section 3.

"This is My beloved Son, in Whom I am well pleased."
Hic est Filius meus dilectus in quo mihi bene complacui.
These words are the greatest revelation that God has made
to the world, they are like the very echo of the life of the
Father. The Father, inasmuch as He is Father, lives to beget
His Son; this begetting which has neither beginning nor
end constitutes the very property of the Father. In eternity,
we shall see with wonder, admiration and love, this procession of the Son begotten in the bosom of the Father. This
procession is eternal: *Filius meus es tu, ego hodie genui te.*[4]
This "to-day," this *hodie,* is the now of eternity.

When He tells us that Jesus is His beloved Son, the Father
reveals to us His life; and when we believe in this revelation,
we participate in the knowledge of God Himself. The Father
knows the Son in endless glory; as for us, we know Him in
the shadows of faith whilst awaiting the light of eternity.
The Father declares that the Babe of Bethlehem, the Youth
of Nazareth, the Preacher of Judea, the Victim of Calvary
is His Son, His well-beloved Son; our faith is to believe this.

It is an excellent thing in the spiritual life to have this
testimony of the Father ever present, as it were, before the
eyes of the heart. Nothing upholds our faith so powerfully.
When we read the Gospel, or a life of our Lord, when we
celebrate His mysteries, when we visit Him in the Blessed
Sacrament, when we prepare ourselves to receive Him in our
hearts in Holy Communion, or when we adore Him after
having received Him, in our whole life, in fine, let us try to
have these words habitually before us: "This is My beloved
Son, in Whom I am well pleased."

And let us then say: "Yea, Father, I believe these words,
I will repeat them after Thee: this Jesus Who is within me
through faith, through Communion, is Thy Son; and because Thou hast said it, I believe it; and because I believe it,

[4] Ps. ii, 7.

I adore Thy Son, so as to render Him my homage; and by Him, in Him, so likewise to render to Thee, O Heavenly Father, in union with Thy Spirit, all honour and all glory."

Such a prayer is extremely pleasing to our Father in Heaven; and when it is true, pure, frequent, it makes us the object of the Father's love; God includes us in the delight that He takes in His own Son Jesus. Our Lord Himself tells us so: "The Father Himself loveth you, because you have . . . believed that I came out from God," [5] that I am His Son. And what happiness for a soul to be the object of the love of the Father, of this Father from Whom comes down "every perfect gift" [6] to rejoice the heart!

Christ in His Mysteries, Part II, chapter 12, section 3.

2. PATERNITY OF DIVINE ADOPTION

To the divine filiation, necessary and eternal, of His Only-begotten Son, the Father willed to add, by an act of love, infinitely free, a filiation of grace: He adopts us as His children, to the point that one day we shall share in the beatitude of His inmost life. This is an inexplicable mystery; but faith tells us that when a soul receives sanctifying grace at baptism, it participates in the Divine nature: *Divinae consortes naturae.*[7] This soul becomes truly the child of God, *Dii estis et filii excelsi omnes.*[8] St. John speaks of a divine birth: *Ex Deo* NATI *sunt,* not in the proper sense of the word, by nature, as the Word is begotten in the bosom of the Father, but by something analogous: *Voluntarie* GENUIT *nos verbo veritatis.*[9]

[5] Joan. XVI, 27.
[6] Jac. I, 17.
[7] II Petr. I, 4.
[8] Ps. LXXXI, 6; Joan, X, 34.
[9] Jac. I, 18.

In a very real, very true sense, we are divinely begotten by grace. With the Word, we can say: "O Father, I am Thy son, I came out from Thee." The Word says it necessarily, by right, being essentially God's own Son; we only say it by grace, as adopted sons. The Word says it from all eternity; we say it in time, although the decree of this predestination is eternal. For the Word, this language denotes a relation of origin with the Father; for us, there is added a relation of dependence. But for us, as for Him, there is a true sonship: we are, by grace, God's children. The Father wills that despite our unworthiness, we should give Him the name of "Father." *Quoniam estis filii, misit Deus Spiritum Filii sui in corda vestra clamantem: abba, Pater.*[10] "God hath sent the Spirit of His Son" for that. This cry pleases our Heavenly Father. It is ineffable, but it is the truth. "Behold," says St. John, "what manner of charity the Father hath bestowed upon us, that we should be called, and should be the sons of God": *Videte qualem caritatem dedit nobis* PATER *ut filii Dei nominemur et* SIMUS.[11]

Christ in His Mysteries, Part I, chapter 3, section 3.

Realised in Adam from the dawn of creation, then crossed by the sin of the first of human kind, who drew after him into disgrace all his race, this decree of love is to be restored by a marvellous invention of justice and mercy, of wisdom and goodness. The Son of God, Who dwells eternally in the Bosom of the Father, unites Himself in time, to a human nature, but in so close a manner that this nature, while being perfect in itself, belongs entirely to the Divine Person to Whom it is united. The Divine life, communicated in its fulness to this humanity, makes it the very humanity of the Son

[10] Gal. IV, 6.
[11] I Joan. III, I.

of God: that is the wonderful work of the *Incarnation*. It is true to say of this Man Who is called Jesus, the Christ, that He is God's own Son.

But this Son, Who by nature is the only Son of the Eternal Father, *Unigenitus Dei Filius,* appears here below only to become the Firstborn of all who shall receive Him, after having been redeemed by Him: *Primogenitus in multis fratribus.*[12] Alone born of the Father in eternal splendour, alone Son by right, He is constituted the head of a multitude of brethren, on whom, by His redeeming work, He will bestow the grace of Divine life.

So that the same Divine life which proceeds from the Father into the Son and from the Son into the humanity of Jesus, will circulate, through Christ in all who will accept it; it will draw them even into the Bosom of the Father, where Christ has gone before us,[13] after having paid, with His Blood, the price of this divine gift.

Hence all holiness is to consist in this: to receive the Divine life from Christ and by Christ, Who possesses its fulness and Who has been constituted the One Mediator; to keep this Divine life and increase it unceasingly by an ever more perfect adhesion, an ever closer union with Him Who is its source.

Holiness then is a *mystery of Divine life communicated and received:* communicated in God, from the Father to the Son by an ineffable generation;[14] communicated by the Son to humanity, which He personally unites to Himself in the Incarnation; then restored to souls by this humanity, and received by each of them in the measure of their special pre-

---

[12] Rom. VIII, 29.

[13] *Ascendo ad Patrem meum et Patrem vestrum . . . In domo Patris mei mansiones multæ sunt . . . Vado parare vobis locum.* Joan. XIV, 2; XX, 17.

[14] Isa. LIII, 8.

destination: *secundum mensuram donationis Christi*,[15] so
that Christ is truly the life of the soul because He is the
source and giver of life.

Communication of this life will be made to men within
the Church until the day fixed by the eternal decrees for the
achievement of the Divine work upon earth. On that day,
the number of the children of God, of the brethren of Jesus,
will have reached its perfection. Presented by Christ to His
Father,[16] the innumerable multitude of these predestined
souls will surround the throne of God, to draw an endless
beatitude from the fountains of life, and to exalt the splendours of the Divine goodness and glory. Union with God
will be eternally consummated, and "God will be all in all."

Christ, the Life of the Soul, Part I, chapter 1, section 1.

The Eternal Father makes known to us that Jesus is His
Son; Jesus is also "the Firstborn amongst many brethren." [17]
Having taken a human nature, He makes us partakers, by
His grace, of His Divine Sonship. If He is God's own Son by
nature, we are so by grace. Jesus is one of ourselves by His
Incarnation; He makes us like to Him in bestowing upon
us a participation in His Divinity, so that we make with Him
only one mystical body. That is the Divine adoption: *Ut filii
Dei nominemur et simus.*

In declaring that Jesus is His Son, the Father declares that
those who, by grace, are partakers of His Divinity, are
equally, although by another title, His children. It is through
Jesus, the Incarnate Word, that this adoption is given to us:
Genuit nos verbo veritatis.[18] And in adopting us as His chil-

15 Ephes. IV, 7.
16 I Cor. XV, 24–28.
17 Rom. VIII, 29.
18 Jac. I, 18.

dren, the Father gives us the right of one day sharing His divine and glorious life. That is the "perfect adoption," *adoptio perfecta.*

On God's part, it is perfect, for the seal of infinite wisdom is set upon all His works: *Domine, omnia in sapientia fecisti.*[19] See indeed what incomparable riches God heaps upon His adopted children: sanctifying grace, the infused virtues, the gifts of the Holy Spirit, the actual graces granted to us daily: all that constitutes the supernatural domain for us here below. And to assure us of all these riches, there is the Incarnation of His Son, the infinite merits of Jesus applied to us in the Sacraments, the Church with all the privileges which the title of Bride of Christ confers upon her. Yes, this adoption, on God's part, is perfect.

But on our part? Here below it cannot be perfect. It ever goes on developing from the day when it was given to us in baptism; it is a germ which has to grow, an outline which has to be filled in, a dawn which must reach its full noontide. We shall attain perfection when, after we have been perseveringly faithful, our adoption comes to its fruition in glory: *Si filii et heredes, heredes quidem Dei, coheredes autem Christi.*[20]

> *Christ in His Mysteries,* Part I, chapter 12, section 3.

[19] Ps. CIII, 24.
[20] Rom. VIII, 17.

2 *Prostrate in Humble Adoration at Thy Feet*

1. THE SOURCE OF OUR ADORATION: GOD'S SUPREME AND INFINITE MAJESTY

When, in prayer, we contemplate the perfections and works of God, when a ray of Divine light reaches us, what is the first movement of the soul touched by grace? It is one of self-abasement; the soul is lost in adoration. This attitude of adoration is the only "true" one that the creature, as such, can have before God.

What is adoration? It is the avowal of our inferiority before the Divine perfections; it is the acknowledgment of our absolute dependence in face of Him Who, alone, is of Himself, the plenitude of Being; it is the homage of our subjection in face of the infinite Sovereignty. When a creature does not remain in this attitude, it is not in the truth.

In Heaven, the Blessed are locked in God's embrace, an embrace surpassing all that the most ardent love can imagine; they are possessed by God, they possess Him in the essence of their soul; God is all in them; and yet they do not cease to be lost in deep reverence, the expression of their adoration: *Timor Domini sanctus permanens in saeculum saeculi.* Should not the annihilation of self be likewise our law here below? When faith, which is the prelude to the Beatific Vision, makes us touch something of God's unfathomable perfections, we at once cast ourselves down in adoration. The soul understands, under a strong inner light, what a close contact there may be between itself and God; it beholds the infinite contrast of the two terms: littleness and lowliness contrasted with greatness and majesty; greatness and majesty contrasted with littleness and lowliness.

The soul may moreover concentrate its attention the more upon the one or other of these two terms of the relation. Is it upon the term: "God"? It tends to *adore* Him. Is it the term of "self"? The soul tends to *humble* itself. It is at the precise instant of our self-annihilation in presence of the Divine Majesty that humility is born in the soul. As soon as reverence towards God fills the soul, it is like the source whence humility springs up: *Humilitas causatur ex reverentia divina.*[1] If this cause is lacking, humility cannot exist. This is a point which cannot be too much insisted upon. We see how eminently humility is a "religious" virtue, permeated, as has been very well said,[2] with religion, and therefore essentially proper to our state.

We understand too, how important it is, in order to strengthen humility, to give ourselves up to the contemplation of the Divine perfections. God is Almighty: "He spoke and all things were made." With a word, He drew out of nothing a wonderful creation; and this creation which is so

[1] II–II, q. CLXI, a. 4 ad 1.
[2] D. O. Lottin, in *L'Ame du Culte, la vertu de religion.* (Louvain, 1920, p. 40 sq.) In this little opuscule of condensed teaching, the author, an enlightened theologian, has shown "how after having linked humility to temperance and obedience to the observance, St. Thomas is brought by evidence of the reality, to relate these virtues to religion. The affinity is indeed undeniable. It was perceived by the ancient ascetical authors. The Rule of St. Benedict, for example, ignores the word *Religio;* but it is all embued with the spirit of religion. It is sufficient, in order to be convinced of this, to read the chapters 5–7 upon obedience, the spirit of silence and humility." (P. 49, n.)

beautiful, these legions of angels, these nations of human beings, so great and numerous, are in regard to Himself, like an atom, as if they existed not: *Omnes gentes quasi non sint, sic sunt coram eo.*[3] He is eternal; all creatures pass away or pay their tribute to the order of succession, while He remains immutable in the full and sovereign possession of His perfections. So perfect is He that He has no need of anyone. His infinite wisdom attains all His designs with strength and sweetness; His adorable justice is equity itself; His goodness and power are unequalled; He has but to open His hand to fill every living creature with blessings.[4]

And what accents would have to be found to celebrate the Divine works in the supernatural order? We have many times spoken of the magnificence of the Divine Plan. God wills to make us His children by making us partakers of the very filiation of His Son Jesus,[5] and thus cause us to draw eternal beatitude at the very fountainhead of the Divinity. The Masterpiece of the eternal thoughts which is Christ, the wonderful mysteries of the Incarnation, the Passion, the Resurrection and the triumph of Jesus, the institution of the Church and the Sacraments, grace, the virtues, the gifts of the Holy Spirit, all this marvellous supernatural order has come forth from this movement of the Heart of God so as to make us His children: *Ut adoptionem filiorum reciperemus.*[6] It is an admirable order, a work of power, of wisdom and love of which the spectacle ravished St. Paul.

When our souls contemplate these Divine perfections and works, not according to a philosophy that would make of it an abstract, cold and dry study, but in prayer, and, when God touches us with His light, all terrestrial superiorities are

[3] Isa. XL, 17.
[4] Ps. XCLIV, 16.
[5] Cf. Eph. I, 5.
[6] Galat. IV, 5.

effaced, all created perfections appear as nothingness, all human greatness fades away like smoke. Before this omniscient, this sovereign wisdom, this absolute power, this august sanctity, this justice into which not the least movement of passion enters; before this boundless goodness, this inexhaustible tenderness and mercy, the soul cries out: "Who is like to Thee, O my God?" *Quis sicut Dominus Deus noster, qui in altis habitat?* [7] And how profound are Thy thoughts! An intense reverence seizes us to the very depths of our souls, and we are lost in our nothingness: what are we, what are the celestial spirits, what are the human multitudes, in face of this wisdom, this power, this eternity, this holiness? *Omnes gentes quasi non sunt sic sunt coram eo.*

> *Christ, the Ideal of the Monk*, Part II, chapter 11, section 3.

2. ADORATION SHOULD BE ACCOMPANIED BY LOVE

This sense of reverence in the soul, while yet being very intense and real, is not distinct from those of confidence and love. Humility does not contradict any of the aspects of the truth. God is to be contemplated in all His perfections and in all His works; He is at once Lord and Father; we are at once creatures and adopted children; it is from this *total* contemplation in the Almighty Power of a sovereign Lord and the Supreme Goodness of a Father full of tenderness, that reverence towards God, the root of humility, ought to arise.

Reverence towards God ought to make a soul lost in self-abasement, and at the same time, through this very self-abasement, yielded up to the loving accomplishment of the Heavenly Father's desires. If forgetful of our nothingness we come before God, full of confidence, but with little rever-

[7] Ps. CXII, 5.

ence; or, if, on the contrary, we are penetrated with fear, but
have only a slight confidence, our relations with God are not
what they ought to be. The self-abasement of the creature
should not be to the detriment of the confidence of the child;
the quality of child ought not to cause forgetfulness of the
condition of creature and sinner.

> *Christ, the Ideal of the Monk,* Part II,
> chapter 11, section 3.

Christ, indeed, knows better than anyone what our relations with God ought to be, He knows the divine secrets. If
we listen to Him we do not run any risk of going astray: He
is Truth itself. Now, what attitude does He want us to have
with God? Under what aspect does He want us to contemplate and adore Him? Undoubtedly, He teaches us that God
is the Supreme Master Whom we must adore: "It is written:
Thou shalt adore the Lord thy God, and Him only shalt
thou serve." But this God Whom we must adore is a Father:
*Veri adoratores adorabunt Patrem in spiritu et veritate, nam
et Pater tales quaerit qui adorent eum.*[8]

Seated upon the edge of Jacob's well, He speaks with the
Samaritan woman. This woman has just acknowledged that
He Who speaks to her is a prophet, one sent by God, and at
once she asks Him (it was the subject of lively contestation
between her compatriots and the Jews) if God must be
adored on the mountains of Samaria or at Jerusalem. And
what does Christ reply? "Woman, believe Me that the hour
cometh, when you shall neither on this mountain, nor in
Jerusalem, adore the Father . . . the hour cometh, and now
is, *Et nunc est,* when the true adorers shall adore the Father
in spirit and in truth. For the Father also seeketh such to
adore Him." Note how our Lord lays stress on the name of
Father. At Samaria, as you know, false gods were adored,

[8] Joan. IV, 23.

and that is why Christ says it is "in truth," that is to say, it is the true God that must be adored. At Jerusalem, the true God was adored, but not "in spirit"; the religion of the Jews was altogether material in its expression and in its aim. It is the Incarnate Word Who inaugurates—*et nunc est*—the new religion, that of the true God, adored in spirit, the spirit of the divine, supernatural, and spiritual adoption, whereby we are made children of God; and that is why our Lord insists upon this term of "Father." "The *true adorers* shall adore *the Father* in spirit and in truth." Doubtless, as we are adoptive children, and as God, while making us His children, diminishes nothing of His Divine Majesty nor of His absolute sovereignty, we must adore Him, prostrate ourselves before Him; but it is in spirit and in truth we must adore Him, that is to say, in the truth and spirit of the supernatural order whereby we are His children.

Adoration is therefore not the only disposition which we ought to have in our heart; it does not constitute the one attitude which we must have towards this Father Who is God. No, Christ Jesus adds thereto love, and a love that is full, perfect, without reserve or restriction. When Jesus was asked which was the greatest of the commandments what did He answer? "Thou shalt love" [9]—love of complacency towards this Lord of such great majesty, towards this God of such high perfection; love of benevolence which seeks to procure the glory of the One Who is the object of this love; love of reciprocity towards a God Who "hath first loved us." [10]

And so as to safeguard within us these two dispositions of reverence and love, which may seem contradictory, God communicates to us the Spirit of His Son Jesus, Who, by His gifts of fear and piety, harmonises within us, in the pro-

[9] Marc. XII, 30.
[10] I Joan. IV, 10,

portion that they require, the most intimate adoration and most tender love: *Quoniam estis filii, misit Deus spiritum Filii sui in corda vestra.*[11]

According to the teaching of Jesus Himself, this Spirit ought to govern and direct all our life: it is "the Spirit of adoption" of the New Covenant, which St. Paul contrasts with "the spirit of bondage" of the Old Law.

You will perhaps ask the reason of this difference. It is because, since the Incarnation, God sees all humanity in His Son Jesus; on account of Him, He envelops entire humanity in the same look of complacency of which His Son, our Elder Brother, is the object. This is why He wishes that like Him, with Him, through Him, we should live as His "most dear children": *Sicut filii carissimi.*[12]

> *Christ in His Mysteries,* Part II, chapter 19, section 5; and *Christ, the Life of the Soul,* Part II, chapter 10, section 1.

[11] Gal. iv, 6.
[12] Ephes. v, i.

3 We Consecrate Our Whole Being to the Glory of Thy Son Jesus

These words comprise the essential point of the Consecration. The Father's sole desire is for the glorification of His only Son, the object of His infinite pleasures. Christ said to the Jews: ". . . but hath given all judgment to the Son, that all men may honour the Son, as they honour the Father. He who honoureth not the Son, honoureth not the Father, Who hath sent Him."

In His prayer after the Last Supper, Jesus asked His Father to glorify Him so that He, His Son Jesus, might glorify the Father, for They are one. So also for us; the glory which we offer to the Son is referred to the Father and makes us pleasing to Him. This consecration to the glory of the Son is linked up with the first petition of the Lord's prayer: "Father, hallowed be Thy name."

1. THE SUPREME WILL OF THE FATHER IS TO GLORIFY AND TO BEHOLD HIS SON JESUS GLORIFIED

In the Blessed Trinity, says St. Paul, the Word is the splendour of the Father's glory, the figure of His substance, the reflection of His eternal light: *Splendor gloriae et figura substantiae ejus.*[1] He is, as the Greek term indicates, the "character," the adequate expression of God, and like the impression of the seal upon the wax. The Eternal Father, in looking upon the Son, sees in Him the perfect reproduction of His divine attributes; the Son perfectly reflects, like a spotless mirror, *speculum sine macula,*[2] all that the Father gives Him.

And this is why the Father, in contemplating His Son, sees in Him all His own perfections; and ravished at this sight, He declares to the world that this Son is the object of all His dilection: *Filius dilectus in quo mihi* BENE *complacui.*[3]

> *Christ in His Mysteries,* Part I, chapter 3, section 2.

You know that the voice of the Father has only been heard three times by the world,[4] and each time it was to tell us that Christ is His Son, worthy of all love and all glory: *Hic est filius meus dilectus . . . ipsum audite:* "Hear ye Him." That was, according to our Lord's own words, the testimony of God to the world when He gave it His Son: *Qui misit me Pater, ipse testimonium perhibuit de me.*[5] And to confirm this testimony, God gave His Son the power of working miracles; He raised Him from the dead. Our Lord Himself tells us that life everlasting depends for us upon the full acceptation of this testimony: *Haec est autem voluntas Patris mei qui misit me, ut omnis qui videt Filium et credit in eum, habeat vitam aeternam.*[6]

> *Christ, the Life of the Soul,* Part II, chapter 1, section 2.

[1] Hebr. I, 3.
[2] Sap. VII, 26.
[3] Matth. XVII, 5.
[4] Matth. III, 17; XVII, 5, and Joan. XII, 25.
[5] Joan. V, 37. See all the passage from V, 31.
[6] *Ibid.,* VI, 40; cf. XVII, 21.

During Christ's mortal life—except on the day of the Transfiguration—this glory was veiled and hidden. The Word willed to unite Himself to a humanity feeble like our own, to a humanity subject to infirmity, suffering and death.

Jesus entered into possession of this resplendent glory on the dawn of His resurrection; His Humanity is henceforth glorious, and impassible. But it still remained here below, in a place of corruption where death reigns. To attain the summit, the full expansion of this glory, the Risen Jesus had need of an abode that responded fittingly to His new condition; He needed the heights of heaven, whence His glory and His power might henceforth radiate in their fulness upon the entire company of the elect.

As God-Man, Son of God, equal to His Father, Jesus has the right of sitting at His right hand, of sharing with Him the Divine glory, the infinite beatitude and almighty power of the sovereign Being.

The second reason of this supreme glorification is its being a recompense for the humiliations that Jesus underwent out of love of His Father and charity for us.

In entering into this world, Christ yielded Himself up entirely to the will of the Father. *Ecce venio ut faciam, Deus, voluntatem tuam.*[7] He accepted to accomplish to the full all the abasements that had been foretold, to drink to the dregs the bitter chalice of sufferings and of untold ignominies; He annihilated Himself even to the malediction of the Cross. And why was this? *Ut cognoscat mundus quia diligo Patrem.*[8] "That the world may know that I love the Father," His perfections, and His glory, His might and His good pleasure.

Christ in His Mysteries, Part II, chapter 16, section 2.

[7] Hebr. x, 9; cf. Ps. xxxix, 8.
[8] Joan. xiv, 31.

2. WE CONFORM TO THE FATHER'S WILL TO GLORIFY HIS SON, FIRST, IN PROCLAIMING, WITH LIVELY FAITH, THE DIVINITY OF JESUS

At the beginning of his Gospel, after having extolled the glory of the Divine Word, St. John says that the Word came into this world, and that this world which He had created, which was His domain, which was "His own," received Him not. But, he adds, all such receive Him as believe in His name: *Quotquot autem receperunt eum . . . qui credunt in nomine ejus . . .* We receive the Incarnate Word, by faith; by faith, we accept the Divinity of Jesus: "Thou art the Christ, the Son of the living God." [9]

Such is the attitude that the Eternal Father requires of us. "This is His commandment," says the same St. John, "that we should believe in the name of His Son Jesus Christ": *Et hoc est* MANDATUM *ejus: ut credamus in nomine Filii ejus Jesu Christi.*[10] He has Himself told us so: "This is My beloved Son . . . hear ye Him." [11] These words which were heard on Thabor, when the splendour of the Divinity filled the Sacred Humanity of Jesus with its rays, are but the echo, in the created world, of the words that the Heavenly Father utters in the heavenly sanctuary, *in splendoribus sanctorum,*[12] "Thou art My Son, this day have I begotten Thee."

Thus we are very pleasing to our Heavenly Father when, accepting His testimony, we profess that Jesus is His own Son, that He is co-eternal with the Father and shares with Him the Divine glory: *Tu solus altissimus Jesu Christe . . . in gloria Dei Patris . . .*

The mystery of the self-abasement of the Word-made-Flesh plunges St. Paul in such admiration that he can

[9] Matth. XVI, 16; Joan. XI, 27.
[10] I Joan. III, 23.
[11] Matth. XVII, 5; Marc. IX, 6; Luc. IX, 3.
[12] Ps. CIX, 3.

scarcely find terms wherewith to express the glory that, according to the very thoughts of God, these abasements will procure to Jesus. Listen to what he says: "Who being in the form of God, thought it not robbery to be equal with God; but emptied Himself, taking the form of a servant, being made in the likeness of men, and in habit found as a man. He humbled Himself, becoming obedient unto death, even the death of the cross. For which cause God also hath exalted Him, and hath given Him a name which is above all names. That in the name of Jesus every knee should bow, of those that are in heaven, on earth and under the earth; and that every tongue should confess that the Lord Jesus Christ is in the glory of God the Father." *Et omnis lingua confiteatur quia Dominus Jesus Christus in gloria est Dei Patris.*[13]

We ought often to unite ourselves in mind and heart with the will of the Eternal Father to glorify His Son: *Clarificavi et iterum clarificabo.* Before opening the Gospel or preparing ourselves to celebrate the mysteries of Jesus, let us first enter into God's views, confessing, by an act of intense faith, that this Christ Whom we are about to contemplate, He to Whom we would pray and unite ourselves, is God like the Father and the Holy Spirit.

That is why the more Christ humbles Himself in becoming a little Child, in choosing the hidden life of Nazareth, in bearing such of our infirmities as are compatible with His dignity, in submitting Himself to the death of the gibbet like a criminal, *Cum sceleratis,* in veiling Himself in the Eucharist; the more His divinity is attacked and denied by unbelievers—the more too ought we to place Him high in the glory of the Father, and in our hearts to yield ourselves to Him in a spirit of intense reverence and entire submission to His Person, and to labour for the extension of His reign in souls.

[13] Philipp. II, 6–11.

This disposition of soul is extremely fruitful because it elevates us to the divine level and makes us pleasing to the Father (*Pater amat vos . . . quia credidistis ego a Deo exivi;* "The Father loves you . . . because you have believed that I came from Him")—pleasing to the Father because all His wishes—and they are infinite—consist in desiring the glory of His Son.

Let us cast ourselves down at the feet of Jesus, and say to Him: "O Christ Jesus, Incarnate Word, Who camest down from heaven to reveal to us the secrets that Thou, the Only-begotten Son of God, dost ever contemplate in the bosom of the Father, I believe and I confess that Thou art God, like the Father, equal to Him; I believe in Thee; I believe in Thy works; I believe in Thy Person; I believe that Thou art come forth from God, that Thou art one with the Father; that he that seeth Thee, seeth the Father; I believe that Thou art the Resurrection and the Life. I believe this and, believing it, I adore Thee and consecrate to Thy service, all my being, all my activity, all my life."

Christ in His Mysteries, Part I, chapter 4, section 3.

3. WE ALSO GLORIFY CHRIST, THE WORD INCARNATE, BY HAVING AN UNLIMITED CONFIDENCE IN THE INFINITE VALUE OF HIS MERITS

God has made us an immense gift in the Person of His Son Jesus. Christ is a tabernacle wherein are "hidden all the treasures of divine wisdom and knowledge" that He has there stored up for us. Christ Himself, by His Passion and death, merited to communicate them to us, and He is always living, interceding with His Father for us.

But we must know the value of this gift and how to use it: *Si scires donum Dei!* Christ with the plenitude of His sanctity and the infinite value of His merits and credit is this gift; but this gift is only useful to us according to the measure of our faith. If our faith is great, intense, profound, and reaching to the height of this gift as far as is possible for a creature, there will be no limit to the divine communications made to our souls by the holy Humanity of Jesus. If we have not a boundless esteem for Christ's infinite merits, it is because our faith in the Divinity of Jesus is not intense enough; and those who doubt this divine efficacy do not know what is the humanity of a God.

We ought often to exercise our faith in the satisfactions and merits acquired by Jesus for our sanctification.

When we pray, let us come before the Eternal Father with an *unshaken confidence* in the merits of His Son. Our Lord has paid all our debt; He has gained all for us, and He unceasingly intercedes with His Father for us: *Semper vivens ad interpellandum* PRO NOBIS.[14] Let us then say to God: "I know, O my God, that I am altogether wretched; that I only add to my faults every day; I know that before Thy infinite holiness I am, of myself, like mud before the sun; but I prostrate myself before Thee; through grace, I am a member of Thy Son's mystical body; Thy Son has given me this grace, after having redeemed me by His Blood; now that I belong to Him, do not reject me from before Thy divine face!"

No, God cannot reject us when we thus rely on the credit of His Son; for the Son treats with Him as equal with equal. When we thus acknowledge that of ourselves we are weak and miserable, that we can do nothing, *Sine me nihil potestis facere,* but that we hope for everything from Christ, all that we need in order to live by the divine life, *Omnia possum in eo qui me confortat,* we acknowledge that this Son is everything for us, that He has been established as our Chief and High Priest. That is, says St. John, to render very acceptable homage to the Father "Who loves the Son," Who wills that

---

[14] Hebr. VIII, 25.

everything should come to us through the Son because He
has given Him all power of life for souls. The soul that has
not this *absolute* confidence in Jesus does not fully acknowledge Him for what He is—the beloved Son of the Father,
and hence does not render to the Father that honour which
He absolutely requires: *Pater enim diligit Filium, ut omnes
honorificent Filium sicut honorificant Patrem. Qui non
honorificat Filium, non honorificat Patrem qui misit illum.*[15]

When we often make such acts of faith in the power of
Christ, in the value of His merits, our life becomes by the
very fact, like a perpetual song of praise to the glory of this
supreme High Priest, this universal Mediator, Who gives us
every grace; and this is to enter deeply into the eternal ideal,
the divine plan; it is to adapt our souls to the sanctifying designs of God at the same time as we associate ourselves with
His will by glorifying His beloved Son: *Clarificavi et adhuc
clarificabo.*

> *Christ, the Life of the Soul,* Part II,
> chapter 1, section 5.

4. BY CONSECRATING OURSELVES ENTIRELY TO HIS SERVICE WITH ARDENT LOVE

The word "devotion" comes from the Latin word *de-
vovere:* to devote or consecrate oneself to a person beloved.
Devotion towards God is the highest expression of our love.
"Thou shalt love the Lord thy God, with thy whole heart,
and with thy whole soul, and with thy whole mind, and
with thy whole strength": *Diliges Dominum Deum tuum
ex* TOTO *corde tuo, et ex* TOTA *anima tua, et ex* TOTA *mente
tua.*[16] This *totus* denotes devotion: to love God with *all oneself,* without reserving anything; to love Him constantly; to

---

[15] Joan. v, 20–24.
[16] Marc. xii, 30.

love Him to the point of giving oneself to His service with promptitude and ease, such is devotion in general; and, thus understood, devotion constitutes perfection: for it is the very flower of charity.[17]

Devotion to Jesus Christ is the devotion of all our being and all our activity to the Person of the Incarnate Word, abstraction made of such or such particular state of the Person of Jesus or of such or such special mystery of His life. By this devotion to Jesus Christ, we strive to know, to honour, to serve the Son of God manifesting Himself to us through His Sacred Humanity.

Christ in His Mysteries, Part II, chapter 19, section 1.

Devotion is not only to have been consecrated to Christ in baptism, but it is to vow all one's energies and works with ease and promptitude to His service and the glory of His Father.[18]

That is what the Church frequently asks for us: "Grant us, O Lord, ever to have a will devoted to Thee, and to serve Thy Majesty with a sincere heart": *Fac nos tibi semper et devotam gerere voluntatem et majestati tuae sincero corde servire.*[19] Elsewhere the Church makes us ask to be devoted in good works to the glory of God's name: *In bonis actibus nomini tuo sit devota.*[20]

To have no other principle than grace in the exercise of our activity, no other end than the accomplishment of the will of God Who has made us His children, no other supreme spring of action than the love of God and the interests

---

[17] Cf. S. Thom. II–II, q. 82, a. I.

[18] *Devotio est quidam voluntatis actus ad hoc quod homo prompte se tradat ad divinum obsequium.* S. Thom. II–II, q. LXXXII, a. 3.

[19] Collect for the Sunday in the Octave of the Ascension.

[20] Collect for the 21st Sunday after Pentecost.

of His glory—that is, as St. Paul says, to "walk worthy of
God, in all things pleasing to Him; being fruitful in every
good work, and increasing in the knowledge of God." *Ambuletis digne Deo per omnia placentes; in omni opere bono
fructificantes et crescentes in scientia Dei. . . .*[21]

Listen to this magnificent text of Our Lord: *Pater non
reliquit me solum, quia quae placita sunt ei facio semper.*
"My Father is with Me, and hath not left Me alone, for I do
always the things that please Him."[22] Each one of us ought
to do the same. O Heavenly Father, it is solely to please Thee,
for Thy glory and that of Thy Son that I do this action.
Christ Jesus, it is in union with Thee I wish to accomplish
this act so that Thou mayest sanctify it by Thy infinite
merits!

The love for His Father that filled the Heart of Christ
ought to become the motive power of the action of His
members as it was of His own action. The glory of His Father was the constant thought of Christ in all His works;
may it also be ours through our continual union with the
grace and charity of Christ! That is why Holy Church
makes us ask God to render our actions conformable to His
good pleasure; by remaining united to "the Son of His love,"
we shall deserve to abound in good works.[23] "Walk in love
as Christ also hath loved us," says St. Paul;[24] and then you
will be fully in accord with your Head: *Hoc enim sentite in
vobis quod et in Christo Jesu.*[25]

> *Christ, the Life of the Soul,* Part II,
> chapter 6, sections 6 and 8.

---

[21] Col. I, 10.

[22] Joan. VIII, 29.

[23] *Omnipotens sempiterne Deus, dirige actus nostros in beneplacito tuo, ut in
nomine dilecti Filii tui mereamur bonis operibus abundare.* Prayer for the Sunday
within the Octave of the Nativity.

[24] Ephes. V, 2.

[25] Philipp. II, 5.

July, 1899.

Holiness in God consists in the perfection with which He glorifies Himself.

The Word is the substantial glory of the Father; this is why we say of Jesus: "Thou only art holy," for He alone perfectly glorifies the Father.

The more we are united to Jesus, the more we glorify the Father.

Mid-December, 1899, Octave of the Immaculate Conception.

This very day, the Good God made me see that the great object of my life ought to be the glory of Jesus, as it is His own: this is also the object of all Mary's desires. I was very struck by these words: "God so loved the world, as to give His Only-begotten Son." The gift of God is worthy of Himself: it is His own Son. Oh! "if thou didst know the gift of God!" From all eternity, the Father finds His delights in the Son, "the Only-begotten Son Who is in the Bosom of the Father."

This same Son is "in our bosom" by Eucharistic Communion and by faith. Christ, says Saint Paul, dwells in our hearts by faith.[26] By faith, we ought to find all our delights in Jesus, as the Father finds them in Him: "This is My Beloved Son, in Whom I am well pleased." But it is by faith that we do this: "According to your faith be it done unto you."

January 4, 1900.

At the beginning of this year I feel a strong attraction of grace to take as the aim of my life that which God has established: the glory of His Son Jesus. I offer myself to the Father and to Mary with this intention.

[26] Eph. III, 17.

February 25, 1900.

To-day, while meditating on the faith of Abraham, I felt a strong movement of grace urging me to consecrate all my life and all my energies to the glorification of Jesus Christ in myself and in others, imitating in that the Father Who gives us His Son; He tells us to hear Him.

Abbot Columba Marmion: A Master of the Spiritual Life, chapter 8.

4 *The Word Incarnate*

1. CHRIST, THE WORD INCARNATE, IS BOTH PERFECT GOD AND PERFECT MAN

"In the beginning was the Word, and the Word was with God, and the Word was God . . . And the Word was made flesh, and dwelt among us."

Christ is the Incarnate Word. Revelation teaches us that the second Person of the Holy Trinity, the Word, the Son, took a human nature in order to unite Himself personally to it. This is the mystery of the Incarnation.

Jesus is God and Man; if we want to know His Person, and to share in His states, we must try to understand not only that He is the Word, but also that He is the Word-made-Flesh; if we would know Him worthily, it is as necessary for us to acknowledge the reality of His human nature as it is to adore the Divinity to which this nature is united.

According to faith, what are we to see in Christ? Two natures, the human and the divine; He is at once God and Man, perfect God and perfect Man.

Open the Gospel and on each page you will see that in all that He does the Incarnate Word shows Himself as God and man; everywhere the Divinity and Humanity are manifested, each according to its nature and properties.

Christ is born of a woman, but He wills that His Mother shall be a Virgin and shall so remain. In the manger, He is an infant Who needs a little milk to nourish Him, but the Angels celebrate His coming as that of the Saviour of the world. He is laid upon straw in a stable, but a marvellous star leads the Eastern Magi to His feet. Like every Jewish boy, He undergoes circumcision, but at the same time He receives a name that comes from Heaven and marks a divine mission. He grows in age and wisdom, but at twelve years old He throws the doctors of the Law themselves into admiration by His wonderful answers. He wills to receive baptism from John the Precursor as if He needed to do penance, but at that same moment the heavens open, and the Eternal Father attests that He is His beloved Son. In the desert, He is hungry, but the angels come to minister to Him. During His journeys throughout Palestine, He suffers weariness, thirst and want, but, by His own authority, He makes the paralytics walk, cures the lame and halt, and multiplies the loaves to feed the multitude. Upon the Lake of Genesareth, sleep closes His eyelids while His disciples struggle against the tempest, but, the next instant, awakened by the terrified apostles, He stills the furious waves with a single gesture. At the tomb of Lazarus, He is moved, He sheds tears, true human tears, but, with a word, He raises to life His friend who had been dead four days. In the Garden of Gethsemani, after an agony full of weariness, distress and anguish, He allows Himself to be taken by His enemies, but the declaration that He is Jesus of Nazareth is sufficient to make them fall to the ground. Upon the Cross, He dies like the last of men, but all nature proclaims by the upheaval it undergoes that it is a God Who dies.

Thus, according to St. Leo's beautiful words, "majesty is allied to lowliness, power to weakness, that which is mortal to that which is eternal . . . an inviolable nature to a passible nature. . . . The true God is born in the integral and perfect nature of a true man, entirely with all that is His, entirely too with all that is ours": *Totus in suis, totus in nostris.*

Everywhere, from the entering of Jesus into this world, the union of the Divinity and Humanity is manifested in Him; a union which takes away nothing of the divine perfections and leaves intact the reality of the human nature: the Incarnation is an ineffable union.

O Eternal Wisdom, how deep are Thy thoughts, how wonderful Thy works!

Christ in His Mysteries, Part I, chapter 4, section 1.

2. THE WONDERFUL UNITY OF TWO NATURES IN THE PERSON OF THE WORD

That which further makes this mystery ineffable is the way wherein the union of natures is realised.

The divine nature and the human nature are united in one Person, the Eternal Person of the Word, of the Son.

In us, the soul and body united together form a human person. In Christ, it is not the same. The human nature, altogether integral, altogether perfect in its essence, in its constitutive elements, has, however, existence only through the Word, in the Divine Person of the Word. The Word gives to the human nature its reality of existence, which, in this case, means its personal "subsistence." There is then in Jesus but one Person, that of the Only-begotten Son of God.

Yet, as you know, however intimately they be united, the two natures keep their particular energies and their specific operations; there is neither blending nor confusion between them: *Non commixtionem passus;* inseparably united in the one Person of the Word, each preserves its own activity.

In fine, the human nature is rooted in the Divinity. It is a human activity, truly human and authentic, which is manifested in Jesus; but it has its ultimate principle in the Divinity. The Divine Person of the Word is the source of all Christ's perfections. In the Holy Trinity, the Word expresses the perfections of the Father by an infinitely simple act; in uniting Himself to the Sacred Humanity, the Word expresses through this Humanity all these perfections by manifold and varied acts conformed to human nature. It is thus that a ray of light in passing through a prism emerges in a variety of different shades of colours. The virtues of the Sacred Humanity of Jesus—His patience, sweetness, goodness, meekness, His kindness, zeal and love—are virtues accomplished by His human nature, but which are deeply rooted in the Divinity, and at the same time manifest the perfections of the invisible God to our earthly gaze. Human in its outward expression, the life of Jesus is Divine in its source and principle.

What is the consequence of this doctrine? You know it, but it is extremely useful to return to it.

It is that all the actions of Jesus are the actions of a God. The actions of the Sacred Humanity are finite actions, bounded by time and space, in the same way as human nature is bounded.

But the moral value of these actions is divine. Why is this? Because every action, although it be accomplished by such or such a faculty of nature, is attributed to the person. In Christ, it is always God *Who* acts, but sometimes *through* His divine nature, sometimes *through* His human nature. It is then true to say that it is a God Who toiled, Who wept, Who suffered, Who died—although all these actions were accomplished through the human nature. All Jesus Christ's human actions, however small they may be in their physical reality, have a divine value.[1]

And this is why Christ's whole life is so pleasing to His Father. The Father finds in Jesus, in His person and in His acts, in His most humiliating states as in His most glorious mysteries, all His delight, because He ever sees the Person of His Only-begotten Son. The Father sees Christ Jesus as no creature can ever see Him. If I may thus speak, He alone can appreciate the value of all that His Son does. As our Lord Himself said: "No one knoweth the Son, but the Father." [2] We may raise our souls and meditate upon the mysteries and states of Jesus, but we shall never arrive at appreciating them as they deserve. Only God can worthily know and recognize that which a God does. But in the Father's sight, the least acts of the Humanity of Jesus, the least movements of His Sacred Heart were a source of delight.

Christ in His Mysteries, Part I, chapter 4, section 2.

3. OUR ATTITUDE IN THE PRESENCE OF THE WORD INCARNATE

Adoration. It is true that this Humanity is a created humanity like unto our own. We do not adore it for its own sake; we must, however, adore it *in* itself, *on account of its union* with the Son of God. Our adoration goes to His Humanity, but the Divine Person to Whom it is substantially united is the term of this adoration.

Next, absolute confidence. God has willed to make Christ's Humanity the instrument of grace. It is through His Humanity that grace flows into us. It is not of the Word in the bosom of the Father, but truly of the Incarnate Word that

[1] In theological terms these actions are called *theandric,* from two Greek words which signify: human and divine.

[2] Matth. XI, 27; Luc. X, 22.

St. John speaks when he says that He was "full of grace . . . and of His fulness we have all received."

During His earthly life, Our Lord, being God, could have wrought all His miracles and given grace to men simply by an act of His Divine will. Each time that the sick were brought to Jesus to be healed or the dead to be raised to life, He could, by a single interior act of His Eternal will, have wrought the miracle demanded. But He did not do so. Read the Gospel and you will see that He willed to touch the eyes of the blind, the ears of the deaf, the tongue of the dumb; that He willed to touch the bier of the son of the widow of Naim, to take the daughter of Jairus by the hand, to give the Holy Ghost to His Apostles by breathing upon them. It was, then, by the contact of His Sacred Humanity that Christ performed miracles and gave grace: the Humanity served as the instrument united to the Word. And this wonderful and touching law is observed in all the mysteries of Jesus.

Now this order, willed by God Himself, always subsists because the union of natures in Jesus Christ remains indissoluble. Hence, when we read the pages of the Gospel or follow the Church in her liturgy, when we unite ourselves to the Sacred Humanity of Jesus by an act of faith, when, above all, we receive His Body in the Eucharist, this Sacred Humanity, inseparable from the Divine Word, serves as the instrument of grace for our souls.

And if you reflect, you will agree that all the economy of the spiritual life is based upon this truth. The Church, the Sacraments, the Holy Sacrifice, the preaching of the Word of God: these are so many means whereby God leads us to Himself.

We see how important and necessary it is for us to remain united to the Sacred Humanity of Jesus: in it dwells the very plenitude of the Divinity, and it is from the Word, through the instrumentality of the Humanity, that we receive every grace: *Verbum caro factum est* . . . *et vidimus eum plenum gratiae et de plenitudine ejus nos omnes accepimus*. The Humanity of Jesus is the divinely established means for transmitting grace to souls.

It is also the means whereby souls come to the Divinity. This is a no less important truth which we ought never to forget. We ought not to stop at the Sacred Humanity as at the final term. In fact, you might say: "As for me, all my devotion consists in giving myself to Christ Jesus, in yielding myself up to Him." That is good, it is excellent, nothing is better than to give ourselves up to Christ. But what is it to give ourselves to Our Lord? It is to unite our will to His. Now the will of Jesus is to bring us to His Father. In that lies all His work; the Father is the term. "I am the way," said Christ Himself in speaking of His Humanity. This Humanity is the one way, it is true, but only a way. The supreme end to which this way leads is the Eternal Father: *Nemo venit* AD PATREM *nisi per me.*[3] By the Humanity we come to the Word, and by the Word to the Father.

This is what St. Paul said to the Christians of his time: *Omnia vestra sunt, vos autem Christi, Christus autem Dei.*[4] By these simple words the great Apostle expressed the degrees of the Divine work upon earth: "For all things are yours . . . and you are Christ's, and Christ is God's."

By the Humanity of Jesus we belong to the Word, to the Son; by the Son, we go to the Father. Christ thus leads us *in sinu Patris*. This is, in what concerns us, the intimate reason of the ineffable mystery of the God-Man.

"O Jesus Christ, Incarnate Word, I prostrate myself before Thee, because Thou art the Son of God, equal to Thy Father. Thou art truly the Son of God, *Deum de Deo, lumen de lumine, Deum verum de Deo vero*. Thou art the Father's

---

[3] Joan. XIV, 6.
[4] I Cor. III, 22–23.

well-beloved Son, in Whom He is well pleased. I love Thee
and I adore Thee."

> *Christ in His Mysteries,* Part I, chapter
> 4, section 4.

April 9, 1903.

I have been praying a great deal for you, for Our Lord
always gives me the longing for your perfection. It seems to
me that, for you, the cult of Jesus in His Divinity and in His
Humanity is the synthesis of perfection. In His *Divinity:*
adoration, utter humility, boundless confidence in His
power, His goodness, His faithfulness. In His *Humanity:* to
find in Him all that our human hearts can ask of love, affection, and sympathy, for He is as truly man, *Filius hominis,*
as He is God. And as His human nature is really distinct
from His Divine nature and remains, without being confounded, in the unity of His Divine Person, so His human
love is truly distinct from His Divine love, although in perfect accord with it, being the expression, under a human
form, of His Divine love.

The humanity of Jesus is the door whereby we enter into
the sanctuary of His Divinity: *Ego sum ostium;* [5] it is the
translation, in human and intelligible words, of that Infinite
and incomprehensible Word: *Unigenitus qui est in sinu
Patris, ipse enarravit.* [6] Love unifies all this in one single act.
Here then is all there is to say: "Love Jesus Christ."

You will ask me, my child, like the disciples to St. John:
"Why do you always repeat the same thing to me?" It is because this is all I know, and this contains everything: *Non
enim judicavi me scire aliquid inter vos, nisi Jesum Christum
et hunc crucifixum.* [7]

> *Union with God,* chapter 2, section 4.

[5] "I am the Door (of the sheep)." John x, 7.

[6] "The only begotten Son Who is in the bosom of the Father." John i, 18.

[7] "I judged not myself to know anything among you, but Jesus Christ, and
Him crucified." I Cor. ii, 2.

5 *Thou Hast Established Him King of Our Souls*

The reason for our consecration: the kingship of Jesus, which the Father wishes us to recognize. This phrase is connected with the second petition of the Our Father—"Thy kingdom come."

1. ORIGIN AND MAGNIFICENCE OF CHRIST'S KINGSHIP

Christ is King. He is so by His Divinity, *Rex Regum et Dominus dominantium;* [1] He rules over all creatures brought out of nothing by His almighty power: *Venite adoremus, et procidamus ante Deum* [2] . . . *Ipse fecit nos et non ipsi nos.* [3]

He will be so likewise as the Incarnate Word. The sceptre of the world had been foretold to Jesus by His Father. The Messias says: "I am appointed king by Him over Sion, His holy mountain, preaching His commandment. The Lord hath said to Me: Thou art My Son, this day have I begotten Thee. Ask of Me, and I will give Thee the Gentiles for Thine inheritance, and the utmost parts of the earth for Thy possession." [4]

[1] Apoc. xix, 16.
[2] Ps. xciv, 6.
[3] *Ibid.,* xcix, 2.
[4] *Ibid.,* ii, 8.

The Word became Incarnate in order to establish "the
Kingdom of God." This expression often occurs in the
preaching of Jesus. In reading the Gospel you will have re-
marked an entire group of parables—the pearl of great price,
the hidden treasure, the sower, the grain of mustard seed,
the murderous vine-dressers, the guests invited to the wed-
ding-feast, the tares, the servants awaiting their Master, the
talents, etc.—which group is intended to show the greatness
of this kingdom, its origin, its development, its extension to
the pagan nations after the reprobation of the Jews, its laws,
its conflicts, its triumphs. Christ organises this kingdom by
the election of the Apostles, and the foundation of the
Church to which He entrusts His doctrine, His authority,
His sacraments. It is a wholly spiritual kingdom wherein is
nothing temporal or political such as was dreamt of by the
carnal minds of most of the Jews; a kingdom into which
every soul of good will enters; a wonderful kingdom of
which the final splendour is altogether heavenly and the
beatitude eternal. . . .

Finally, Christ is King by right of conquest. After the
combat, it is with joy that earthly princes reward the valiant
captains who have defended their prerogatives, won the victory over the enemy, and by their conquests widened the
boundaries of the kingdom.

Was it not this that took place in heaven on the day of the
Ascension, though with an incomparable glory? With supreme fidelity, Jesus had accomplished the work that His
Father had given Him to do: *Quae placita sunt ei facio semper* . . . *Opus consummavi;* abandoning Himself to the action of Divine justice, as a holy Victim, He had descended
into an incomprehensible abyss of sorrows and humiliations.
And now all was expiated, the price was paid and redemption accomplished, the powers of darkness were defeated, the
perfections of the Father were acknowledged and His rights

avenged, and the gates of the kingdom of heaven were opened to all the human race. If we may thus lisp about such mysteries, what joy for the Heavenly Father, to crown His Son after the victory gained over the prince of this world! What divine gladness to call the Sacred Humanity of Jesus to the enjoyment of the splendour, the beatitude and power of an eternal exaltation!

And what still further enhanced this divine gladness, was that Jesus, when about to consummate His sacrifice, has asked of His Father that glory which was to extend that of the Father: "Father, the hour is come: glorify Thy Son, that Thy Son may glorify Thee."

Yea, Father, the hour is come. Thy justice has been satisfied by expiation; may it be so likewise by the glory that comes to Thy Son Jesus, because of the love that He has manifested to Thee in His sufferings. O Father, glorify Thy Son! Establish His reign in the hearts of those who love Him; bring under His sceptre the souls that have turned away from Him; draw to Him those who, sitting in darkness, do not yet know Him. Father, glorify Thy Son, so that in His turn, Thy Son may glorify Thee in manifesting to us Thy Divine Being, Thy perfections, Thy will!

But the Father has already replied to us: "I have glorified Him and again shall I glorify Him"—*Clarificavi et iterum clarificabo*. We hear Him saying to Christ Himself these solemn words predicted by the Psalmist: "Thou art My Son. . . . Ask and I shall give Thee the nations as heritage. . . . Sit on My right hand and I will make Thy enemies Thy footstool."

Such is the order, the plan ordained from all eternity; Jesus was established Head and King over all God's heritage because it is He Who, by His blood, has regained for us the rights to this heritage. "The Father has placed all things in His hands." *Omnia dedit Pater in manu ejus*. We dwell in

Him by faith and love; He dwells in us by His grace and merits; He offers us to His Father and His Father finds us in Him.

St. John extols the magnificence of this kingdom. He shows us the elect falling prostrate before their Divine Head, Christ Jesus, and proclaiming that He has redeemed them in His Blood, out of every tribe, and tongue, and people, and nation, and has made of them a kingdom to the glory of His Father: *Et fecisti nos Deo nostro regnum.*

> *Christ in His Mysteries,* Part I, chapter 5, introduction; Part II, chapter 16, section 2.

We must all be partakers of this kingdom. Christ excludes no one from the life He has brought, and, by it, He renders us children of God: *Pro omnibus mortuus est Christus;* Christ has re-opened the gates of eternal life to all humanity. As St. Paul says: He is the first-born, but of a multitude of brethren: *In multis fratribus.*[5] The Eternal Father wishes to constitute Christ His Son, Head of a Kingdom, the Kingdom of His children. The Divine Plan would not be complete if Christ was isolated. It is His glory, as it is the glory of the Father, *In laudem gloriae gratiae suae,*[6] to be at the head of an innumerable company, which is His complement, πλήρωμα, and without which, so to say, He would not be complete.

St. Paul distinctly says this in his Epistle to the Ephesians, where he traces out the Divine Plan: God has made Christ to sit "on His right hand in the heavenly places, above all principality and power and virtue and dominion, and every name that is named not only in this world, but also in that which is to come: And He hath subjected all things under

---

[5] Rom. VIII, 29.
[6] Ephes. I, 6.

His feet, and hath made Him head over all the Church which is His body." [7] It is this company, this Church that Christ has acquired, according to the words of the same Apostle, that it may be at the last day, without "spot or wrinkle, but holy and without blemish": *Ut exhiberet ipse sibi gloriosam Ecclesiam, non habentem maculam, aut rugam, aut aliquid hujusmodi, sed ut sit sancta et immaculata.*[8] This Church, this Kingdom is being formed even here below. It is only entered by Baptism. On earth we live in it by grace, in faith, hope, and charity, but the day will come when we shall contemplate its perfection in heaven; that will be the kingdom of glory in the light of vision, the rejoicing in unending possession and union. That is why St. Paul said that "the grace of God is life everlasting, in Christ Jesus, our Lord."

This is the great mystery of God's design. *Si scires donum Dei!* If you but knew the gift of God!

> *Christ, the Life of the Soul,* Part I, chapter 1, section 6.

2. FEELINGS OF THE SOUL ADMITTED BY BAPTISM INTO CHRIST'S KINGDOM

There is one affection which we ought chiefly to have in presence of the Person and mysteries of Jesus; it is that of admiration. This way of loving and honouring Him in His mysteries is acceptable to our Lord. Did He not Himself give us the example when He exulted with holy enthusiasm at the sight of His Father's adorable perfections and His wonderful ways with souls? *Exsultavit Spiritu Sancto.*

> *Christ, the Ideal of the Monk,* Part II, chapter 17, section 8.

[7] *Ibid.,* i, 20–23.
[8] *Ibid.,* v, 27.

Let us also offer continual thanksgiving to God "Who hath delivered us from the power of darkness, and hath translated us into the kingdom of the Son of His love," [9] that is to say, into His Church.

The call to the faith is a signal benefit because it contains in germ the vocation to the eternal beatitude of the Divine vision. Never let us forget that this call was the dawn of all God's mercies towards us, and that for man all is summed up in fidelity to this vocation; faith is to bring us to the Beatific Vision.

Not only ought we to thank God for this grace of the Christian faith, but we ought each day to render ourselves more worthy of it by safeguarding our faith against all the dangers that it encounters in our age of naturalism, scepticism, indifference, human respect, and by living a life of faith with constant fidelity.

Moreover, let us beseech God to grant this precious gift of the Christian faith to all the souls who yet "sit in darkness, and in the shadow of death"; let us beseech Our Lord that the star may shine upon them; that, through His tender mercy, He Himself will be the Sun to visit them from on high: *Per viscera misericordiae Dei nostri in quibus visitavit nos, Oriens ex alto.*[10]

This prayer is very pleasing to Our Lord; it is, in fact, to beseech Him that He may be known and exalted as the Saviour of all mankind and the King of kings.

It is likewise pleasing to the Father, for He desires nothing so much as the glorification of His Son. Let us then often repeat, during these holy days, the prayer that the Incarnate Word Himself has put upon our lips: "O Heavenly Father, 'Father of Lights,' Thy Kingdom come, that kingdom

[9] Col. I, 13.
[10] Luc. I, 78–79.

whereof Thy Son Jesus is the head. *Adveniat regnum tuum!*
May Thy Son be more and more known, loved, served, glorified, so that in His turn He may, by manifesting Thee the
more to men, glorify Thee in the unity of the Holy Ghost:
Pater, clarifica Filium tuum ut Filius tuus clarificet te!"

Christ in His Mysteries, Part II, chapter
8, section 1.

To prayer we must join the works of zeal which are compatible with the condition wherein Providence has pleased
us. By frequent contact with the furnace of substantial Love,
the soul is set on fire for God's interests and glory, and for
the extension of Christ's reign in hearts. The true inner life
makes us give ourselves to souls as well as to God: it is the
fount of zeal. When one truly loves God, one desires that He
be loved, that His name be hallowed, His Kingdom come in
souls and His will be done in us: *Sanctificetur nomen tuum,
adveniat regnum tuum, fiat voluntas tua sicut in caelo et in
terra!* The soul that truly loves God, deeply resents the in-
juries that are done to the object of its love; "a fainting takes
hold of it because of the wicked that transgress the divine
law": *Defectio tenuit me pro peccatoribus dereliquentibus
legem tuam.*[11] It suffers at seeing the empire of the prince of
darkness extended by sin; for Satan "as a roaring lion goeth
about seeking whom he may devour,"[12] and he has accom-
plices into whom he breathes an incessant ardour, a zeal of
hatred against the members of Jesus Christ.

The soul that loves God sincerely is also devoured with
zeal, but it is for the glory of the house of the Lord: *Zelus
domus tuae comedit me.*[13]

What in fact is zeal? It is an ardour that burns and is com-

---

[11] Ps. cxviii, 53.
[12] I Petr. v, 8.
[13] Ps. lxviii, 10; Joan. ii, 17.

municated, that consumes and is spread abroad; it is the
flame of love—or of hatred—manifested by action. The soul
inflamed with holy zeal spends itself for the interests of God
without counting the cost, it strives to serve them with all
its powers. And the more glowing this inward fire is, the
more it radiates outwardly. This soul is animated with that
fire which Christ Jesus came to cast upon earth, and so ardently desires to see kindled in us.

Christ, the Ideal of the Monk, Part II,
chapter 17, introduction.

6 *Submit to Him Our Souls, Our Hearts, Our Bodies*

This petition is the logical outcome of faith in the king-ship of Jesus, Son of God. If Christ has been established King of our souls, by the Father, it is for the purpose of rul-ing them and governing them. The kingdom of Jesus is real-ized practically in our souls only by submission to His wishes, which are at the same time the Father's wishes. We must not proclaim this Kingship with our lips only but ac-knowledge it by our works. This prayer is linked up with the third petition of the Pater; the Father's name is glorified only by the establishment of His reign in us and His reign is established in us only by submitting our whole being to His will.

In the following extracts, Dom Marmion cites this text of the Psalmist (VIII, 8) applied by St. Paul to Jesus: "The Father has subjected all things under His feet" (Hebr. II, 8 and Ephes. I, 22). This text recurs often in the preaching of Dom Marmion at the time of his stay at Louvain; it even comprises the theme of several conferences, so familiar is this thought to him; it is found again in his spiritual notes of the

*same period and in a letter of December 2, 1908, some weeks
before the writing of the Consecration.*

1. SUBMISSION TO THE PERSON OF CHRIST THROUGH FAITH AND LOVE

Christ must reign in our hearts, and all within us must be
subject to Him. Since the day of Christ's triumph, He gloriously lives and reigns in God, in the bosom of the Father:
Vivit et regnat Deus. Christ only lives where He reigns, and
He lives in us in the same degree as He reigns in our soul.
He is King as He is High Priest. When Pilate asked Him if
He was a King, Our Lord answered him: *Tu dicis quia rex
sum ego;* [1] "I am, but My kingdom is not of this world."
"The kingdom of God is within you": *Regnum Dei intra
vos est.* [2] This dominion of Christ must, day by day, be ex-
tended in our souls; it is this that we ask of God: *Adveniat
regnum tuum!* Oh, may it come, Lord, that day when, truly,
Thou wilt reign in us by Thy Christ!

And why has not that day already come? Because so many
things in us, self-will, self-love, our natural activity are not
yet subject to Christ, because we have not yet done what the
Father desires: *Omnia subjecisti sub pedibus ejus,* [3] we have
not yet put all things beneath the feet of Christ. That is a
part of the glory which the Father wills henceforth to give
to His Son Jesus: *Exaltavit illum et donavit illi nomen ... ut
in nomine Jesu omne genu flectatur.* [4] The Father wills to
glorify Christ, because Christ is His Son, because He
humbled Himself; the Father wills that every knee should
bend at the name of Jesus; all in creation is to be subject to
Jesus; in heaven, upon earth, in hell; all, too, in each one of
us: will, intelligence, imagination, energies.

[1] Joan. XVIII, 37.
[2] Luc. XVII, 21.
[3] Ps. VIII, 8.
[4] Philipp. II, 9–10.

Jesus came in us as King on the day of our baptism, but sin disputes this dominion with Him. When we destroy sin, infidelities, attachment to the creature; when we live by faith in Him, in His word, in His merits; when we seek to please Him in all things, then Christ is Master, then He reigns within us; as He reigns in the bosom of the Father, so He lives in us. He can say of us to the Father: "Behold this soul: I live and reign in her, O Father, that Thy name may be hallowed."

Christ in His Mysteries, Part II, chapter 15, section 5.

In receiving Jesus Christ in Communion, we receive Him wholly: His Body, His Blood, His Soul, His Humanity, His Divinity. Christ makes us sharers of His thoughts, and His sentiments; He communicates His virtues to us, but above all, He enkindles in us the fire that He came to cast upon earth,[5] the fire of love, of charity: that is the result of this transformation produced by the Eucharist. . . . The coming of Christ in us tends, of its nature, to establish between His thoughts and ours, between His sentiments and our sentiments, between His Will and our will, such an exchange, such a correspondence and similitude that we have no other thoughts, no other sentiments, no other will than those of Christ: *Hoc enim sentite in vobis, quod et in Christo Jesu.*[6]

This operates through our whole being, all our energies, so that, by the faith we have in Him, by the love we bear towards Him, it may be really His life, and no longer our *ego* that is the principle of our life. This is very clearly shown in a prayer which the Church makes the priest recite after Communion: "Grant, O Lord, that the operation of Thy heavenly Gift may possess both our minds and bodies,

[5] Luc. XI, 49.
[6] Philipp. II, 5.

that its effect, and not our senses, may ever have dominion within us."

Christ, the Life of the Soul, Part II, chapter 8, section 3.

October 28, 1902.

More and more I feel myself drawn to lose myself, to hide myself in Jesus Christ: *Vivens Deo* IN *Christo Jesu.* He Himself becomes, it seems to me, the eye of my soul, and my will is blended with His. I am drawn to desire nothing *outside* of Him, that I may abide *in Him.*

December 26, 1902.

It seems to me that my inner life becomes more and more simple; it tends to unify my will with that of the Eternal Father through Jesus Christ, and I feel inwardly invited to cut off every desire, except that of fulfilling the *known will of God,* with all the energy of my soul; and as for the good pleasure of God that *I do not know,* to abandon myself, without plan or desire, to His wisdom and goodness.

August 3, 1903.

Once it is thoroughly understood that the will of God is the same thing as God Himself, we see that we ought to prefer His adorable will to all besides, and take it, in what it does, in what it ordains, in what it *permits,* as the one *norm* of ours. Let us keep our eyes fixed upon this holy will, and not upon the things that cause us pain and trouble.

Abbot Columba Marmion: A Master of the Spiritual Life, chapter 8.

2. FROM CHRIST, OUR SUBMISSION MUST EXTEND TO THE CHURCH, HIS SPOUSE

St. Paul tells us that God "hath subjected all things under His feet, and hath made Him head over all the Church, which is His body and the fulness of Him Who is filled all in all": *Omnia subjecit sub pedibus ejus (Christi), et ipsum dedit caput supra omnem Ecclesiam, quae est corpus ipsius et plenitudo ejus.*[7]

By these words, in which he speaks of the Church, the Apostle completes the description of the economy of the mystery of Christ.

We cannot have a full conception of Christ considered apart from the Church. Jesus has the glory of His Father in view, as the foundation of all His life, of all His acts, but the masterpiece by which He is to procure this glory is the Church. Christ comes on earth to create and constitute the Church; it is the work to which all His existence converges, and He confirms it by His Passion and Death. His love for His Father led Jesus Christ to the mountain of Calvary, but it was there to form the Church, and make of her, by purifying her in His Divine Blood, a spotless and immaculate Bride: *Dilexit Ecclesiam et seipsum tradidit pro ea ut illam sanctificaret.* . . .

When Christ came into this world, the only means of going to the Father was to submit oneself entirely to His Son, Jesus: *Hic est Filius meus dilectus, ipsum audite.* In the beginning of the public life of the Saviour, the Eternal Father showed His Son to the Jews, and said to them: Hear Him because He is My Only Son; I send Him to reveal to you the secrets of My Divine life and My will, *Ipse enarravit* . . . *ipsum audite.*

But since His Ascension Christ has left His Church on earth, and this Church is like the extension of the Incarnation amongst us. The Church—that is to say, the Sovereign Pontiff, and the Bishops, with the pastors who are subject to them—speaks to us with all the infallible authority of Jesus Christ Himself.

[7] Ephes. I, 22–23.

While He was upon earth, Christ contained infallibility in Himself: *Ego sum veritas.* "I am the truth; I am the life; he that followeth Me, walketh not in darkness, but shall have the light of life." Before leaving us, He confided these powers to His Church: *Sicut misit me Pater, et ego mitto vos.* "As the Father hath sent Me, I also send you; he that heareth you heareth Me, and he that despiseth you, despiseth Him that sent Me." *Qui vos audit, me audit: et qui vos spernit, me spernit. Qui autem me spernit, spernit eum qui misit me.* "In the same way that I hold My doctrine from My Father, so the doctrine that you teach, you hold from Me; whosoever receives this doctrine, receives My doctrine, which is that of My Father; whosoever despises it, in whatever degree or measure it may be, despises My doctrine, despises Me, and despises My Father."

See then this Church, possessing all the power, all the infallible authority of Christ, and understand that the absolute submission to the Church of all your being, intelligence, will, and energies is the only means of going to the Father. Christianity in its true expression, only exists by means of this absolute submission to the doctrine and laws of the Church.

This way is safe, for Our Lord is with His Apostles until the consummation of the world, and He has prayed for Peter and his successors that their faith should not fail.[8]

Let us then have great confidence in this Church which Jesus has left to us. We have the happiness of belonging to Christ, in belonging to this society which is one, Catholic, Apostolic and Roman. We ought to rejoice greatly, and ever thank God for having "translated us into the Kingdom of the Son of His love."[9] Is it not an immense assurance to be able to draw grace and life at their authentic and official sources, through our incorporation with the Church?

[8] Matth. xxviii, 20.
[9] Col. i, 13.

Moreover, let us give to those who have jurisdiction over us, the obedience which Christ demands of us. This submission of our intelligence and will must be given to God in the person of a man, otherwise God does not accept it. Let us give to those who govern us, above all to the Sovereign Pontiff, Vicar of Christ, to the Bishops who are in union with him, and who possess the lights of the Holy Spirit [10] to guide us, that inward submission, that filial reverence, that practical obedience which make of us true children of the Church.

The Church is the Bride of Christ, she is our Mother; we ought to love her because she brings us to Jesus and unites us to Him. We ought to love and revere her doctrine, because it is the doctrine of Jesus Christ; to love her prayer and associate ourselves with it because it is the prayer of the Bride of Christ, and there is none safer for us, none more pleasing to Our Lord. In a word, we ought to attach ourselves to the Church, to all that comes from her as we should have been attached to the very Person of Jesus and to all that came to us from Him, if it had been given us to follow Him during His earthly life.

Such is the Church as a visible society. St. Paul compares her to an edifice "built upon the foundation of the Apostles, Jesus Christ Himself being the chief cornerstone." *Ipso summo angulari lapide Christo Jesu.*[11] We live in this house of God, "no more strangers and foreigners, but fellow-citizens with the Saints."

> *Christ, the Life of the Soul,* Part I, chapter 5, introduction and sections 1 and 2.

[10] *Spiritus Sanctus posuit episcopos regere Ecclesiam Dei.* Act. xx, 28.
[11] Ephes. II, 19–22.

7 *And May Nothing Within Us Move Without His Order, Without His Inspiration*

1. THE FULNESS WHICH OUR SUBMISSION TO CHRIST, KING OF OUR SOULS, SHOULD ATTAIN

The Kingdom of God is first of all within us; it is established in us in the very measure that we strip ourselves of every creature and of self. All our spiritual life consists in the imitation of Christ Jesus. The Word, being the Son of God, proceeds entirely from His Father, He lives by Him, He lives for Him: *Ego vivo propter Patrem;* [1] this sums up the whole life of Jesus, the Incarnate Word. It will be proportionately the same for us; the more that our life and aims flow from God, the more that our activity finds the source of its inspirations in the will of God—the higher and more supernatural will our life too become. We need great abnegation in order to establish this disposition in us and never to seek the principle of our actions save in God; for the natural instinct of man urges him to make himself his own centre and to seek the principle of his life in himself alone,

[1] Joan. VI, 58.

in that which is personal and proper to himself. On the contrary the life of our soul must be entirely subject to the Divine good pleasure and must have no movement that does not come from the Holy Spirit.

This is what we ask of our Lord each morning at Prime, on beginning the day. "O Lord our God, King of heaven and earth, vouchsafe this day to direct and sanctify, to rule and govern our hearts and our bodies, our feelings, our words, and our works, according to Thy Law, and in the doing of Thy commandments . . . O Saviour of the world, Who livest and reignest, world without end": *Dirigere et sanctificare, regere et gubernare dignare, Domine Deus, Rex caeli et terrae, hodie, corda et corpora nostra, sensus, sermones et actus nostros, in lege tua, et in operibus mandatorum tuorum.* We here ask the Word to direct, to take in hand all that is in us; our thoughts, our feelings, our actions, all that we are, all that we have, all that we do. All that is ours will then come from God through Jesus Christ and His Spirit, and will return to God. We shall bring our personality into subjection to Christ Jesus, in order to destroy what is bad in us, and to make all that is good converge towards the doing of His Divine will: then without ceasing to remain ourselves, we shall do everything under the impulsion, by the action of His grace and of His Spirit. It will be no longer in our self-love, our self-esteem, nor our self-will, that we shall seek the mainspring of our thoughts, words, and deeds, but in the love of Christ's will, in cleaving to His law: *In lege tua et in operibus mandatorum tuorum.* We shall have laid down our personality to put on Christ: *Christum induistis.* Doubtless, in this union of ourselves with the Word, two distinct persons always remain, for this union is only moral, but we can strive to subject our personality in the order of activity so perfectly to the Word, that this personality will disappear as far as possible leaving to the Divine Word all the initiative of our life.

Christ, the Ideal of the Monk, Part II,
chapter 10, section 5.

If I may thus express myself, we ought to make all our activity proceed from God; to lay down at His feet all our own thoughts, all our own judgment, our self-will so as no longer to think, judge, will or act save as He wills. Was it not thus that Jesus acted? "The Son cannot do anything of Himself, but what He seeth the Father doing," [2] the Incarnate Word said of Himself. All proportion guarded, it ought to be the same with us. We ought to immolate to God whatever is ill-regulated in the need we experience of being something of ourselves and of relying only on ourselves. And for this, before all that we do, let us implore the help of our Father in Heaven, as Jesus did.

This is the practical homage whereby we acknowledge our dependence upon our Father Who is likewise our God, and whereby we proclaim, like Jesus, that all that we have is from the Father: *Omnia quae dedisti mihi abs te sunt. . . .*[3]

This Sacred Humanity belonged and was so absolutely yielded up to the Word, that it had no proper personality: this is one of the essential aspects of the mystery of the Incarnation.

All proportion being kept, it ought to be so with us, for Jesus Christ is our Model in all things. His Humanity only acted as subject to the Word in Whom it subsisted, to the Word Who gave this Humanity existence. Let there be no movement in us that does not come from God, no desire that is not according to the Divine good pleasure, no action that does not tend to serve as an instrument to His glory. A

[2] Joan. v, 19.
[3] *Ibid.,* xvii, 7.

soul that is in such dependence of love, of will and of action upon God can say in all truth: "The Lord ruleth me," *Dominus regit me.*

And the sacred writer adds: *Et nihil mihi deerit,* "And I shall want nothing." And so it is that because this soul is wholly given up to the Word, the Word says to His Father: "This soul is Mine, it is therefore also Thine, O Father," *mea omnia tua sunt.* The Word gives this soul to the Father in order that the Father may send His most perfect gifts down upon it.

Christ in His Mysteries, Part I, chapter 3, section 3; chapter 4, section 3.

December 2, 1908.

The Good God gives me a great desire to make Jesus the Supreme Master of my inner life and the one and only source of my activity. I am no doubt *very far* from this ideal, because of my self-love and my numberless infidelities. However, I have great confidence that one day I shall be able to say in truth: I live, no, not I, but Christ lives in me. Then according to His promise He will reveal to me the secrets of His divinity: "If anyone loveth Me," He has said, "I will *manifest* Myself to him. . . ."

November 8, 1910.

Our Lord gives me a great attraction for this way: the complete and *continual* laying down of my whole self at the feet of the Incarnate Word. I want to imitate the Sacred Humanity of Jesus in Its unity (with the Word), in Its submission and absolute dependence on the Word. Help me, my daughter, to realise this ideal, for all lies in that. Once the Father sees a soul thus *one* with His Word, there are no graces or favours which He will not give to it.

The Sacred Humanity of Jesus is the "way." Its power to

unite us to the Word is infinite. Let us then glorify Him by being saints: *In hoc clarificatus est Pater meus ut fructum plurimum afferatis.*

February 16, 1913.

I do hope I may henceforth live for God *alone.* I feel our Lord wants me to live as He did: *propter Patrem,* and that in two senses: (1) That all my inspiration may come from Him; (2) all my activity be employed for Him.

December 13, 1913.

Our Lord has been drawing me very strongly for some time to a life more united with Him. My great longing is to see Jesus *reign* and *live* in such a manner in my soul that all my powers, all my faculties, all my desires, may be perfectly subject to Him.

> *Abbot Columba Marmion: A Master of the Spiritual Life,* chapters 8 and 16.

2. THE GRACE OF JESUS IS THE SOURCE OF THIS TOTAL SUBJECTION

Christ, in His personal and physical reality, is perfect, but He forms, with His Church, a mystical body which has not yet reached its complete perfection. This perfection is attained gradually in the course of the centuries by the sanctification of souls, "according to the measure of the giving of Christ." [4] In a body there are many members and all have not the same function and the same nobility. This mystical body makes only one with Jesus Christ, Who is its Head; through grace we make part of this body; but we must become perfect members, worthy of the Divine Head; that is what we must have in view in our supernatural progress.

And because He is the Head, Christ is the first source of

[4] Ephes. IV, 7.

this progress. Never forget this: Jesus Christ, having taken
our nature, has sanctified all our actions, all our feelings: His
human life was like to ours, and His Divine Heart is the
centre of every virtue. Jesus Christ exercised every form of
human activity; we must not think of Our Lord as living
rapt in ecstasy; on the contrary, He found the motive power
of His activity in the beatific vision of the perfections of His
Father; He willed to glorify His Father by sanctifying in
His Person the forms of activity we ourselves have to exert.
We pray: He passed the nights in prayer; we work: He
toiled in labour till the age of thirty; we eat: He sat at table
with His disciples; we suffer contradictions on the part of
men: He has known them; did the Pharisees ever leave Him
in peace? We suffer: He has shed tears. He suffered for us,
before us, both in His body and soul, as none other has ever
suffered. We experience joy: His holy soul felt ineffable joy;
we take rest: sleep has likewise closed His eyelids. In a word,
He has done all we do. And why has He done all this? Not
only to set us the example, since He is our Head; but also by
all these actions, to merit for us the power of sanctifying all
our acts: to give us that grace which renders our actions
pleasing to His Father. This grace unites us to Him, makes
us members of His body; and in order to grow up in Him,
to attain our perfection as His members, we have but to let
this grace take possession, not only of our being, but of all
our activities.

Christ dwells in us with all His merits, so as to vivify all
our actions; when, therefore, by an upright and pure intention, often renewed, we unite all the actions of our day to
the same human actions that Jesus accomplished here below,
the Divine virtue of His grace exercises a constant influence
over us.

Christ, the Life of the Soul, Part II,
chapter 6, section 8.

Each morning, when, after Holy Communion, we make
but one with Him, let us renew our disposition of wishing
to belong entirely to Him. O Jesus, I wish to live by Thy life,
through faith and love; I wish Thy desires to be my desires,
and, like Thee, out of love for Thy Father, I wish to do all
that may be pleasing to Thee: I have placed "Thy law in the
midst of my heart": *Et legem tuam in medio* CORDIS MEI.[5] It
is pleasing to Thee when I faithfully keep the prescriptions
of the Christian law which Thou hast established and those
of the monastic code which I have accepted; as proof of the
delicacy of my love for Thee, I wish to say as Thou hast said
Thyself: Neither a jot nor a tittle shall be taken away by me
from Thy law: *Iota unum aut unus apex non praeteribit a
lege donec omnia fiant;*[6] grant me Thy grace that I may not
let the least thing pass that could give Thee pleasure, in order
that, according to Thine own word, being faithful in small
things, I may likewise become so in great things;[7] grant
above all that I may ever act out of love for Thee and for
Thy Father: *Ut cognoscat mundus quia diligo Patrem;*[8] my
sole desire is to be able to say like Thee "I do always the
things that please Him."

> *Christ, the Ideal of the Monk,* Part II,
> chapter 7, section 5.

3. THE PRECIOUS FRUITS OF PERFECT SUBMISSION

We must give ourselves entirely to Jesus Christ, surrender
to Him our soul, our understanding, our will, our body:
everything in us ought to be subject to Him; all that is withdrawn from the action of His Spirit is withdrawn from the
Divine order. Outside the light of the Word, there is only

[5] Ps. xxxix, 8–9.
[6] Matth. v, 18.
[7] Cf. Luc. xvi, 10.
[8] Joan. xiv, 31.

darkness; outside the way which is Himself, we find only error; without His grace, there is only powerlessness. And indeed what peace can be given to us by darkness, error and powerlessness to go to God, the only true Good, the only true End of our life?

Let us then yield ourselves up to Our Lord by an act of living faith, of deep adoration, of perfect submission and entire abandonment. Let us ask Him to direct all our life, to be the object of all our aspirations, the principle of all our actions. He is "the Prince of Peace," "the pacific King": *Rex pacificus:* may He be really the King of our souls. We say to God every day: "Thy Kingdom come": *Adveniat regnum tuum.* What is this Kingdom of God which we desire? It is the Kingdom of Christ, for God has appointed Him King upon earth and in heaven: *Postula a me, et dabo tibi gentes hereditatem tuam!* [9]

When we thus submit ourselves entirely to Christ Jesus, when we abandon ourselves to Him, when our soul only responds, like His own, with a perpetual *Amen* to all that He asks of us in the name of His Father; when, after His example, we abide in this attitude of adoration before all the manifestations of the Divine Will, in face of the least permissions of His Providence, then Christ Jesus establishes His peace in us: His peace, not that which the world promises, but the true peace which can only come from Himself: *Pacem meam do vobis; non quomodo mundus dat, ego do vobis.* [10]

Indeed, such adoration produces in us the unity of all desires. The soul has but one thing in view: the establishing in her of Christ's Kingdom. Christ Jesus, in return, satisfies this desire with magnificent plenitude. The soul possesses the perfect contentment of her deepest tendencies because

[9] Ps. ii, 8.
[10] Joan. xiv, 27.

the satisfaction of her supernatural desires has been reduced
to one; she is in the right order of things; she lives in peace.

Happy the soul who has thus understood the order established by the Father, that soul who seeks only to be conformed by love to His admirable order, where all leads up
to Christ Jesus: she tastes peace, a peace of which St. Paul
says that it surpasses all understanding and defies all expression.

> *Christ, the Ideal of the Monk,* Part II,
> chapter 18, section 2.

December 15, 1894.

There will never be any peace for you except in the *complete abandonment* of yourself in the hands of your Heavenly Father. It is always necessary to come back to this point,
for Our Lord requires of you this testimony of your confidence and love. Each time then that you feel troubled and
distrustful, you should try *quietly* by prayer and through
union with Jesus, to bring your will to this *absolute submission,* to this complete abandonment of yourself, of your
future and of everything, into God's hands.

April 3, 1908.

What gives simplicity and peace to our lives is the sincere
and complete abandon of oneself to God for His glory. To
abandon ourselves is to give to God all that we are and all
that we have in order to be *His thing* of which He can dispose at will.

Jesus says, "Father, all My things are Thine," and the
Father took Him at His word and delivered Him to unheard-
of torments. Many people speak of abandon, but very few
keep their word with God. They give themselves to God to
be His property, and as soon as ever God begins to dispose
of this property for His Glory and according to the designs

of His Wisdom, they cry out, they murmur, and let it be seen that their abandon was not serious, it was only a meaningless word.

When we have made our religious profession, we become so much God's "thing," His property, that each time we try to arrange our life, our occupations for ourselves and according to our own views we are using something that belongs to God and hence comes the loss of His gifts and graces. The chief thing for you is to *scrutinize very closely* the movements of your heart, your motives (of action), this kingdom of God which is within you. All the beauty of the King's daughter is within, and this beauty consists in that perfect simplicity of love which in everything only considers God and His interests.

Union with God, chapter 4, section 3.

8 *So That United to Him We May Be Carried to Thy Bosom*

Jesus Christ, the Word Incarnate, the only begotten Son, is in the bosom of His Father. Thus speaks St. John in his Gospel (1, 18). The Son lives with the very life of the Father in an ineffable unity. This "bosom of the Father," to which we are invited by our predestination, is not, strictly speaking, a place, but a state, a permanent condition of supernatural life, implying an idea of intimacy, of tenderness.

It is solely by our union with the only Son, Jesus, Who always dwells there, that we can enter into the bosom of the Father, the sanctuary of divinity. To be united to Jesus in order through Him and in Him to become the object of the Father's pleasure, tenderness and blessings is indeed a high aspiration. The ardent faith which Dom Marmion had in the Father's love for us and in the merits of Jesus intensified this aspiration and made him familiar with it.

This aspiration is already outlined in an undated letter, which may however be fixed in 1886: "Our Lord is master of His gifts; and, as He is infinite Wisdom, we go straight to the Father when we depend on Him." It becomes explicit in the letter of December, 1899, cited above. But it is especially from 1906 that this thought seizes his soul and that he lives by this aspiration; it forms the subject matter of spiritual conferences given by him in April, June and October of that year.

1. JESUS CHRIST HAS THE POWER TO BRING US INTO THE BOSOM OF THE FATHER

The Apostle St. James tells us that every gift, every grace, comes down to us from our Heavenly Father; and he at once adds: "Of His own will hath He begotten us by the word of truth": *Voluntarie genuit nos verbo veritatis.* The divine adoption by grace which makes us children of God is wrought by the Son, by the Word.

This truth is one of those to which St. Paul returns most often. Like St. James, he declares that all blessings come from the Father and that they are all related to the decree of our adoption in Jesus Christ, His beloved Son. In the eternal plan, we become God's children only in Jesus Christ, the Incarnate Word: *Elegit nos in ipso.*[1] The Father will only recognise us as His children if we bear in us the features of His Son Jesus: *Praedestinavit* [*nos*] . . . *conformes fieri Filii sui.*[2] So that it is only as joint-heirs with Christ that we are one day to be *in sinu Patris*.

Such is the divine decree. Let us now see the realisation, in time, of this eternal design, or rather the manner wherein the divine plan, which was crossed by Adam's sin, has been restored.

The Eternal Word is made flesh. The Psalmist says of the Word that He "hath rejoiced as a giant to run the way": *Exsultavit ut gigas ad currendam viam.* It is from the heights

[1] Eph. I, 3–4.
[2] Rom. VIII, 29.

of heaven that He comes forth: *A summo caelo egressio ejus;* and it is to this sublime summit that He ascends: *Et occursus ejus usque ad summum ejus.*[3] This *egressio a summo caelo,* is the eternal birth in the bosom of the Father: *Exivi a Patre;* His return is His ascension towards the Father: *Relinquo mundum, et vado ad Patrem.*[4]

But He does not ascend alone. This giant came to seek lost humanity; He has regained it; and, in an embrace of love, He bears it away with Himself in His course to place it near Him *in sinu Patris:* "I ascend to My Father Who is also your Father, and I go to prepare a place for you in My Father's house."

Such is the work of the Divine Giant: to lead back fallen humanity into the bosom of the Father, the source of all beatitude whilst restoring to this humanity the grace of adoption by His life and His sacrifice.

Christ in His Mysteries, Part I, chapter 3, section 4.

You know that between God and us, between the Creator and the creature, the gulf is infinite. "I am Who am," the Being subsisting by Myself: *Ego sum qui sum.*[5] Every other being is taken out of nothingness. Who is going to throw a bridge across this gulf? Christ Jesus. He is preeminently the Mediator, the Pontiff. It is through Jesus Christ alone we can be raised up to God. The Incarnate Word tells us decisively: *Nemo venit ad Patrem nisi per me.*[6] "No man cometh to the Father, but by Me." It is as if He said: "You will never attain to the Divinity save in passing through My Humanity." Never forget He is the Way, the only way. Christ alone, God and Man, raises us up to His Father. We

[3] Ps. xviii, 6–7.
[4] Joan. xvi, 28.
[5] Exod. iii, 14.
[6] Joan. xiv, 6.

here see how important it is to have a living faith in Christ Jesus. If we have this faith in the power of His Humanity, as being the Humanity of a God, we shall be assured that Christ can make us enter into contact with God. For, as I have often told you, the Word in uniting Himself to human nature, has, in principle, united us all to Himself. And if we are united to Him by grace, Christ bears us with Him *In sancta*,[7] as St. Paul says, into "the Holy of holies," the sanctuary of the Divinity where, as Word, He is before all ages: *Et Verbum erat apud Deum*.[8]

> *Christ, the Life of the Soul*, Part II, chapter 10, section 7.

Oh! let us say with the Apostle: "Blessed be the God and Father of our Lord Jesus Christ, Who hath blessed us with spiritual blessings" through His Son, in His Son, and hath made us sit with Him in those heavenly splendours where, in the midst of eternal felicity, He begets the Son of His dilection! *Consedere fecit nos in caelestibus*. Yes, blessed be God! And blessed be the Divine Word Who was made flesh for us, Who by the shedding of His Blood has restored to us the heavenly inheritance. O Jesus, beloved Son of the Father, to You be all praise and all glory!

> *Christ in His Mysteries*, Part I, chapter 3, section 4.

2. HERE ON EARTH WE MAY BE IN THE FATHER'S BOSOM BY OUR UNION WITH HIS SON JESUS

If the Eternal Father has decreed that we should be His children, but only so in His Son Jesus: *Praedestinavit nos in adoptionem filiorum* PER JESUM CHRISTUM;[9] if He has made

[7] Hebr. ix, 12.
[8] Joan. i, 1.
[9] *Ibid.*, i, 5.

us partakers of the heritage of His beatitude only through His Son, we can realise this divine plan and consequently assure our salvation, only by remaining united to the Son, to the Word. Never let us forget this: there is no other way for us to go to the Father: *Nemo venit ad Patrem, nisi per me!* [10] No man, *nemo,* can hope to come to the Father otherwise than by the Son. And to go to the Father, to reach Him, is not that all salvation and all holiness?

Now, how are we to remain united to the Word, to the Son?

First of all *by faith.* "In the beginning was the Word, and the Word was with God, and the Word was God. . . . All things were made by Him. . . . He was in the world, and the world was made by Him, and the world knew Him not. He came unto His own, and His own received Him not. But as many as received Him, He gave them power to be made the sons of God, to them that believe in His name," and thus "are born . . . of God."

The Eternal Father presents His Word to the world: "This is My beloved Son. . . . Hear ye Him." If we receive Him by faith, that is to say, if we believe that He is the Son of God, the Word makes us partakers of the best that He has: His Divine Sonship; He shares with us His condition of Son, He gives us the grace of adoption: *Dedit eis potestatem filios Dei fieri;* He gives us the right of calling God our Father.

All our perfection consists in our faithful imitation of the Son of God. Now, St. Paul tells us that all paternity comes from God: *Ex quo omnis paternitas nominatur.*[11] We can say too of the Son: *Ex quo omnis filiatio nominatur.* It is the Son alone Who, by His Spirit, teaches us how we may be sons: *Quoniam estis filii, misit Deus spiritum* FILII SUI *in corda vestra clamantem:* ABBA, PATER.[12]

[10] *Ibid.,* xiv, 6.
[11] Ephes. iii, 15.
[12] Gal. iv, 6.

We are to receive the Son Himself; to see ever in Him, whatever be the state wherein we contemplate Him, the Word co-eternal with the Father. Then we are to receive His teachings, His doctrine. He is in the bosom of the Father: and by His words He reveals to us that which He knows: *Ipse enarravit.* Faith is the knowledge that we have, through the Word, of divine mysteries. Whatever be the page of the Gospel that we read or that the Church sets before us in the course of the celebration of the mysteries of her Bridegroom, let us say to ourselves that these words are those of the Word: *Verba Verbi,* of Him Who expresses the thoughts, the desires, the will of our Father in Heaven: *Ipsum audite.*[13] Let us sing *Amen* to all that we hear from the Word, to each page that, in her liturgy, the Church detaches from the Gospel to propose to our faith. Let us say to God: O Father, I do not know Thee, since I have never seen Thee; but I accept all that Thy Divine Son, Thy Word, reveals to me of Thee.

This prayer is excellent; and often, when it is made with faith and humility a ray of light comes down from on high [14] which throws a light upon those texts that we read and makes us penetrate into their depths so that we find therein principles of life.

For the Word is not only the expression of the perfections of His Father, but, moreover, of all that the Father wills. All that the Word commands us in His Gospel or by His Church is the expression of the adorable will and desires of our Father in Heaven. And if we fulfill, above all through love, the precepts that Jesus gives us, we shall remain united to Him, and through Him, to the Father: *Si praecepta mea servaveritis,* MANEBITIS *in dilectione mea . . . Qui autem diligit me, diligetur a Patre . . .*[15]

13 Matth. xvii, 5; Luc. ix, 35.
14 Cf. Jac. i, 17.
15 Joan. xv, 10; xiv, 21.

Here is all the formula of holiness: to adhere to the Word, to His doctrine, to His precepts, and, through Him, to the Father Who sends Him and gives to Him the words that we are to receive. . . .[16]

If then we would go to God, let us strive to have boundless faith in the power that Jesus has to unite us to His Father. What indeed does Our Lord say? "Father, I will that where I am, they also whom Thou hast given Me may be with Me": *Pater, volo ut ubi sum ego, et illi sint mecum.*[17] And where is Christ? "In the bosom of the Father."

When our faith is intense, and we give ourselves wholly to Jesus, He draws us with Him *In sinu Patris.*[18] For Jesus is at the same time the Way and the End. He is the Way by His Humanity, *via qua imus;* He is the End by His Divinity, *patria quo imus.*[19] It is this that makes the great security of this way: it is perfect, and contains in it the term itself.

It is an excellent thing in prayer to make acts of faith in the almighty power that Jesus has of leading us to His Father.

O Christ Jesus, I believe that You are true God and true Man, that You are the Divine Way, the Way of an infinite efficacy for making me bridge the gulf that separates me from God; I believe that Your sacred Humanity is perfect and so powerful that, despite my miseries, my shortcomings, my weaknesses, it can bring me thither where You are in the Father's bosom.

Christ in His Mysteries, Part I, chapter 3, section 5; Part II, chapter 20, section 3.

February, 1906.

Our Lord's words: "This is the work of God, that you be-

[16] Cf. Joan. xvii, 8.
[17] *Ibid.,* xvii, 24.
[18] *Ibid.,* i, 18.
[19] S. Aug. *Sermo* xcii, c. 3; *Sermo* cxxiii, c. 3.

lieve in Him Whom He hath sent," make me see still more
clearly that we have all in Jesus Christ. He who yields himself up unreservedly to Jesus Christ through faith fulfils perfectly with Him, in Him, and by Him all His duty towards
the Father. Jesus is *one* with the Father: "I and the Father
are one." He is "in the bosom of the Father," and he who is
united, by faith, to Jesus, does, *in unity,* what Jesus does for
His Father. The member does according to its function
what the body does: "You are the Body of Christ and members one of another." When we are united by faith with
Jesus Christ and, in the darkness of faith, lay down our in-
tellect at the feet of Christ, accepting with love all that He
does in our name in the full vision of His Father, our prayer
is of a high degree, and made "in spirit and in truth." Sometimes at these moments the Spirit of Christ draws us to rest
in silence and in adoration at the feet of Jesus; at other times
He urges us to unite ourselves to His oblation, to His submission towards His Father. We must follow these movements.

*Abbot Columba Marmion: A Master of
the Spiritual Life,* chapter 8.

3. WE ARE THERE ABOVE ALL BY OUR UNION WITH CHRIST IN THE EUCHARIST

The reception of the Eucharist unites us, in the first place,
to Christ's holy humanity, and this union becomes operative
through faith. When you believe that the humanity of Jesus
is the humanity of the Son of God, the very humanity of the
Word; and that in Him there is only one Divine Person;
when with the whole strength and fulness of your faith, you
adore this holy humanity, you then enter into contact with
the Word through it; it is the way which leads you to the
divinity.

For we do not unite ourselves only to Christ. Christ is but
one with the Father: *Ego et Pater unum sumus,* one in the

unity of the Holy Spirit. Communion unites us at the same
time with the Father and the Holy Spirit. Christ, the Word
Incarnate, belongs altogether to His Father; when we communicate, He takes us, He unites us to His Father, as He
Himself is united to Him; Jesus said to His Father at the
Last Supper, after having instituted the Blessed Eucharist:
"And not for them [My Apostles] only do I pray but for
them also who through their word shall believe in Me; that
they may be one, as Thou, Father, in Me, and I in Thee;
that they also may be one in Us . . . that they may be one,
as We also are One: I in them, and Thou in Me": *Ego in
eis et tu in me.*

What a mystery! He Whom I receive in Communion is
the Son begotten from all eternity, the beloved Son to Whom
the Father communicates His life, His Divine life, the fulness of His Being and His infinite beatitude. How much
reason had Our Lord to say: "As the Living Father hath
sent Me, and I live by the Father, so He that eateth Me the
same also shall live by Me": *Et qui manducat me, et ipse
vivet propter me;* he . . . "abideth in Me, and I in him":
In me manet et ego in illo.

If we ask Our Lord what we can do that is most pleasing
to His Sacred Heart, it is certain that He will tell us, before
all else, to be like Him, the child of God. If then we want to
please Him, let us receive Him every day in the Eucharistic
Communion, and say to Him: "O Jesus, You are the Son of
God, the perfect, adequate image of Your Father; You know
Your Father, You are wholly His, You behold His Face; increase within me the grace of adoption which makes me the
child of God; teach me to be, by Your grace and by my virtues, like You and in You, a worthy child of the Heavenly
Father." It is certain that if we ask this grace with faith, the
Word will give it to us.

He has told us: "The Son cannot do anything of Himself,
but what He seeth the Father doing: for what things soever

He doth, these the Son also doth in like manner." He wills only what the Father wills. Hence the Son enters fully into the views of His Father, and when He gives Himself to us, it is in order to establish, preserve, and augment the grace of adoption within us. All His Divine personal life is to be *ad Patrem;* in giving Himself to us, He gives Himself as He is, seeking in all things His Father and the glory of His Father; and so our entire turning towards the Father is wrought when we receive the Word with faith, confidence and love. What we ought to ask and constantly seek after is that all our thoughts, all our aspirations, all our desires, all our activity, should tend, by the grace of our filiation and by love, to our Heavenly Father in His Son Jesus: *Viventes Deo in Christo Jesu.*

> *Christ in His Mysteries,* Part II, chapter 18, section 5; Part I, chapter 3, section 5.

I love to think after Communion that the Eternal Word Who is *in sinu Patris* is likewise in me *in sinu peccatoris.* And this thought throws me into adoration and thanksgiving.

When I possess Jesus in my heart after the Mass, I am united to Jesus. Faith tells me that He is in Me and I in Him. Jesus is in the bosom of the Father, and I, poor sinner, am there with Him. Then I say to the Father: "I am the *Amen* of Jesus. Amen! that Your Beloved Son, the Word, say for me all that ought to be said; He knows me, He knows all my miseries, my needs, my aspirations, my desires." What confidence this thought begets!

> *Abbot Columba Marmion: A Master of the Spiritual Life,* chapter 18.

November 19, 1910.

God has poured forth all "the treasures of His Wisdom and of His Science" on the Sacred Humanity of Jesus Christ because of its union with the Word, and *the measure of His gifts to us is the degree of our union with this same Word.* Now this union with the Word is effected by the power and *efficacy of the Sacred Humanity, especially in Holy Communion.* What we have to do is to maintain ourselves, through the Sacred Humanity in an habitual state of absolute adoration and SUBMISSION to the Word, Who resides within us. Our life must be an *Amen* ever echoing the wishes and designs of that Word on us. A soul once arrived at that state, becomes the object of God's best gifts.

Union with God, chapter 2, section 4.

4. THE CONDITIONS REQUIRED OF THE SOUL THAT WISHES, WHILE ON EARTH, TO LIVE WITH JESUS IN THE BOSOM OF THE FATHER

We give here a page taken from the personal notes of Dom Marmion dating from his stay in Louvain, together with some contemporary and later texts. This aspiration to dwell in "the bosom of the Father" is still fervently maintained in his soul.

The conditions required for this intimate life in God through Jesus are logically and closely connected with the object of the two preceding petitions: "Submit our souls, our hearts to Him"; "May nothing within us move without His orders, without His inspirations."

April 22, 1906, Low Sunday.

After a week of dryness and powerlessness, I have had a moment of union with Jesus.

Saint Paul tells us: Christ "hath raised us up together, and hath made us sit together in the heavenly places." Each state of Our Lord works in us, like a Sacrament, according to our faith, and produces the effects corresponding to this state. But there is a *fundamental state* of Jesus which underlies all the others: "The Only-begotten Son Who is in the *bosom of the Father.*" That is His sanctuary which He never leaves. In the manger, at Nazareth, upon the cross, even at the moment when He cried out: "My God, My God, why hast Thou forsaken Me?" He was always in the bosom of the Father.

One with Jesus, we are *in sinu Patris.* This is the life of *pure love* which supposes the effort of doing always what is most pleasing to the Father: [20] "He hath not left Me alone: for I do always the things that please Him." Our weaknesses, our miseries do not prevent us from being *in sinu Patris,* for it is the bosom of infinite love and mercy, but it supposes a deep abasement and contempt of ourselves, so much the greater in that we are so near to this infinite holiness. It supposes, too, that we lean upon Jesus, "Who of God is made unto us wisdom, and justice, and sanctification, and redemption." All that is done *in the bosom of the Father, with the spirit of sons of adoption,* is of immense price. But this state supposes the absence of all deliberate fault, and of all refusal to follow the inspirations of the Holy Spirit. For if Jesus takes upon Himself our infirmities and our miseries, He does not accept the least deliberate sin: "Which of you shall convince Me of sin?" In this sanctuary graces are received, and often the repose of contemplation.

At times the thought of our weakness, of our stains, of our unworthiness may come to alarm us. This thought ought to humiliate us and make us abase ourselves before God, but not frighten us, for if we are *in sinu Patris,* it is with Jesus and in Him that we are there, and the greater our miseries the more our faith and our confidence in Him, *honour Him.* For Jesus identifies Himself so much with us that, in us, He is sick and feeble, and even clad in our miseries, and when,

---

[20] In a spiritual lecture given eight days afterwards (April 30), Dom Marmion shows that therein lies the "secret of dwelling in the bosom of the Father," to always do what pleases the Father.

in the strength of our faith, we come before God in the *name of Jesus,* it is His Beloved Son Whom He sees poor, weak and miserable (such as He was in His Passion) in us.

December 21, 1908 (four days before writing the Consecration).

Ask for me that I may become the humble and faithful servant of Jesus, that all in me may be *subjected* to Him: *omnia subjecisti sub pedibus ejus,* and that He will bear me there where He is: *in sinu Patris.*

> *Abbot Columba Marmion: A Master of the Spiritual Life,* chapter 8.

August 31, 1909.

The Incarnate Word did all things for His Father, and He says, *Mea omnia tua sunt:* "All My things are Thine, O Father." That is why if you lay yourself down *entirely* at His feet, He will take you with Him "into the bosom of the Father," *in sinu Patris. Pater, quos dedisti misi volo ut ubi sum ego et illi sint mecum.* "Father, I will that where I am, they also whom Thou hast given Me may be with Me." Now Jesus is always *in sinu Patris.* For that, my daughter, it needs great and continual abnegation, in order that Jesus may become the only mainspring of all your movements: *Vivo ego, jam non ego, vivit vero in me Christus.* Here we have the perfect union of the Bridegroom with the bride, a union to which He destines you if you are faithful. Then one becomes the object of a love of predilection on the part of the Father from Whom cometh down every good and perfect gift.

> *Union with God,* chapter 5.

December, 1913.

Let *Jesus* be the absolute Master of your inner life, and He will teach you all the secrets of His love. He has said,

"Neither doth anyone know *the Father,* but the Son, and he to whom it shall please the Son to reveal Him." Think well on that, for our Heavenly Father is the supreme End of the spiritual life.

Union with God, chapter 2, section 4.

July 20, 1914.

United to Jesus, we enter by right into the *sanctuarium exauditionis* where all petitions are heard. My daughter, when you are weak and suffering, you are like Jesus *in sinu Patris,* but upon the cross. Jesus on the cross, in agony, in weakness, forsaken by His Father, was ever *in sinu Patris* and never dearer to the Father, never nearer to the Father.

Abbot Columba Marmion: A Master of the Spiritual Life, chapter 11.

June 5, ——.

You are rich in infirmities and were you to lean on Christ alone, doing all, suffering all in His name, united with Him, He would render you more and more agreeable to His Father. He would bring you with Him into that sanctuary which He calls *sinus Patris,* His Father's bosom, and there, under God's eye, you would constantly try to please Him by doing what you feel is *most* pleasing to Him. Those alone dwell in God's bosom who have an immense confidence in His fatherly goodness and mercy which are infinite, and who try their best to please Him in all things.

Union with God, chapter 4, section 2.

9 *And Consumed in the Unity of Thy Love*

This invocation completes the prayer to the Father and is concerned with the final end of God's thought for us. Begun here below, in confident faith and generous love, our union is consummated forever in the beatitude of heaven, in the Father's bosom, where God will be entirely in us.

1. THE DIVINE PLAN OF OUR GLORIOUS BEATITUDE

"I have glorified Thee on earth. I have finished the work which Thou gavest Me to do. And now glorify Thou Me, O Father, with Thyself, with the glory which I had, before the world was, with Thee. . . . Father, I will that where I am, they also whom Thou hast given Me may be with Me; that they may see My glory which Thou hast given Me." [1]

These words form the beginning and the end of the ineffable prayer that Jesus addressed to His Father at the Last Supper, when about to crown His mission of salvation upon earth by His redeeming Sacrifice.

Christ Jesus first asks that His holy Humanity may share in that glory which the Word possesses from all eternity.

[1] Joan, XVII, 4, 24.

Then, as Christ never separates Himself from His Mystical Body, He asks that His disciples and all those who shall believe in Him, may be associated with Him in that glory. It is His will that we should be "where He is." And where is He? *In gloria Dei Patris:* "in the glory of God the Father." [2] There is the final term of our predestination, the consummation of our adoption, the supreme completion of our perfection, the plenitude of our life.

Let us hear how St. Paul sets forth this truth. After having said that God, Who wills us to be holy, has predestined us to be made conformable to the image of His Son, in order that this Son may be the firstborn amongst many brethren, He immediately adds: "And whom He predestinated, them He also called. And whom He called them He also justified. And whom He justified, them He also glorified." These words point out the successive phases of the work of our sanctification: namely, our predestination and vocation in Christ Jesus, our justification by grace, which makes us the children of God, and our supreme glorification assuring eternal life to us.

We have seen God's plan for us; how Baptism is the sign of our supernatural vocation, the Sacrament of our Christian initiation, and how we are justified, that is to say, rendered just, by the grace of Christ. This justification can go on being made more and more perfect, according to the degree of our union with Jesus Christ, until it finds its final term in glory. *Quos justificavit, illos et glorificavit.* Glory in this Divine inheritance which comes to us from the fact of our being the children of God: *Si filii et haeredes, haeredes Dei;* an inheritance Christ has merited to give us, which He Himself already possesses, and wills to share with us: *cohaeredes autem Christi.* The same inheritance which is Christ's is to become ours—eternal life, glory and beatitude in the possession of

[2] Philipp. ii, 11.

God. The term of the Divine life in us is not to be found
here on earth. It is, as Jesus says, with the Father: *apud te
. . . in gloria Patris.*

The life of Christ within us by grace here below is only a
dawn; it does not reach full noon—a noon, however, without decline—unless it blossoms in glory; Baptism is the source
whence springs the divine river, but the goal of this river,
which delights the city of souls, is the ocean of eternity.

You know how earnestly St. Paul prayed for the faithful
of Ephesus, that they might understand the mystery of
Christ, and that it might be granted them to comprehend
the sublimity and depth of this mystery. But the great
Apostle is also careful to point out that this mystery is only
crowned in eternity, and that is why he ardently desires that
this thought should occupy the minds of his disciples. "I do
not cease," he writes to them, "to make commemoration of
you in my prayers that the God of our Lord Jesus Christ, the
Father of glory, may enlighten the eyes of your heart that
you may know what is the hope of your calling, and what
are the riches of the glory of His inheritance in the saints."
*Ut sciatis quae sit spes vocationis ejus et quae divitiae gloriae
hereditatis ejus in sanctis.*

> *Christ, the Life of the Soul,* Part II, chap-
> ter 13, introduction.

2. THIS ETERNAL CONSUMMATION IN THE FATHER'S BOSOM IS THE FRUIT OF A PROMISE MADE BY JESUS

Our Father in Heaven "knoweth what is needful" for us.
If He calls us, He likewise gives us the grace to come to Him.
He gives us His Son in order that His Son may be our Way,
that He may bring us Truth, and communicate Life to us.
It suffices that we remain united to this Son by grace and by

our virtues for us one day to be partakers of His glory *in sinu Patris*.

Christ Jesus said one day: *Ego si exaltatus fuero a terra omnia traham ad meipsum.* "When I shall be lifted up from the earth, upon the Cross, My power will be such that I shall be able to lift up to Me those who have faith in Me. Those who looked upon the brazen serpent, in the desert, were healed; thus those who look upon Me with faith and love will be drawn to Me, despite their sins, their wounds and their unworthiness, and I will lift them as high as Heaven. I, Who am God, consented for love of thee to hang upon the Cross as one accursed. In return for this humiliation I have power to raise with Me even to the heavenly splendours whence I descended, those who believe in Me. I came down from Heaven, I shall ascend thither taking with Me those who hope in My grace. This grace is so powerful that it can unite thee to Me, and unite thee so indissolubly that no one can snatch out of My hands those whom My Father has given Me, those whom I have, through pure mercy, redeemed with My precious Blood."

Praecursor pro nobis introivit Jesus.[3] He has gone before us, but so that we may follow Him thither, for our life here below is only a passage, a probation: "In the world you shall have distress,"[4] said Jesus. There will be inward contradictions to be suffered, temptations to be borne from the prince of this world, disappointments arising from the course of events; for "the servant is not greater than his Master."[5] But, He added: "Let not your heart be troubled," do not be discouraged. "Believe in God, believe also in Me,"[6] Who am likewise God. "I am with you all days even to the con-

[3] Hebr. VI, 20.
[4] Joan. XVI, 33.
[5] *Ibid.*, XV, 20.
[6] *Ibid.*, XIV, 1.

summation of the world." [7] "Your sorrow shall be turned
into joy." [8] The hour will arrive when "I will come again,
and will take you to Myself, that where I am you also may
be" in My Father's kingdom: *Accipiam vos ad meipsum ut
ubi sum ego et vos sitis.*[9]

O divine promise, given by the Uncreated Word, by the
Word in person, by the infallible Truth; promise full of
sweetness: "I will come Myself! . . ." We shall belong to
Christ, and through Him to the Father, in the bosom of
beatitude. "In that day," says Jesus, "you shall know"—no
longer *in umbra fidei,* in the shadows of faith, but in the full
radiance of eternal light, *in lumine gloriae*—"you shall know
that I am in My Father, and you in Me, and I in you." [10]
You shall see My glory as the Only-begotten Son,[11] and this
vision shall be for you an ever living source of ineffable joy.

> *Christ in His Mysteries,* Part I, chapter
> 3, section 6; and *Christ, the Ideal of the
> Monk,* Part II, chapter 11, section 10.

3. THE FULL CONSUMMATION OF OUR LIFE IS REALISED IN THE VISION OF GOD FACE TO FACE, IN IMMUTABLE LOVE AND ENDLESS BEATITUDE

In heaven, we shall *see* God. To see God as He sees Himself is the first element in this participation in the Divine
nature that constitutes the life of blessedness. It is the first
vital act in glory. Here below, as St. Paul tells us, we only
know God by faith, in a dim manner, but then "face to face."
"Now," he says, "I know in part, but then I shall know even
as I am known." [12] What this vision is in itself, we cannot

---

[7] Matth. xxviii, 20.
[8] Joan. xvi, 20.
[9] *Ibid.,* xiv, 3.
[10] *Ibid.,* xiv, 20.
[11] *Ibid.,* i, 14.
[12] *Ibid.,* 12.

know now, but the soul will be confirmed in grace by "the light of glory" which is the unfolding of grace in heaven. We shall see God with all His perfections; or, rather, we shall see that all His perfections are but one infinite perfection, which is the Divinity. We shall contemplate the inner life of God. We shall enter, as St. John says, into fellowship with the Holy and Blessed Trinity, Father, Son, and Holy Spirit.[13] We shall contemplate the fulness of Being, the fulness of all truth, of all holiness, all beauty and all goodness. We shall contemplate, and that for ever, the Humanity of the Incarnate Word; we shall see Jesus Christ, in Whom the Father is infinitely well pleased; we shall see Him Who has willed to become our "Elder Brother": we shall contemplate the Divine features, henceforward glorious, of Him Who has delivered us from death by His bitter Passion, Who has given us to live this immortal life. To Him we shall sing the song of gratitude: "Thou hast redeemed us, O Lord, in Thy Blood, and hast established us in Thy Kingdom; to Thee be praise and glory." [14]

We shall *see* God. Is that all? No; to see God is the first element of eternal life, the first source of beatitude, but if the intelligence is divinely satisfied by the Eternal Truth, must not the will also be so by the Infinite Goodness? We shall love God.[15] "Charity," says St. Paul, "never falleth away." [16] We shall love God, no longer with a weak, vacillating love, so often turned aside by creatures, and exposed to fall away, but with a love that is powerful and pure, perfect and eternal. In this vale of tears where we must pain-

[13] I Joan. i, 3.

[14] Apoc. v, 9–10, and 13.

[15] According to St. Thomas (I–II, q. iii, a. 4), beatitude consists essentially in the possession of God contemplated face to face. This Beatific Vision is, above all, an act of intelligence. From this possession of God by the intelligence proceeds, as a property, the beatitude of the will which finds its complete satisfaction and repose in the possession of the beloved object rendered present by the intelligence.

[16] I Cor. XIII, 8.

fully struggle to preserve the life of Christ in us, love is
already so strong and intense in certain souls as to draw
from them such words as those of the Apostle: "Who shall
separate us from the love of Christ? shall tribulation? or distress? or persecution? . . . Neither death nor life . . . nor
height nor depth, nor any other creature shall be able to
separate us from the love of God." What then will this love
be when it embraces, never more to lose it, the Infinite
Good? What loving aspirations towards God ceaselessly satisfied! And this unending love will express itself in acts of
adoration, complacency and thanksgiving. St. John shows us
the saints prostrating themselves before God, and making
Heaven resound with their praise: "Glory, honour and
power to our God for ever and ever." [17] That is the expression of their love.

Finally, we shall *enjoy* God. You have read in the Gospel
how Our Lord Himself compares the Kingdom of Heaven
to a wedding feast that God has prepared to honour His
Son. "He will gird Himself and make them sit down to
meat, and passing, will minister to them." [18] What does this
signify if not that God will be our joy? The Psalmist exclaims: "[Thy elect] shall be inebriated with the plenty of
Thy house: and Thou shalt make them drink of the torrent
of Thy pleasures. For with Thee is the fountain of life."
Quoniam apud te est FONS VITAE.[19] God says to the soul that
seeks Him: "I Myself will be thy reward exceeding great."
EGO *ero merces tua magna nimis.*[20] It is as if He said: "I have
loved thee so much that I have not willed to give thee a
natural bliss: I have willed to bring thee into My own house,
to adopt thee as My child, that thou mayest partake of My
beatitude. It is My will that thou shouldst live of My very

17 Apoc. VII, 12.
18 Luc. XII, 37.
19 Ps. XXXV, 9.
20 Gen. XV, 1.

life, that My beatitude should become thine. Here below, I
have given thee My Son; become mortal by His humanity,
He delivered Himself up to merit for thee the grace of being
and remaining My child. He has given Himself to thee in
the Eucharist under the veil of faith; now, it is I in glory
Who give Myself to thee to make thee share in My life, and
to be thy endless beatitude." *Seipsum dabit quia seipsum
dedit; seipsum dabit immortalibus immortalem, quia seipsum dedit mortalibus mortalem.* Grace here below, glory
above; but it is the same God Who gives us both and, as I
have said, glory is only the unfolding of grace: the Divine
adoption, on earth, is hidden and imperfect, in Heaven, it is
revealed and consummated.

> *Christ, the Life of the Soul,* Part II, chap-
> ter 13, section 1.

PART 2. *The Son*

"O Jesus." This title is sufficient, for it is the name designated by the Father Himself, before the birth of Christ, to signify His mission of salvation here below.

"Unite us to Thee." It is only through union with Christ that we are saved and carried to the Father's bosom; therefore this union becomes the essential object of our prayer to the Son.

Union with His all-holy life, *because it is the model of our life which should be, like His, entirely consecrated* to the Father and to souls.

Christ is not only the pattern of our holiness but its very source. According to a saying of St. Paul, Christ has become, by the Father's will, our wisdom, justice, sanctification, redemption—in a word, our all.

It is thus the divine plan is realized in us. Our holiness is founded on the truth *of the eternal thoughts of God concerning us.*

10 *O Jesus*

1. SIGNIFICANCE OF THE NAME OF JESUS AND HOW THE INCARNATE WORD REALISED IT

When "the fulness of time" fixed by the eternal decrees had come, says St. Paul, "God sent His Son, made of a woman, that He might redeem them who were under the law." [1] It was then that "the grace of God our Saviour hath appeared to all men . . . that He might redeem us from all iniquity." [2]

Such is the essential mission of the Word Incarnate, signified by His very name. "Thou shalt call His name Jesus," says the Holy Gospel—Jesus: that is to say, Saviour—"for He shall save His people from their sins." [3] Therefore, adds St. Peter, "There is no other name under heaven given to men, whereby we must be saved"; [4] this name is unique as the Redemption wrought by it is universal.

And from what does Christ deliver us? From the yoke of sin. What did Jesus say at the time of His Passion when about to consummate His Sacrifice? *Nunc princeps hujus mundi ejicietur foras.* "Now shall the prince of this world

[1] Gal. IV, 4–5.
[2] Tit. II, 11 and 14.
[3] Matth. I, 21.
[4] Act. IV, 12.

be cast out. And I, if I be lifted up from the earth, will draw
all things to Myself." [5]

It was indeed by His immolation upon Mount Calvary
that our King destroyed Satan's reign. St. Paul tells us that
Christ, snatching from the devil's hands the sentence of our
eternal bondage, destroyed it, "fastening it to the cross":
*Delens quod adversum nos erat chirographum decreti . . .
affigens illud cruci.*[6] His death is the ransom of our deliverance. What is the song that resounds in the holy splendour
of heaven from the innumerable choir of the redeemed? To
Thee, O Lord, be all honour, praise and glory, for it is by
Thy immaculate Blood, O Divine Lamb, that we have become Thy Kingdom! [7]

Christ delivers us from eternal damnation in order to bring
us to the Father and reconcile us with Him. He is "the one
Mediator between God and men": *Unus mediator Dei et
hominum homo Christus Jesus.*[8]

Son of God, God Himself, enjoying all the prerogatives of
the Godhead, Christ, the Word Incarnate, can treat as an
equal with the Father. When about to shed His Blood as
the price of our redemption, He asks His Father that we
may be united to Him. *Volo, Pater;*[9] "I will, O Father."
The absolute character of this prayer shows the oneness of
the Divine Nature in which Jesus, as the Word, lives with
the Father and their common Spirit.

He is also Man: the human nature bestows on Jesus the
power of offering to the Father all the satisfaction that love
and justice demand: *Holocautomata . . . non tibi placuerunt, corpus autem aptasti mihi, ecce venio ut faciam, Deus,*

---

[5] Joan. XII, 31–32.
[6] Col. II, 14.
[7] Cf. Apoc. IV, 11; V, 9.
[8] I Tim. II, 5.
[9] Joan. XVII, 24.

voluntatem tuam.[10] The sacrifice of this Divine Victim appeases God, and makes Him propitious to us: *Pacificans per sanguinem crucis ejus.*[11] As Mediator, Christ Jesus is Pontiff; as Man-God, He forms the bridge over the gulf made by sin between heaven and earth. He binds us to God through His Manhood wherein "dwelleth all the fulness of the Godhead corporeally."

St. Paul also tells us that "God indeed was in Christ, reconciling the world to Himself": *Deus erat in Christo mundum reconcilians sibi,*[12] so that we "who some time were afar off, are made nigh by the blood of Christ": *Vos qui aliquando eratis longe, facti estis prope in sanguine Christi.*[13] At the foot of the Cross, justice appeased and peace restored give each other the kiss of reconciliation: *Justitia et pax osculatae sunt.*[14]

Rightly does the Apostle conclude by saying: *In quo [Christo] habemus fiduciam et accessum in confidentia per fidem ejus.*[15] Through faith in Christ we may indeed have the boldness to draw near to God with confidence. How can we lack confidence when Christ, the Son of the Father, having become our Surety and the Propitiation for our iniquities, has expiated and paid off all? Why should we not draw near to this High Priest, Who, like unto us in all things, sin excepted, chose to experience all our infirmities, to drink of the chalice of all our sufferings, to find, in the experience of sorrow, the power of compassionating our miseries more deeply?

> *Christ, the Ideal of the Monk,* Part I, chapter 2, section 2.

[10] Hebr. x, 5–7.
[11] Col. i, 20.
[12] II Cor. v, 19.
[13] Eph. ii, 13.
[14] Ps. xxxiv, 11.
[15] Eph. iii, 12.

2. THE INFINITE POWER OF THIS NAME WITH THE HEAVENLY FATHER

St. Paul has celebrated the divine glorification of Jesus, in magnificent terms, in his Epistle to the Ephesians. "What is the exceeding greatness of [God's] power towards us, who believe, according to the operation of the might of His power, which He wrought in Christ, raising Him up from the dead, and setting Him on His right hand in the heavenly places. Above all principality, and power, and virtue, and dominion, and every name that is named, not only in this world, but also in that which is to come. And He hath subjected all things under His feet, and hath made Him head over all the Church." [16]

Henceforward Christ Jesus is and remains for every soul the one source of salvation, of grace, of life, of benediction; henceforward, says the Apostle, His name has become so great, so resplendent, so glorious that every knee shall bow before it, in heaven, on earth, and in hell, and every tongue shall confess that Jesus lives and reigns "in the glory of God the Father." [17]

Consider how, in very truth, since that blessed hour, the countless multitudes of the elect in the Heavenly Jerusalem, of which the Lamb that was slain is the eternal light, cast their crowns at His feet, and fall down before Him; proclaiming in a chorus like the sound of many waters, that He is worthy of all honour and glory because their salvation and beatitude have their beginning and their end in Him. [18]

Since that hour, upon all the face of the earth, every day, during the holy action of the Mass, the praise and supplication of the Church ascend to Him Who alone can sustain

[16] Ephes. i, 19–22.
[17] Philipp. ii, 10–11.
[18] Apoc. *passim.*

her in her conflicts, because He is the one source of all
strength and of all virtue: "Thou Who sittest at the right
hand of the Father, have mercy on us. For Thou only art
holy, Thou only art the Lord: Thou only, O Jesus Christ
with the Holy Ghost, art most high in the glory of God the
Father": *Tu solus Altissimus, Jesu Christe . . . in gloria Dei
Patris.*

Again since that hour, the princes of darkness, from
whom the victorious Christ has snatched their prey for ever:
Captivam duxit captivitatem,[19] are filled with terror at the
very name of Jesus, and constrained to flee, and bow down
their pride before the victorious sign of the cross. . . .

I believe, Lord Jesus, but increase my faith! I have full
confidence in the reality and plenitude of Your merits, but
strengthen this confidence! I love You, O Jesus, You Who
have manifested Your love in all Your mysteries, *in finem,*
but make my love ever greater.

> *Christ in His Mysteries,* Part II, chapter
> 16, section 1; and Preliminary Confer-
> ence I, section 5.

3. DO ALL THINGS IN THE NAME OF JESUS

*This is St. Paul's expression (Coloss. III, 17) and means:
to accomplish all our actions, not only by being united to
Jesus through sanctifying grace, but also by inspiring ourselves with the feelings of Jesus, by acting as disciples of
Christ, or, as Dom Marmion, who often commented on this
text, says, in our capacity as members of the Mystical Body of
Christ, with the dispositions of the Heart of Jesus, according
to His designs, for the glory of the Father. (I Cor. XI, 31.)
The name of Jesus was given to Christ the eighth day fol-*

---

[19] Ephes. IV, 8.

lowing His birth. This day actually coincides with the be-
ginning of the civil year. Dom Marmion has left two texts
in his spiritual notes relating to this evangelical episode, one
on January 1, 1899, a few months before his departure for
Louvain, the other, revealing more profound thought, on
January 1, 1906.

January 1, 1899.

The Church begins the year with the name of Jesus. Let
us place this name on our lips and in our heart. Our efforts
are weak, but united with Him and His merits, they are of
great value in the eyes of God: By Him, and with Him and
in Him, be to the Father all honour and glory.

Merchants and business men draw up a balance sheet at
the end of the year in order to see their way for the future.
Let us do the same. *Expenditure:* 365 days. Physical and
moral forces. Sufferings. *Receipts:* God, and what is done
for God: "Their works follow them," all the rest is lost.

For this year, let us do all for God. However, our best
works are so imperfect! In the eyes of God, says Holy Scripture, all our justices are as filthy rags. The more light we
have the more we see our imperfections: "in many things
we all offend."

But Jesus Christ supplies for us. He is ours. He came
down from heaven for us and for our salvation. His riches
are ineffable and innumerable. He dwells in our heart. Let
us do all in union with Him. He has sanctified all our
actions. This is why St. Paul tells us to do all things in His
name: "Do all in the name of the Lord Jesus Christ."

January 1, 1906.

The Church imprints the adorable name of Jesus upon the
whole year: "Thou shalt call His name Jesus." I feel a great

desire to imprint this blessed name upon my whole being, upon all my actions, that I "may deserve to abound in good works in the name of the Beloved Son."

I see more and more that the Father beholds all in His Son, loves all in His Son; for He is altogether His. We are pleasing in His eyes in so far as He sees us in His Son: "He that abideth in Me, and I in him, the same beareth much fruit." A small thing done in the name of Jesus is greater in God's eyes than the most remarkable things done in our own name.

I will strive to disappear so that Jesus may live and act in me: "He must increase, but I must decrease." Saint Paul was filled with this spirit: "I count all things to be but loss"— the actions done in our own name—"that I may gain Christ: and may be found in Him, not having my justice, which is of the law, but that which is of the faith of Christ Jesus." This is why he tells us: "All whatsoever you do in word or in work, do all in the name of the Lord Jesus Christ, giving thanks to God and the Father by Him." That is to say, to act as members of Christ, in the same dispositions, according to His designs.

> *Abbot Columba Marmion: A Master of the Spiritual Life,* chapter 8.

October 21, 1908.

Try, my dear daughter, to do each action with great love, and in the name—not of Helen [her name before she entered the religious life]—but in the name of Jesus . . . God bless you and make you *all His own.*

> *Union with God,* chapter 2, section 1.

11 *Unite Us to Thee*

*The first petition which Dom Marmion makes to Christ
is for union with Him. The degree of our holiness is measured by our union with Christ, the model and source of all
holiness. This is the essential condition under which we are
borne to the Father's bosom.*

1. SANCTIFYING GRACE, THE PRINCIPLE OF UNION WITH JESUS

The Last Supper is over. Our Divine Saviour leaves the
Cenacle with His disciples to go to the Mount of Olives. On
the way, outside Jerusalem, He passes over a little hill covered with vineyards. In pointing them out to His Apostles
He says: "I am the Vine; you the branches: he that abideth
in Me, and I in him, the same beareth much fruit: for without Me you can do nothing. . . . As the branch cannot bear
fruit of itself unless it abide in the vine, so neither can you,
unless you abide in me." In the same way as the branch
cannot bear fruit unless it remains united to the trunk, so is
it with us, if we do not remain united to Christ by grace.

Grace is the sap that rises from the root to the branches.
It is not the root or the trunk that bears fruit: it is the branch;
but the branch united by the trunk to the root, and drawing
from the root the sap that nourishes. Break off the branch,

separate it from the trunk, and, no longer receiving the sap, it withers and becomes dead wood, incapable of producing the least fruit.

It is the same with the soul that does not possess grace: it is not united to Christ, it does not draw from Him the sap of sanctifying grace which would make it supernaturally living and fruitful. Do not forget that Christ alone is the source of our spiritual life; all our activity, all our existence have no value for eternal life unless we are united to Christ by grace. If we are not, it is in vain that we exert and spend ourselves, and accomplish the most brilliant actions in the sight of men; in God's sight all this activity is devoid of supernatural profit and without merit for eternal life.

Christ, the Life of the Soul, Part II, chapter 5, section 2.

St. Paul has thrown great light on this truth. This is what he says: "If I speak with the tongues of men and of angels, and have not charity, I am become as sounding brass or a tinkling cymbal. And if I should have prophecy, and should know all mysteries, and all knowledge, and if I should have all faith, so that I could remove mountains, and have not charity, I am nothing. And if I should distribute all my goods to feed the poor, and if I should deliver my body to be burned, and have not charity, it profiteth me nothing." In other words, the most extraordinary gifts, the highest talents, the most generous undertakings, the most splendid actions, the most strenuous efforts, the greatest sufferings, are of no merit for eternal life without charity, that is to say, without that supreme love of the soul for God, considered as He is in Himself, that supernatural love which is born of sanctifying grace, as the flower arises from its stem.

Let us then refer all our life to God, our Last End and Eternal Beatitude: the charity of God that we possess with

sanctifying grace must be the mainspring of all our activity.
When we possess Divine grace within us, we fulfil the wish
of Our Lord: we "abide in Him," *manete in me,* and He
"abides in us," *et ego in vobis;* He abides with the Father
and the Holy Spirit: *Ad eum veniemus et mansionem apud
eum faciemus.* The Holy Trinity, dwelling truly within us
as in a temple, does not remain inactive, but unceasingly
sustains us so that our soul may exercise its supernatural
activity.

> *Christ, the Life of the Soul,* Part II,
> chapter 5, section 2. Cf. *Christ in His
> Mysteries,* Part II, chapter 19, section 3.

2. WHEN WE CONTEMPLATE CHRIST WITH FAITH HE UNITES HIMSELF TO US

Christ still acts in us by the contact we have with Him in
faith.

In order to understand this, let us read again an episode
related by St. Luke. In one of His apostolic journeys, Our
Divine Saviour is surrounded and pressed by the multitude.
A sick woman, desiring to be healed, approaches Him, and,
full of confidence, touches the hem of His garment. Immediately, Our Lord asks those who surround Him: "Who is
it that touched Me?" And Peter answers: "Master, the multitude throng and press Thee, and dost Thou say, Who
touched Me?" But Jesus insists: "Somebody hath touched
Me; for I know that virtue is gone out from Me." And at
that very instant the woman was healed: and this, on account of her faith: *Fides tua te salvam fecit.*

It is certain that those who lived in Judea with Christ and
had faith in Him, received an abundant share in those graces
which He merited for all men; the Gospel assures us of this.
Christ had not only, as I have shown you, power to cure

corporal infirmities, but also the power to sanctify souls. See for example how He sanctified the woman of Samaria who, after having spoken with Him, believed Him to be the Messias; how He purified Magdalen who, considering Him to be a prophet, one sent by God, came to pour her perfumes over His sacred feet. The contact of the Son of God becomes, for the souls who have faith in Him, the source of life: *Fides tua te salvam fecit.* Consider how, during His Passion, by one look of His, He gives to Peter, who has thrice denied Him, the grace of repentance; consider at His death, the good thief; he recognizes Jesus as the Son of God, since he asks Him for a place in His kingdom; and immediately the Saviour, on the point of expiring, grants him the remission of his crimes: "To-day thou shalt be with Me in Paradise."

We know this, we are so convinced of it that sometimes we say: "Oh, if it had been given to me to live with Our Lord in Judea, to have followed Him like the Apostles, to have approached Him during His life, and to have been present at His death, I should have been so surely sanctified!" And yet, however, hear what Jesus says: "Blessed are they that have not seen, and have believed." BEATI *qui non viderunt et crediderunt.*[1]

Does not this make us understand that contact with Him by faith alone is still more efficacious, and more advantageous to us? Let us then believe in these words of Our Divine Master: His words are "spirit and life":[2] let us be persuaded that the power and virtue of His holy humanity are the same for us as for His contemporaries; for Christ lives always: *Christus heri, et* HODIE, *ipse et in saecula.*

Christ, the Life of the Soul, Part I, chapter 5, section 4.

[1] Joan. xx, 29.
[2] *Ibid.,* vi, 64.

Dominica in Albis, 1900.

Everything to-day speaks to us of faith: "Blessed are they that have not seen, and have believed." "It is the foundation and root of all justification." [3] It is by a living faith, the conviction of the Divinity of Jesus Christ that we live the divine life.

1. It is by faith that this divine life begins: Those who believe in His name . . . *are born of God.*[4] "Whatsoever is born of God, overcometh the world. . . . Who is he that overcometh the world, but he that believeth that Jesus is the Son of God?" This intimate conviction of the Divinity of Jesus Christ makes us throw ourselves at His feet like the man born blind: "The just man liveth by faith." "He that believeth in Me, although he be dead, shall live."

2. By this faith, we identify ourselves in some way with Jesus Christ:

(a) *In our thoughts:* "He that believeth in the Son of God, hath the testimony of God in Himself." We have the same thoughts as those of Jesus Christ: "He who is joined to the Lord is one spirit" with Him.

(b) *In our desires:* "Let this mind be in you, which was also in Christ Jesus."

(c) *In our words:* "If any speak let him speak as the words of God." Christ becomes the mainspring of all our [projects]: "That Christ may dwell BY FAITH in your hearts."

(d) *In our actions:* "All whatsoever you do in word or in work, do all in the name of the Lord Jesus Christ, giving thanks to God and the Father by Him."

Then comes to pass the: "I live, now not I; but Christ

[3] Council of Trent.
[4] John 1, 12–13.

liveth in me . . . I live *in the faith* of the Son of God, Who
loved me, and delivered Himself for me."

Abbot Columba Marmion: A Master of
the Spiritual Life, chapter 8.

3. LOVE IS THE MEASURE OF UNION

October 4, 1900.

Do all your actions as far as possible out of *pure love of*
God, and in union with the perfect dispositions of the Sacred
Heart of Jesus.

November 21, 1900.

I want you, my child, to apply yourself with order and
attention to act *solely* out of love for God in all that you do.
Each action done out of pure love is an act of pure love of
God.

But where are we to find this pure love? We have it
neither of ourselves, nor in ourselves. We shall find it in the
Sacred Heart of Jesus Which is an infinite furnace of love,
and as you receive this Sacred Heart so often in Holy Communion, you have only to place your heart in the centre of
this Divine Heart in order to love with Its love. Oh yes, my
child, the Sacred Heart is an *infinite* treasury of Divine love,
and this Heart *is ours, It abides always in us.* "He that eateth
My flesh, and drinketh My blood, abideth in Me, and I in
him." Unite yourself then very often with the Sacred Heart,
and love with It and by It.

This is *a great secret.* Yes, Jesus came upon this earth for
that alone.

March 28, 1904.

On rising, in union with the Sacred Heart of Jesus, Whose
first movement was an impulse of love by which He offered

Himself without reserve to His Father, say, *Ecce venio ut faciam Deus voluntatem tuam.* "Behold, I come to do Thy will, O God."

On beginning the day, on entering the oratory, *unite* your heart closely with the Heart of Jesus. This Heart was a glowing centre of love, for Jesus loved His Father *with all His Heart.*

This love of your heart ought to shine out in the love *of your whole soul,* by employing your soul and all its faculties in prayer and the Divine Praise. Jesus loved His Father with all His Soul.

During the day, this love of your heart ought also to shine out in the work of obedience done *with all your strength.* Jesus worked for love of His Father with all His strength.

Finally, *throughout* the day, let your love urge you to occupy your mind with the thought of God, with studying His perfections, and with all that relates to His service. That is loving God *with all one's mind.* The Spirit of Jesus was ever plunged in the contemplation of His Father.

During the day, be faithful to "direct" your different actions according to the prescriptions of your holy Rule.

Often go back, by a spiritual Communion, to that centre of love which is the Sacred Heart of Jesus. All *our* life ought to be passed in this sweet intercourse with *the Spouse of our souls, Jesus.*

1907 (date not mentioned).

Your union with Our Lord depends much more on Him than on you. He has said, *Pater non reliquit me solum quia quae placita sunt ei facio semper,* "My Father hath not left me alone: for I do always the things that please Him." Meditate a little on these words, my dear child. Look at God in all that you do, and do all for love—prayer, work, school, recreation, etc. Then Our Lord will come to you, "If any one love Me, my Father will love him, and We will come to him, and make Our abode with him."

This union with Our Lord is not incompatible with our occupations. The more I see of souls, the more I am assured that exterior circumstances cannot hurt this union.

Union with God, chapter 2, section 4.

12 *In Thy All-holy Life*

We ask to be united to Jesus in His all-holy life because He is the model of all holiness and because we are predestined by the Father to conform to the image of His wellbeloved Son. We must first of all contemplate this life.

1. AS REVEALED IN THE GOSPELS

Everything in Jesus is holy. He Himself is the Saint of saints: *Tu solus sanctus,* we sing at Mass in the *Gloria.* And all His mysteries are holy. His birth is holy: *Quod nascetur ex te sanctum;* all His life is holy; He does "always the things that please" His Father; and none can convince Him of sin. His Passion is holy; true it is that He dies for the sins of men, but yet the Victim is sinless, He is the spotless Lamb. The High Priest Who immolates Himself is "holy, innocent, undefiled, separated from sinners." And the Church calls His resurrection "holy."

Christ in His Mysteries, Part II, chapter 15, introduction.

The knowledge of Jesus and of His states is to be derived first of all from the Gospel.

These sacred pages, inspired by the Holy Spirit, describe

the life of Jesus upon earth and contain His teachings. It is
sufficient for us to read these pages, so simple and so sublime—but to read them with faith—in order to see and hear
Christ Himself. The soul who, in prayer, often has recourse
to this unrivalled book, comes little by little to the knowledge of Jesus and of His mysteries, penetrates into the secrets
of His Sacred Heart and understands that magnificent revelation of God to the world which is Jesus: *Qui videt me,
videt et Patrem.* For this book is inspired; light and power
go out from it to enlighten and strengthen souls that are upright and sincere. Happy are they who open it every day!
They drink at the very well-spring of living waters.

Christ in His Mysteries, Preliminary
Conference II, section 1.

Jesus is perfect God, the sole-begotten Son of God: *Deum
de Deo;* but He is also perfect Man; He belongs authentically to our race. You know that from His two-fold nature
flows a two-fold activity; a divine activity, and a human activity, but these two activities are not confounded, any more
than the two natures are confounded, although ineffably
united in one and the same Person.

Christ is the revelation of God adapted to our weakness;
He is the manifestation of God under a human form. "He
that seeth Me," Christ has said, "seeth the Father also": *Qui
videt me, videt et Patrem.*[1] He is God living amongst us and
showing us by this tangible human life how we ought to
live in order to please our Father in Heaven.

All that Jesus accomplished was perfect, not only because
of the love wherewith He accomplished it, but also in the
manner He brought it to fruition; and all that Jesus did,
even His least actions, were the actions of a God and infinitely pleasing to His Father: they are consequently for us

[1] Joan. XIV, 9.

examples to be followed, models of perfection: *Exemplum dedi vobis ut quemadmodum ego feci ita et vos faciatis.*[2] In imitating Christ Jesus, we are sure of being, like Him, although under a different title, pleasing to His Father. "The life of Christ," said a holy monk who spoke from experience, "is an excellent book for the learned and the ignorant, the perfect and the imperfect, who desire to please God. He who reads it carefully and frequently, attains high wisdom, and easily obtains . . . spiritual light, peace and quietness of conscience, and a firm confidence in God in sincere love." [3]

Let us then contemplate in the Gospel the example of Jesus: it is the norm of all human sanctity. If we remain united to Jesus by faith in His doctrine, by the imitation of His virtues, especially His religious virtues, we shall surely attain to God. It is true that there is an infinite distance between God and us; God is the Creator, and we are creatures, the last rung on the ladder of intellectual creation; God is spirit, we are spirit and matter; God is unchanging, we are ever subject to change; but with Christ we can bridge this distance and establish ourselves in the immutable, because, in Jesus, God and the creature meet in an ineffable and indissoluble union. In Christ we find God.

For it is to the Father that Jesus leads us. Listen to what He says on leaving His disciples: "I ascend to My Father and to your Father, to My God and to your God"; the Word has come down from Heaven to take upon Himself our flesh and to redeem us; His work accomplished, He ascends to Heaven, but He does not ascend alone; He virtually takes with Him all who believe in Him. And why? In order that —in Him again—the union of all with the Father should be accomplished: *Ego in eis et tu in me.* Is not this Jesus' supreme prayer to His Father? "That I may be in them, O

[2] *Ibid.,* XIII, 15.
[3] Blosius, *The Mirror of the Soul,* ch. x, 7.

Father—by My grace—as Thou in Me, that they may contemplate, in the Divinity, the glory which Thou hast given
Me."

Christ, the Ideal of the Monk, Part I,
chapter 2, section 1.

2. AS REPRESENTED BY THE CHURCH, THE SPOUSE OF CHRIST, IN HER LITURGY

Christ is God's great Revelation; He is God translated to
our souls. Firstly Jesus makes the divine secrets known to
us; afterwards, He shows us how a God lives amongst men
in order to teach them how to live perfectly; He is the pur-
est and most living manifestation of the divine perfections.
When Philip the Apostle asked Our Lord to show him the
Father, what reply did Christ make? "Who sees Me, sees the
Father"; He and the Father are one: *Ego et Pater unum
sumus.* He is the image of the invisible God. Thus, to be
"filled with the science of God" we need only look upon the
Person of Our Lord, listen to His words, contemplate His
mysteries.

Now, where shall we find the recital of Christ's doings
and sayings? I have told you, in the Gospel.

The Gospel, however, is admirably set out, enframed and
commented upon in the Church's liturgy. From Advent to
Pentecost, the Church unfolds before our gaze the whole life
of Her Divine Spouse, not merely as it is found in the Gos-
pels, but illustrated, if I presume to say so, by the prophecies,
the letters of St. Paul, the commentary of the holy Doctors.
The whole existence of Christ, integral and living, is re-
enacted before our eyes; the Church offers for our contemplation, one by one, under their particular aspect of
splendour, in characteristic relief and according to their sequence, all the mysteries of Jesus; the Church presents,
therein, in its appropriate place, all that He said, all that He

did, all that He realized in His Person, all that He willed
for us. Nowhere else, as in the liturgy, can we become so
well acquainted with the gestures of Jesus Christ, the words
which fell from His lips, the feelings of His Divine Heart;
it is the Gospel relived at each stage of the earthly life of
Christ, Man-God, Saviour of the world, head of His Mystical
Body, and bringing with Him the virtue and grace of all His
mysteries, for our souls' benefit. Nowhere, as in the liturgy,
does there exist such a complete, simple, orderly and deep
exposition of all the marvels which God has performed for
our sanctification and salvation; it is both the most perfect
expression of Revelation and that most adapted to our souls'
needs, it is an exposition which appeals both to the eyes of
the body and of the imagination and which moves the attentive soul to its depths.

The liturgical cycle is an incomparable source of supernatural light. Moreover—and this is an essential truth for our
sanctification—we may derive from it the special fruit which
Our Lord willed to attach to each of His mysteries when, as
our head, He lived with them here below.

For although it is always the same Saviour, the same
Jesus, pursuing the same work of our sanctification, each
mystery, however, is a fresh manifestation of Christ for us;
each has its special beauty, its particular splendour, as likewise its own grace. The grace that flows for us from the
Feast of the Nativity has not the same character as that
which the celebration of the Passion brings us; we ought to
rejoice at Christmas, to feel sorrow for our sins when we
contemplate the unspeakable sufferings whereby Christ expiated them. In the same way, the inward joy that floods
our souls at Easter arises from another source and has another splendour than that which thrills us when we celebrate
the coming of our Saviour upon earth.

It is said of Jesus that when He was upon earth "virtue

went out from Him, and healed all": *Virtus de illo exibat et sanabat omnes.* Christ Jesus is ever the same; if, with faith, we contemplate His mysteries, either in the Gospel or in the liturgy that the Church sets before us, the grace that He merited for us when He lived these mysteries is produced within us. In this contemplation we see how Jesus, our Exemplar, practised virtue; we share the particular dispositions of His Divine Heart in each of these states; but above all we find in Him the special graces that He then merited for us.

The mysteries of Jesus are states of His Sacred Humanity; all His graces came from His Divinity in order to be communicated to His Humanity, and, through His Humanity, to each member of His Mystical Body: *Secundum mensuram donationis Christi.* In taking a human nature from our race, the Word, so to speak, espoused all humanity to Himself, and every soul shares—in a measure known to God, and proportioned, in what regards ourselves, to the degree of our faith—in the grace that inundates Christ's blessed soul.

Following Christ Jesus in this manner in all His mysteries, uniting ourselves to Him, we share, little by little, but surely, and each time more fully and deeply, in His Divinity and in His Divine life. According to the beautiful words of St. Augustine, that which was formerly brought to pass in a divine reality, is spiritually received in fervent souls by the repeated celebration of these mysteries: *Quod semel factum in rebus veritas indicat, hoc saepius celebrandum in cordibus piis solemnitas renovat.*

While, with the eyes of faith and the love that yearns to give itself, we contemplate Christ's mysteries, the Holy Spirit, Who is the Spirit of Christ, acts within our inmost soul and fashions it, by His sovereignly efficacious touches, in such a way as to reproduce within it, as by a sacramental virtue, the traits of the Divine Model.

This is why the contemplation of the mysteries of Jesus is

so fruitful in itself; this is why the essentially supernatural contact with the states of her Spouse, into which the Church, guided by the Holy Spirit, places us in the liturgy is so vital for us. There is no surer way nor more infallible means for making us one with Christ.

Christ in His Mysteries, Preliminary
Conference II, sections 1 and 2.

3. WHOSE FULNESS IS BEQUEATHED TO US IN EUCHARISTIC COMMUNION

The contemplation of the mysteries of Jesus constitutes one of the elements of our transfiguration into Him; I have already said that when, by a living faith, we place ourselves in contact with Him, Christ produces in us, by the ever efficacious virtue of His holy Humanity united to the Word, that resemblance which is the sign of our predestination.

If that be true of the simple contemplation of His mysteries, how much deeper and more extensive will the action of Jesus be in this domain when He dwells in our souls by sacramental Communion! This union is the greatest and most intimate that we can have here below with Christ, the union that takes place between the bread and the one who takes it. Christ gives Himself to be our Food, but, inversely to what takes place as to corporal food, it is we who are assimilated to Him. Christ becomes our life.

The first property of the manna was to nourish. The specific grace belonging to the Eucharist is to maintain divine life in the soul, by making us participate in the life of Christ.

But like the manna which "was turned to what every man liked," so the life that Christ gives us by Communion, is all His life that passes into our souls to be the exemplar and the form of ours, to produce within us the divers affections of the Heart of Jesus, to make us imitate all the virtues He practised in His states, and to shed within us the special grace which He merited for us when living His mysteries.

Doubtless we must never forget that under the Eucharistic species is found only the substance of the *glorious* body of Jesus, such as it is at present in heaven, and not such as it was, for example, in the crib of Bethlehem.

But when the Father looks upon His Son Jesus in the heavenly splendours, what does He behold in Him? He sees the One Who lived thirty-three years upon earth for us, He beholds all the mysteries that this mortal life contained, the satisfactions and the merits whereof these mysteries were the source; He beholds the glory that this Son gave Him in living each of them. In each of them too He beholds ever the same Son in Whom He was well pleased, although now Christ Jesus sits at His right hand only in His glorious state.

In the same way, it is Jesus born of Mary Whom we receive, Jesus, Who dwelt at Nazareth, Who preached to the Jews of Palestine; it is the Good Samaritan; it is He Who healed the sick, delivered Magdalen from the devil, and raised Lazarus from the dead; it is He Who, wearied, slept in the ship; it is He Who was crushed by anguish; it is He Who was crucified upon Calvary; it is the glorious Jesus risen from the sepulchre, it is the mysterious Pilgrim of Emmaus, Who made Himself known "in the breaking of bread";[4] it is He Who ascended to Heaven to the Father's right hand; it is the eternal High Priest, ever living, Who never ceases to pray for us.

All these states of the life of Jesus are, in substance, given to us in Communion, with their properties, their spirit, their merits and their virtue: under the diversity of states, and the variety of mysteries, is perpetuated the identity of the Person Who lived them and now lives eternally in Heaven.

When, therefore, we receive Christ at the Holy Table, we may contemplate Him and converse with Him in any of His

---

[4] Luc. XXIV, 35.

mysteries; although He is now in His glorious state, we find
in Him the One Who has lived for us and merited for us
the grace that these mysteries contain; dwelling in us, Christ
communicates this grace to us in order to effect little by
little that transformation of our life into Him, which is the
effect proper to the sacrament. It is enough, in order to
understand this truth, to read the "secrets" and "post-com-
munions" of the Mass for the different feasts of our Saviour.
The object of these prayers, which hold a special rank among
those of the Eucharistic Sacrifice, are diversified according
to the virtue of the mysteries celebrated.

We can, for example, unite ourselves to Jesus as living *in
sinu Patris*,[5] equal to His Father, God like Him; the One
Whom we adore within us, we adore as the Word co-eternal
with the Father, the very Son of God, the object of His
Father's good pleasure: Yes, I adore Thee within Me, O Divine Word; by the intimate union that I have at this moment with Thee, grant me to be also with Thee *in sinu
Patris,* now by faith, later in the eternal reality, that I may
live by the very life of God, which is Thy life.

We can adore Him, the Incarnate Word, as Our Lady did
when He lived in her before being manifested to the world.
Only in heaven shall we know with what reverence and love
the Blessed Virgin inwardly adored the Son of God Who,
through her, took our flesh.

Again we can adore Him within ourselves as we would
have adored Him nineteen centuries ago in the stable-cave
of Bethlehem with the shepherds and Magi; He then communicates to us the grace of imitating the special virtues of
humility, poverty and detachment, that we contemplate in
Him in this state of His hidden life.

If we desire, He will be within us the agonising Saviour,
Who, by His wonderful submission to His Father's good

[5] Joan. I, 18.

pleasure obtains for us the grace to bear our daily crosses; He will be the Divine Risen Lord Who grants us to detach ourselves from all that is earthly, to "live unto God" more generously and fully; He will be in us the Victor Who gloriously ascends into heaven and draws us after Him that we may already dwell there by faith, hope and holy desire.

Christ thus contemplated and received, is Christ living His mysteries over again in us; this contemplation is the life of Christ being instilled into ours, and, with all its own beauties, its particular merits and special graces substituting itself for our life: *Deserviens uniuscujusque voluntati.*

Christ in His Mysteries, Part II, chapter 18, section 3.

13 *Thy Life Wholly Consecrated to Thy Holy Father*

The life of Jesus is holy because it is, through love, entirely referred to the Father, devoted to the will and glory of the Father.

1. FROM THE FIRST MOMENT OF THE INCARNATION

In the Trinity, as you know, God the Father has an attribute proper to Himself which is distinctive from His Person: He is the First Principle, proceeding from none: *Principium sine principio.* This is true only of the Father; the Son is a principle, yes; He Himself has told us so: [*Ego*] *principium qui et loquor vobis,* only this is relatively to us; with the Father and the Holy Spirit, He is the fount of all life for every creature. But when we speak of the Three Divine Persons, the Father alone is the Principle proceeding from no other Person; from Him proceeds the Son; and, from the Father and the Son, proceeds the Holy Spirit. This attribute is personal to the Father.

The Son, even as God, holds everything from the Father: *Omnia quae dedisti mihi abs te sunt.* The Son, in beholding His Father, can say to Him that all that He is, all that He has, all that He knows, is from His Father because He pro-

116

ceeds from Him, without there being between the First and
Second Person, either inequality, or inferiority, or succession
of time. This is one side of the mystery.

This sublime truth is especially revealed to us in the Gospel of St. John where Our Lord constantly protests that He
holds everything from His Father.

Christ, the Ideal of the Monk, Part II,
chapter 10, section 4.

It is true that Jesus is God, the true God come forth from
God, the Light arising from the Uncreated Light,[1] the Son
of the Living God, equal to the Father. But He is likewise
man; He is authentically one of us, through His human
nature. And although this human nature is united in an indissoluble way to the Divine Person of the Word, although
the holy soul of Jesus has ceaselessly enjoyed the delights of
the Beatific Vision, although it has been drawn into the divine current which necessarily bears the Son towards the
Father, it remains true to say that Christ's human activity,
which was derived from His human faculties as from its immediate sources, was sovereignly free.

It is in the exercise of this free activity that we can find
in Jesus that which we call the "seeking after God." What
are the innermost aspirations of His soul, those to which He
Himself refers all His mission, and in which He sums up all
His life?

St. Paul tells us; he raises for us a corner of the veil to
enable us to penetrate into the Holy of Holies. He tells us
that the first throb of the soul of Jesus on entering into this
world was one of infinite intensity towards His Father: *Ingrediens mundum, dicit: . . . Ecce venio, in capite libri
scriptum est de me: ut faciam, Deus, voluntatem tuam.*[2]

[1] *Credo* of the Mass.
[2] Hebr. x, 5–7.

And we see Christ Jesus, like a giant, rejoice to run the way, in the pursuit of the glory of His Father. This is His primal disposition. Let us hear how, in the Gospel, He clearly tells us so. "I seek not My own will, but the will of Him that sent Me." [3] To the Jews, He proves that He comes from God, that His doctrine is divine, because He seeks the glory of Him that sent Him. He seeks it to such a degree that He has no solicitude for His own. He has ever these words upon His lips: "My Father"; His whole life is but the magnificent echo of this cry: *Abba [Pater]*. All for Him is summed up in seeking the will and the glory of His Father.

And what constancy in this search! He Himself declares to us that He never deviated from it: "I do always the things that please [My Father]": *Quae placita sunt ei facio semper;* at the supreme hour of His last farewell, at the moment when about to deliver Himself up to death, He tells us that all the mission He had received from His Father was accomplished.

Christ, the Ideal of the Monk, Part I,
chapter 1, section 5.

The Heart of Christ is an immense furnace of love. The great love of Christ is that which He bears towards His Father. All His life can be summed up in these words: "I do always the things that please My Father."

Let us meditate these words in our prayer; only thus shall we be able to penetrate a little into their secret. This unspeakable love, this tending of the Soul of Christ towards His Father is the necessary consequence of His hypostatic union. The Son is altogether *ad Patrem,* as the theologians say: this is, if I may thus express it, His essence: the holy Humanity is carried along by this divine current; having become, by the Incarnation, the Humanity of the Son of God, it therefore belongs entirely to the Father. The funda-

[3] Joan. v, 30.

mental disposition, the primary and habitual sentiment of
the Soul of Christ is necessarily this: I live for My Father, "I
love My Father." It is because He loves His Father that Jesus
gives Himself up to all He wills.

Christ, the Life of the Soul, Part I, chapter 2, section 3.

Our Lord gave His disciples the infallible criterion of
love. "If you keep My commandments, you shall abide in
My love." And He at once gives an example: "As I also
have kept My Father's commandments, and do abide in His
love." Jesus has ever remained in the love of the Father, because He has ever done His will. St. Paul expressly declares
that the first movement of the Word-made-Flesh was a
movement of love: "Behold I come that I should do Thy
will, O God." In this first glance of His earthly existence,
the soul of Jesus saw the whole succession of His mysteries,
the humiliations, the fatigues, the sufferings of which they
were formed; and, by an act of love, He accepted to fulfil
all these things.

This movement of love towards His Father has never
ceased. Our Lord could say: *Quae placita sunt ei facio semper,* "I do always the things that please Him." He fulfils
everything to the last iota; He accepts all that His Father
requires of Him even to the bitter chalice of His agony: *Non
mea voluntas, sed tua fiat;* even to the ignominious death
of the Cross, *Ut cognoscat mundus quia diligo Patrem, sic
facio.* And when all is consummated, the last beat of His
Heart and His last thought are for the Father: "Father, into
Thy hands, I commend My spirit."

The love of Jesus for His Father underlies all His states
and explains all His mysteries.

Christ in His Mysteries, Part I, chapter
3, section 2.

2. IT IS IN HIS PASSION ESPECIALLY THAT THE LOVE OF JESUS FOR HIS FATHER SHINES FORTH

The first act of the holy soul of Jesus in the Incarnation was to dart through the infinite space that separates the created from the divine. Resting in the Bosom of the Father, His soul contemplates face to face His adorable perfections. We cannot picture to ourselves that this contemplation could be, if I may so express myself, only speculative. Far from it. As the Word, Christ loves His Father, in very deed, with an infinite love surpassing all comprehension. But the Humanity of Jesus is drawn into this impetuous current of uncreated love and the Heart of Christ burns with the most perfect love that could ever exist. A member of the human race through His Incarnation, Christ falls moreover under the great precept: "Thou shalt love the Lord thy God, with thy whole heart, and with thy whole soul, and with thy whole mind, and with thy whole strength." Jesus has perfectly fulfilled this commandment. From His first entering into the world, He yielded Himself up through love: *Ecce venio . . . Deus meus volui et legem tuam in medio cordis mei.* I have placed, O Father, Thy law, Thy will "in the midst of My Heart." His whole existence is summed up in love for the Father. . . .

The sorrows and the ignominies of the Passion, even death itself, does not diminish this burning fervour of the Heart of Jesus for His Father's glory; quite the contrary. It is because in all things He seeks the will of the Father, as manifested by the Scriptures, that He delivers Himself, out of love, to the torments of the Cross: *Ut impleantur Scripturae.* The waters of a river do not rush towards the ocean with more majestic impetuosity than the soul of Jesus tended inwardly towards the abyss of sufferings wherein the Passion was to plunge Him. "That the world may know that I love

the Father; and as the Father hath given Me commandment,
so do I": *Et sicut mandatum dedit mihi Pater, sic facio.*

> *Christ, the Ideal of the Monk,* Part II,
> chapter 12, section 9; and Part I, chapter
> 1, section 5.

Behold Him in agony. During three hours, lassitude, sadness, fear, a torrent of agonies inundates His soul, and over-
whelms it to such a degree that blood oozes from His sacred
veins. What an abyss of suffering this agony caused! What
does Jesus say to His Father? "Father, if Thou wilt, remove
this chalice from Me."

Did Jesus no longer accept His Father's will? Certainly
He accepted it. This prayer is but the cry of the sensitivity
of poor human nature crushed by disgust and suffering; at
this moment He is above all *vir sciens infirmitatem,* "a man
acquainted with infirmity." Our Lord feels the terrible
weight of agony pressing on His shoulders; He wishes us
to know this, and that is why He said this prayer.

Listen however to what He adds immediately: "Neverthe-
less, Thy will, not Mine, be done." Here is love's triumph.
Because He loves His Father, He places His Father's will
above all things and He accepts every suffering. Notice that
the Father could have, had He so willed, in His eternal designs, lessened the sufferings of Our Lord and changed the
circumstances of His death; He did not will it. In His justice, He determined that, to save the world, Christ should
submit to every suffering. Did this decree diminish the love
of Jesus? Certainly not; He did not say: "My Father could
have arranged things otherwise"; no, He fully accepts all His
Father wishes; *Non mea voluntas sed tua fiat;* "Thy will,
not Mine, be done."

He will henceforth complete the sacrifice. Some moments
after His agony, at the time of His arrest when St. Peter

wishes to defend Him and strikes with his sword one of
those who come to seize his Master, what does the Saviour
say instantly? "The chalice which My Father hath given Me,
shall I not drink it?"; *Calicem quem dedit mihi Pater, non
bibam illum?*

He is presently arrested as a malefactor; He could deliver
Himself from His enemies who at a single word from Him
are thrown to the ground; He could, if He so willed, ask
His Father Who would have given Him "more than twelve
legions of Angels," but He desires only that His Father's
will, as manifested by the Scriptures, shall be fulfilled to the
letter: *Sed ut adimpleantur Scripturae,* and therefore He
gives Himself up to His mortal foes. He obeys Pilate because,
although a pagan, the Roman governor represents the authority from above. He obeys His executioners; at the moment of expiring, in order to fulfil a prophecy, He cries out:
"I thirst": *Postea, sciens Jesus quia omnia consummata sunt,
UT consummaretur Scriptura dixit: Sitio.* He does not die
until all has been consummated by a perfect obedience:
*Dixit: consummatum est, et inclinato capite, tradidit spiri-
tum.* The *Consummatum est* is the most true and adequate
expression of His whole life of obedience. It echoes the *Ecce
venio* of the moment of His Incarnation. These two phrases
are cries of obedience; the whole earthly existence of Christ
turns around the axis based on these two poles.

> *Christ, the Ideal of the Monk,* Part II,
> chapter 12, section 1 and *passim.*

3. FOLLOWING THE EXAMPLE OF JESUS, THE SON OF GOD, ALL
OUR LIFE SHOULD BE CONSECRATED, IN LOVE, TO OUR HEAVENLY
FATHER

Our holiness is nothing but the full surrender of the
whole of ourselves through love, to the will of the Most
High. Now His will is essentially that we should be His

worthy children. He has predestined us "to be made conformable to the image of His Son": *Praedestinavit* [*nos*]
conformes fieri imaginis Filii sui.[4] All that God enjoins upon
us and asks of us, all that Christ counsels us, has no other
end than to give us the opportunity of showing that we are
God's children and the brethren of Jesus; and when we attain this ideal in everything, not only in our thoughts and
actions, but even in the motives from which we act, then we
reach perfection.

Perfection can indeed be resumed in this inward disposition of the soul seeking to please the Heavenly Father by
living habitually and totally in the spirit of its supernatural
adoption.

Perfection has love for its habitual motive; it embraces the
entire life, that is to say, it makes one think, will, love, hate
and act, not only according to the views of nature vitiated
by original sin, nor yet merely according to nature in so far
as it is upright and moral (although this is certainly always
requisite), but in the spirit of this divine "superaddition"
infused by God: to wit, grace which makes us His children
and friends.

He alone is perfect who lives *habitually* and *totally* according to grace; it is a failing, an imperfection, for a man
adopted as a child of God to withdraw any one of his acts
from the influence of grace and from charity which accom-
panies grace. Jesus has given us the watchword of Christian
perfection: "I must be about My Father's business": *In his
quae Patris mei sunt* OPORTET *me esse.*[5]

The result of this disposition is to render all the actions of
a soul, thus fully living according to the meaning of its
supernatural adoption, pleasing to God, because they are all
rooted in charity.

[4] Rom. VIII, 29.
[5] Luc. II, 49.

Let us listen to St. Paul. "Walk worthy of God," he writes, "in all things pleasing": *Ut ambuletis digne Deo per omnia placentes.*[6] The Apostle tells us we are to do this by walking worthy of the vocation in which we are called. *Ut digne ambuletis vocatione qua vocati estis.*[7] And this vocation is to the supernatural life and the glorious beatitude that crowns it: *Ut ambularetis digne Deo qui vocavit vos in* SUUM *regnum et gloriam.*[8]

So then, to please our Heavenly Father, in order that He be glorified, that His Kingdom be established within us and His will be done by us totally and steadfastly—that is perfection: "Stand perfect, and full in all the will of God": *Ut stetis perfecti et pleni in omni voluntate Dei.*[9]

This attitude towards God avails to make us "fruitful in every good work": *Per omnia placentes, in omni bono opere fructificantes.* And does not Our Lord Himself declare that this perfection is glorious to God? "In this is My Father glorified: that you bear very much fruit": *In hoc clarificatus est Pater meus ut fructum plurimum afferatis.*

> *Christ, the Ideal of the Monk,* Part I,
> chapter 2, section 4.

April 18, Easter Tuesday, 1900.

I have obtained much light in reflecting on these words: "Christ liveth unto God." I have felt the intensity of this life of Jesus *all of God.* The union of our life with this life is the highest form of perfection. Without Him, we can do nothing, but it was just to communicate this life to us that He came: "As the Father hath life in Himself, so He hath given to the Son also to have life in Himself." "I am come that

[6] Col. I, 10.
[7] Eph. IV, I.
[8] I Thess. II, 12.
[9] Col. IV, 12.

they [My sheep] may have life and may have it more abundantly." The Resurrection is the mystery of this life, and Jesus communicates it to us especially in Holy Communion: "Except you eat the flesh of the Son of Man, and drink His blood, you shall not have life in you." This bread is "the life of the world." I feel more and more the desire to associate myself with this divine life, so that Jesus may be glorified in me. For that is the *aim* of His glorious life: He "rose again FOR our justification," and He ever continues this action: "always living to make intercession for us." This life of Jesus is the love of His Father, whence comes the flowering of all the *human virtues* divinised in Him. There is our Model. I have taken the resolution of trying to unite my poor life to this intense and divine life.

> *Abbot Columba Marmion: A Master of the Spiritual Life,* chapter 8.

14 *All Consecrated to Souls*

1. THE LOVE OF JESUS FOR MEN

His love for the Father is not the only love with which Christ's Heart beats; He loves us too and in an infinite manner. It was veritably for us that He came down from Heaven, in order to redeem us and save us from death: *Propter nos et propter nostram salutem;* it was to give us life: *Ego veni ut vitam habeant, et abundantius habeant.* He had no need to satisfy and to merit for Himself, for He is the very Son of God, equal to His Father, at Whose right hand He is seated in the heights of Heaven; but it was for us that He bore everything. For us He became Incarnate, was born at Bethlehem, and lived in the obscurity of a life of toil; for us He preached and worked miracles, died and rose again; for us He ascended into Heaven and sent the Holy Spirit; He still remains in the Eucharist for us, for love of us. Christ, says St. Paul, loved the Church, and delivered Himself up for her, that He might purify and sanctify her and win her to Himself.

> *Christ in His Mysteries,* Preliminary
> Conference I, section 4.

During His public life, this love of Christ for men, His brothers, was manifested in many ways. He loved to give

pleasure. His first miracle was to change water into wine at
the wedding feast of Cana, so as to avoid embarrassment for
His hosts who were short of wine.

A short time afterwards, in the synagogue of Nazareth,
Jesus quoting from Isaias, appropriates to Himself these
words unveiling the plan of His work of love: "The Spirit
of the Lord is upon me. Wherefore He hath anointed me to
preach the Gospel to the poor, He hath sent me to heal the
contrite of heart, to preach deliverance to the captives, and
sight to the blind, to set at liberty them that are bruised, to
preach the acceptable year of the Lord, and the day of reward."

"This day," Jesus adds, "is fulfilled this scripture in your
ears." [1]

And indeed Jesus reveals Himself to all as a King full of
meekness and kindness.[2] I should need to quote every page
of the Gospel if I would show you how misery, weakness,
infirmity and suffering have the gift of touching Him, and
in so irresistible a manner that He can refuse them nothing.
St. Luke is careful to note how He is "moved with compassion": *Misericordia motus*.[3] The blind and the lame, the
deaf and dumb, those with the palsy, lepers come to Him;
the Gospel says that He "healed all": *Sanabat omnes*.[4]

He welcomes them all too with unwearying gentleness.
He allows Himself to be pressed on all sides, continually,
even "after sunset." [5] One day He "could not so much as eat
bread." [6] Another time, on the shore of the Lake of Tiberias,
He is obliged to enter into a ship so as to be more at liberty
to distribute the divine word.[7] Elsewhere the multitude

[1] Luc. IV, 18–19, 21; cf. Isa. LXI, 1.
[2] Matth. XXI, 5.
[3] Luc. VII, 13.
[4] *Ibid.*, VI, 19.
[5] Marc. I, 32–33.
[6] *Ibid.*, III, 20.
[7] *Ibid.*, IV, 1–2.

throng into the house where He is, so that in order to enable a paralytic man lying upon his bed to come near to Him, there is no other resource save to let down the sick man through an opening made in the roof.[8]

The Apostles themselves were often impatient. The Divine Master took occasion of this to show them His gentleness. One day they want to send away the children that are brought to Him. "Suffer the little children to come unto Me," Jesus says, "and forbid them not, for of such is the kingdom of God." And He stays to lay His hands upon them and bless them.[9] Another time, the disciples, being angry because He had not been received in a city of Samaria, urge Him to allow them to "command fire to come down from heaven" to consume the inhabitants: *Domine, vis dicimus ut ignis descendat de caelo?* And Jesus immediately rebukes them: *Et conversus increpavit illos:* "You know not of what spirit you are. The Son of man came not to destroy souls, but to save." [10]

This is so true that Jesus works miracles even to raise the dead to life. Behold how at Naim He meets a poor widow following the mortal remains of her only son. Jesus sees her, He sees her tears; His Heart, deeply touched, cannot bear this sorrow. "O woman, weep not!" *Noli flere.* And at once He commands death to give up its prey: "Young man, I say to thee, arise." The young man sits up, and Jesus restores him to his mother.[11]

> *Christ in His Mysteries,* Part II, chapter 11, section 3.

Christ, says St. Paul, who loves to employ this term, is the very kindness of God appearing upon earth; He is a King,

---

[8] *Ibid.,* II, 4.
[9] *Ibid.,* x, 13–14, 16.
[10] Luc. IX, 54–56.
[11] *Ibid.,* VII, 11–15.

but a King full of meekness, Who bids us forgive and proclaims those blessed who, following His example, are merciful. St. Peter, who had lived with Him three years, says that everywhere He went about doing good, *Pertransiit benefaciendo.* Like the Good Samaritan, whose charitable action He so wonderfully describes, Christ has taken humanity into His arms, He has taken its sorrows into His soul: *Vere languores nostros ipse tulit, et dolores nostros ipse portavit.* He comes "for the destruction of sin," which is the supreme evil, the only true evil; He drives out the devil from the bodies of the possessed; but, above all, He drives him out from souls, in giving His own life for each one of us.

> *Christ, the Life of the Soul,* Part II,
> chapter 11, section 3.

When the hour for achieving His oblation draws near, what does He say to His apostles gathered around Him? "Greater love than this no man hath, that a man lay down his life for his friends," *Majorem hac dilectionem nemo habet, ut animam suam ponat quis pro amicis suis.* And this love which surpasses all love, Jesus is about to show forth to us, for, says St. Paul, "Christ dies for all." He died for us when we were His enemies. What greater mark of love could He give us? None.

> *Christ in His Mysteries,* Part II, chapter
> 13, section 1.

2. THE MERCIFUL LOVE OF JESUS FOR SINNERS

The deepest form of misery is sin. If there is a trait particularly striking in the conduct of the Incarnate Word during His public life, it is the strange preference that He manifests for His ministry towards sinners.

The sacred writers tell us that "as He was sitting at meat . . . behold many publicans and sinners came, and sat down with Jesus and His disciples": *Ecce* MULTI *publicani et pecca-tores venientes discumbebant cum Jesu et discipulis ejus.*[12] Jesus was even called "the friend of publicans and sinners": *Publicanorum et peccatorum amicus.*[13] And when the Phari-sees showed that they were scandalized, far from denying the fact, Jesus confirmed it, in giving the reason that lay at the root of it: "They that are well have no need of a phy-sician, but they that are sick. For I came not to call the just but sinners."[14]

In the eternal plan, Jesus is our Elder Brother: *Praedes-tinavit [nos Deus] conformes fieri imaginis Filii sui, ut sit primogenitus in multis fratribus.* He has taken our nature, sinful in the race, but pure in His Person, *In similitudinem carnis peccati.* He knows that the great mass of mankind fall into sin and need forgiveness; that souls, the slaves of sin, sitting "in the darkness and in the shadow of death," do not understand the direct revelation of divine things; they can only be drawn to the Father by the condescension of the Sacred Humanity. This is why a great part of His teaching and doctrine, and countless acts of benignity and forgiveness towards sinners, tend to make these poor souls understand something of the depths of Divine mercy.

In one of His most beautiful parables, that of the Prodigal Son, Jesus discloses to us an authentic portrait of His Heav-enly Father. He shows first of all the extraordinary goodness of the father, who forgets all the ingratitude, all the baseness of the prodigal, remembering only that his son "was dead and is come to life again; he was lost, and is found." That is why it is necessary to rejoice and prepare a feast imme-diately; for "there shall be joy in heaven upon one sinner

[12] Matth. IX, 10; cf. Marc. II, 15; Luc. V, 29.
[13] Matth. XI, 19; Luc. VII, 34.
[14] Matth. IX, 12–13; Marc. II, 17; Luc. V, 31–32.

that doth penance, more than upon the ninety-nine just who need not penance."

Of itself alone, the parable of the Prodigal Son forms a magnificent revelation of divine mercy. But it pleased Our Saviour to illustrate this teaching and lay stress upon this doctrine by deeds of mercy that deeply charm and move us.

You know the conversation between Jesus and the Samaritan woman. Who was this soul? Certainly, in this locality, there were many to be met with far less corrupted than the sinner whom He willed to save; and yet it is this one whom He now awaits. He knows all the sin, all the shame of this poor woman, and it is she, in preference to all others, to whom He is about to manifest Himself.

There was nothing in the sinful woman of Sichar to distinguish her from others, unless it was the depth of her misery; but she was drawn to Christ by the Father. Then the Saviour receives her, enlightens, sanctifies, transforms her, and makes her His apostle: *Et eum qui veniet ad me non ejiciam foras.* For "this is the will of the Father Who sent Me, that of all that He hath given Me, I should lose nothing; but should raise it up again" to grace here below, whilst awaiting "the last day," when I will raise it up again in glory.

The woman of Samaria is one of the first to be raised up to grace by Jesus. Magdalen is another, but how much more glorious!

Erat in civitate peccatrix: "And behold a woman that was in the city, a sinner." Thus the Gospel begins her story with the attestation of her evil life. For Magdalen's profession was to give herself up to sin, as the profession of a soldier is to bear arms and that of a politician to direct the destinies of the state. Her sinful life was notorious. Seven devils, symbol of the abyss into which she had fallen, made of her soul their abode.

Did Jesus repulse her? Far from it, He permits her to approach Him, to kiss His feet. He defends her before the Pharisees and forgives her all her sins.

Magdalen the sinner has become the triumph of the grace of Jesus, one of the most magnificent trophies of His Precious Blood.

Whom has Christ placed at the head of His Church that He willed to be without "spot or wrinkle, or any such thing; but that it should be holy, and without blemish," and for the sanctification whereof He came to give all His precious Blood? [15] Whom did He choose? Was it John the Baptist, sanctified from his mother's womb, confirmed in grace and of such eminent perfection that he was taken for Christ Himself? No. Was it John the Evangelist, the virgin disciple, he whom Christ loved with a special love, who alone remained faithful to Him even to the foot of the Cross? Again no. Whom then did He choose? Knowingly, deliberately, Our Lord chose a man who was to forsake Him. Is it not remarkable?

Christ, being God, knew beforehand all that was to happen. When He promised Peter that He would build upon him His Church, He knew that Peter, wonderful as was the spontaneity of his faith, would deny Him. Despite all the miracles wrought under his eyes by the Saviour, despite the glory with which he beheld Christ's Humanity resplendent on Thabor, Peter on the very day of his first communion and his ordination, swore saying: "I know not the Man! . . ." [16] And it was he whom Jesus chose in preference to all others. Why was this?

Because His Church would be composed of sinners. Except the most pure Virgin Mary, we are all sinners; we have all need of the divine mercy; and therefore Christ willed

[15] Ephes. v, 25–27.
[16] Matth. xxvi, 72, 74.

that the visible head of His kingdom should be a sinner whose fault would be related in Holy Scripture with every detail showing its cowardice and ingratitude.

Yet once more, why so much condescension? *In laudem gloriae gratiae suae:* [17] to exalt the triumphant glory of His grace in the sight of all.

God wills that "no man may glory" in his own righteousness, but that all should magnify the power of His grace and the wideness of His mercy: *Quoniam in aeternum misericordia ejus.*

Our miseries, our failings, our sins, we know them well enough; but what we do not know—souls of little faith!—is the value of the Blood of Jesus and the power of His grace.[18]

> *Christ in His Mysteries,* Part II, chapter 11, *passim.*

3. THAT WE MUST HAVE A FIRM FAITH IN THE LOVE OF JESUS FOR US

When we consider these mysteries of Jesus, which of His perfections do we see especially shine out? It is love.

Love brought about the Incarnation: *Propter nos . . . descendit de caelis et incarnatus est;* love caused Christ to be born in passible and weak flesh, inspired the obscurity of the hidden life, nourished the zeal of the public life. If Jesus delivers Himself up to death for us, it is because He yields to the excess of a measureless love; [19] if He rises again, it is "for our justification"; [20] if He ascends into heaven, it is to pre-

[17] Ephes. i, 6.

[18] It will be sufficient to note that in the pages which follow this extract Dom Marmion shows that if our confidence has its source in God's mercy towards us, it finds one of its most powerful developments in repentance. The extreme condescension of Jesus towards sinners cannot, according to St. Paul's saying, serve as motive for remaining in sin or falling back into it when once delivered from it.

[19] Joan. XIII, 1.

[20] Rom. IV, 25.

pare a place [21] for us in that abode of blessedness; He sends
the Paraclete so as not to leave us orphans; [22] He institutes
the Sacrament of the Eucharist as a memorial of His love. [23]
All these mysteries have their source in love.

It is necessary that our faith in this love of Christ Jesus
should be living and constant. And why? Because it is one
of the most powerful supports of our fidelity.

Look at St. Paul. Never did man labour and spend himself
as he did for Christ. One day when his enemies attack the
lawfulness of his mission, he is led, in self-defence, to give a
brief outline of his works, his toils and sufferings. However
well we know this sketch drawn from the life, it is always a
joy to the soul to read again this page, unique in the annals
of the apostolate: Often, says the great Apostle, was he
brought nigh to death: "Of the Jews five times did I receive
forty stripes, save one. Thrice was I beaten with rods, once
I was stoned, thrice I suffered shipwreck, a night and a day
I was in the depth of the sea. In journeying often, in perils
of waters, in perils of robbers, in perils from my own nation,
in perils in the city, in perils in the wilderness, in perils in
the sea, in perils from false brethren. In labour and painful-
ness, in much watchings, in hunger and thirst, in fastings
often, in cold and nakedness. Besides those things which
are without: my daily instance, the solicitude for all the
churches." [24] Elsewhere, he applies to himself the words of
the Psalmist: "For Thy sake, we are put to death all the day
long, we are accounted as sheep for the slaughter. . . ."
And yet he immediately adds: "but in all these things we
overcome, because of Him that hath loved us": *Sed in his
omnibus superamus.* [25] And where does he find the secret of

[21] Joan. xiv, 2; Hebr. vi, 20.
[22] Joan. xiv, 18.
[23] Luc. xxii, 19.
[24] II Cor. xi, 23–28.
[25] Rom. viii, 36–37.

this victory? Ask of him how he endures everything, though "weary even of life";[26] how, in all his trials, he remains united to Christ with such an unshaken firmness that neither "tribulation, or distress, or famine, or nakedness, or the sword" can separate him from Jesus.[27] He will reply: *Propter eum qui dilexit nos:*[28] "Because of Him Who hath loved us." What sustains, strengthens, animates and stimulates him is the deep conviction of the love that Christ bears towards him: *Dilexit me et tradidit semetipsum pro me.*[29]

And, indeed, that which makes this ardent conviction strong within him is the sense that he no longer lives for himself—he who blasphemed the name of God and persecuted the Christians[30]—but for Him Who loved him to the point of giving His life for him: *Caritas Christi urget nos ...*[31] "The charity of Christ presseth us," he exclaims. Therefore, I will give myself up for Him, I will spend myself willingly, without reserve, without counting the cost; I will consume myself for the souls won by Him: *Libentissime impendam et superimpendar!*[32]

This conviction that Christ loves him truly gives the key to all the work of the great Apostle.

Nothing urges one to love like knowing and feeling oneself to be loved. "Every time that we think of Jesus Christ," says St. Teresa, "let us remember the love with which He has heaped His benefits upon us. ... Love calls forth love. ..."[33]

Christ Jesus does not change. He was yesterday, He is to-day; His Heart remains the most loving and most love-

---

[26] II Cor. i, 8.
[27] Rom. viii, 35.
[28] *Ibid.,* 37.
[29] Gal. ii, 20.
[30] Cf. Act. xxvi, 9–10; I Cor. xv, 9.
[31] II Cor. v, 14.
[32] *Ibid.,* xii, 15.
[33] *Life Written by Herself,* Chap. xxii.

able that could be met with. St. Paul tells us explicitly that
we ought to have full confidence in Jesus because He is a
compassionate High Priest Who knows our sufferings, our
miseries, our infirmities, having Himself espoused our weaknesses—saving sin. Doubtless, Christ Jesus can no longer
suffer: *Mors illi ultra non dominabitur;* but He remains the
One Who was moved by compassion, Who suffered and redeemed men through love: *Dilexit me et tradidit semetipsum pro me.*

> *Christ in His Mysteries,* Part II, chapter
> 19, introduction and section 2.

4. FOLLOWING THE EXAMPLE OF CHRIST, WE SHOULD LOVE ALL MEN, OUR BROTHERS

The day so ardently desired by Our Lord has come: *De-
siderio desideravi;* [34] He has eaten the Jewish Pasch with His
disciples; but He has replaced the figures and symbols by a
Divine reality; He has just instituted the Sacrament of union,
and given His Apostles the power of perpetuating it. And
now it is that before going to suffer death, He opens His
Sacred Heart to reveal its secrets to His "friends"; it is like
the last will and testament of Christ. "A new commandment
I give unto you," He says, "that you love one another as I
have loved you"; [35] and at the end of His discourse, He renews His precept: "This is My commandment, that you love
one another." [36]

And He holds so much to the observance of this commandment that He asks His Father to bring about this mutual love in His disciples: "Holy Father, keep them in Thy
Name whom Thou hast given Me: that they may be one, as
We also are . . . I in them and Thou in Me, that they may
be made perfect in one." [37]

[34] Luc. XXII, 15.
[35] Joan. XIII, 34.
[36] *Ibid.,* XV, 12.
[37] *Ibid.,* XVII, 11 and 23.

Jesus did not make this prayer only for His disciples, but for us all: "And not for them only do I pray," He says, "but for them also who believe in Me: that they may be all one, as Thou, Father, in Me, and I in Thee, that they also may be one in Us." [38]

So this commandment of the love of our brethren is the supreme wish of Christ: it is so much His desire that He makes of it, not a counsel, but a commandment, *His* commandment, and He makes the fulfilment of it the infallible sign by which His disciples shall be recognised: *In hoc cognoscent omnes quia discipuli mei estis si dilectionem habueritis ad invicem.*[39] It is a sign all can understand, none other is given: *Cognoscent* OMNES: no one can be mistaken as to it: the supernatural love you have for one another will be the unequivocal proof that you truly belong to Me. And, in fact, in the first centuries, the pagans recognised the Christians by this sign: "See," they would say, "how they love one another." [40]

For Our Lord Himself, it will be the sign He will use in the day of judgment to distinguish the elect from the reprobate. It is He Who has said it to us—Christ has become our neighbour, or rather, our neighbour is Christ presented to us in one form or another; He comes before us, suffering in the sick, indigent in those who experience misery, prisoner in the captives, sad in those who weep. But it is faith which thus reveals Him to us in His members; and if we do not see Him in them, our faith is weak; our love is imperfect. For which reason St. John says: "For he that loveth not his brother whom he seeth, how can he love God Whom he seeth not?" If we do not love God under the visible form in which He presents Himself to us, that is, in our neighbour, how can we say that we love Him, Himself, in His divinity?

[38] *Ibid.*, 20–21.
[39] *Ibid.*, XIII, 35.
[40] Tertullian, *Apolog.* c. 39.

Now, the love of Jesus for men is the model of what our love should be: "Love one another as I have loved you"; *Sicut dilexi vos.* What is the deep reason of Our Lord's love for His disciples, and for us in them?

Because they belonged to His Father: *Rogo . . . pro his quos dedisti mihi, quia tui sunt.* It is because souls belong to God and to Christ that we must love them. Our love must be supernatural; true charity is the love of God, enfolding, in the same embrace, God and all that is united to Him. We must love all souls as Christ loves them, even to the supreme degree of giving ourselves: *in finem.*

Let us then endeavour first of all to love God by keeping united to Our Lord: from this Divine love, as from an ardent furnace whence a thousand rays shine forth to give light and warmth, our charity will be extended to all around us, and so much the further according as the furnace is the more ardent. Our charity towards our neighbour is to flow from our love for God.

> *Christ, the Life of the Soul,* Part II,
> chapter 11, sections 1 and 3.

August 27, 1899.

The more we are the image of Jesus, the more we glorify the Father.

Jesus is at once the Son of God and the Saviour of men.

1. As Son of God, He is the splendour and the glory of the Father. "I do not seek My glory," He says in the Gospel, "but that of My Father Who sent Me. At the head of the book [of My life upon earth] it is written: Father, may I do Thy will. May Thy name be hallowed."

2. As Saviour of men. "That the world may know that I love the Father, I fulfil the precept that He has given Me [to deliver Myself up for men]. I came not to do My will, but that of My Father Who sent Me. The will of My Father

is that whoever sees the Son and believes in Him, shall have eternal life. There is no greater love than to give one's life for one's friends." We too ought to give our life for our brethren.

September 29, 1899.

To-day I received a particular grace. I understood that all my perfection should consist in the closest union of myself with Jesus Christ as Son of God and Saviour of men. I clearly understood this after Mass. In this manner, my thanksgiving is divided between the acts of Jesus in regard to His Father and towards my soul and that of others.

June 17, 1901.

In prayer, Our Lord draws me to identify myself with Him, to abide in Him and He in me, and then, He urges me: (1) to make acts of love to His Father, in union with Him; (2) for myself, to abandon myself entirely to Him; (3) to love my neighbour as He has loved him. It is, above all, this last point which has drawn me for some time past. I feel a *great increase* of love for the Holy Church, the Bride of Christ. I have, as it were, an habitual sense that the neighbour is Christ, and I feel urged to a great charity towards all. I see very clearly that true charity embraces all the virtues and requires continual renunciation.

February 23, 1903.

Our Lord gives me more and more a great confidence in the Holy Sacrifice and in the Divine Office. It seems to me that when I celebrate or when I say the Office, I bear the whole world with me, all the afflicted, the suffering, the poor, and all the interests of Jesus Christ. When I give myself to Jesus Christ, it seems to me almost always that He unites me with Him and then with all His members and that He asks me to do like Him, of Whom it is said: "Surely He hath borne our infirmities and carried our sorrows."

January 20, 1904.

It is a curious fact that since I have given myself more to God in prayer I have received a very lively sense of my union with all the members of the Church, and with *some* in particular. It seems to me that I bear the whole Church in my heart, especially at Holy Mass and during Divine Office, and in this way I have no more distractions as in the past.

Abbot Columba Marmion: A Master of the Spiritual Life, chapter 8.

15 *Be Thou Our Wisdom, Our Justice, Our Sanctification, Our Redemption*

Christ is not only the model, but the very source of holiness, because He communicates His wisdom, justice, holiness and redemption to us.

These four words are taken by Dom Marmion from St. Paul (I Cor. I, 27–31) and cited in the order given by the Apostle himself. To grasp the full sense and understand the singular preference of Dom Marmion for this text which is often found in his writings it is necessary to indicate on what occasion St. Paul wrote this letter and also to reproduce the complete text from which the above words are taken.

The Corinthians had an exaggerated respect for human wisdom to the detriment of eternal and divine truth. To this worldly wisdom St. Paul opposes God's wisdom which saves men by preaching Christ crucified. The knowledge of our incorporation in Christ effected by the Cross is the wisdom of God which replaces all human wisdom. "But the foolish things of the world hath God chosen that He may confound the wise, and the weak things of the world hath God chosen

that He may confound the strong, and things that are not,
that He might bring to naught the things that are. That no
flesh should glory in His sight. But of Him are you in Christ
Jesus Who of God is made unto us wisdom and justice and
sanctification and redemption, that as it is written: He that
glorieth, may glory in the Lord."

The supernatural wisdom of which St. Paul speaks is not
purely speculative or theoretical. The words "justice, sancti-
fication and redemption" are in apposition to wisdom and
in a manner explain its content. (*Cf. Allo,* Première Épitre
aux Corinthiens, *p.* xxxix *and pp.* 20–21.)

Dom Marmion has, above all, retained the "nobis"; *it is*
"for us" that Christ became wisdom—He is our *wisdom,* our
justice, our *sanctification,* our *redemption—that is, "through*
the Father," in virtue of our incorporation in Christ, of the
close and sublime solidarity that God the Father Himself
willed to establish between His Son Jesus and us; so much
so that the merits and riches of Christ belong to us, have
become ours.

OUR WISDOM

St. Paul names wisdom first because it is the principal
theme of all this portion of his letter to the Corinthians.

1. WORLDLY WISDOM AND DIVINE WISDOM

The wisdom of the century, purely human wisdom, always wishes to rule itself, to do everything while consulting
only purely rational lights; it intends to arrange existence
in its own way; it is angry with everything which is contrary to what it seeks, contrary to the conceptions which it
itself forms of perfection.

But what is this human wisdom in the eyes of God? "Foolishness," writes St. Paul in his first letter to the Corinthians: *Sapientia enim hujus mundi stultitia est apud Deum.* As regards the laws of supernatural life, this worldly wisdom, this "prudence of the flesh," as the Apostle also names it, is only vanity and error. This wisdom has not understood that God has wished to redeem the world not through riches, nor by brilliant actions, neither by the prestige of science nor of eloquence, but by investing Himself with the weakness of our nature and by leading a poor and hidden life; human wisdom did not understand that God concealed, during thirty years, this ineffable plenitude of perfections which comprises the holy humanity of Jesus; it did not understand that Christ was to die a bloody death on a gibbet. The Cross is "a folly or a scandal." But God, it is still St. Paul who speaks, has willed to confound this wisdom by the "folly" of His impenetrable decisions.

Therefore, whenever we wish to judge of the absolute value of a thing or a work, we should do so by considering it from God's point of view. God alone is truth; truth is the light in which God, Eternal Wisdom, sees everything; these things are as valuable only as God estimates them to be. This is the only infallible criterion of judgment outside of which one falls a prey to self-deception.

We are familiar with the well-known truth that our holiness is of the supernatural order, that is to say, above the rights, exigencies and strength of our nature; therefore everything related to this supernatural order, whose author is God alone, exceeds, by its transcendence, all our human conceptions. "The thoughts of God and the ways of God are not ours." He tells us so Himself: *Non enim cogitationes meae, cogitationes vestrae; neque viae vestrae, viae meae;* "Between our ways and the ways of God lies infinity"; *Sicut exaltantur coeli a terra.* That is why, in order to know the truth about things in the supernatural sphere, we must see them as God does.

God is so magnificent that He will be Himself our light: in Heaven, our holiness will be to contemplate the infinite light, to derive from its splendour the source of all life and all joy: *In lumine tuo videbimus lumen.*

Here below, this light is inaccessible to us on account of its brilliance, our sight is too feeble to bear it. And yet it is necessary for us in order to attain the end. Who will be our light? Christ Jesus. *Ego sum veritas:* "I am the Truth." He alone can reveal the infinite light to us. He is God come forth from God, Light arising from Light: *Deus de Deo, lumen de lumine. . . .* Being true God, He is Light itself, without shadow of darkness: *Deus lux est, et tenebrae in eo non sunt ullae.*

This light has come down into our valleys, tempering the infinite splendour of its beams beneath the veil of the Sacred Humanity. Our eyes, which are so feeble, can contemplate this divine light which is hidden and revealed at the same time under the weakness of passible flesh: *Illuxit in cordibus nostris . . . in facie Christi Jesu;* it "enlighteneth every man that cometh into this world": *Lux vera quae illuminat omnem hominem.*

> *Christ in His Mysteries,* Part II, chapter 20, section 3 and *passim.*

The Word makes us hear the words from on high, which He alone knows because He alone ever dwells in the Father's Bosom: *Qui est in sinu Patris ipse enarravit;* being "One with the Father," He gives us the words which the Father has given to Him, so that the words of Jesus, sent by the Father, are the words of God Himself: *Quem enim misit Deus, verba Dei loquitur.* Manifold words of the One Word, as the human words that translate them are manifold and

likewise the generations that are to hear them in order to
live by them.

These words of God are words of Eternal Life: *Verba
vitae aeternae habes.* Our Lord tells us: "This is eternal life:
that they may know Thee, the only true God, and Him
Whom Thou hast sent." The words of Jesus, the Incarnate
Word, reveal God to us, His Nature, His Being, His Perfections, His Love, His Rights, His Will. Being the utterances
of the Word, the utterances of Wisdom, they make the soul
penetrate into the light from above; they transport us into
these holy splendours where God dwells.

> *Christ, the Ideal of the Monk,* Part II,
> chapter 15, section 7.

2. BEING ETERNAL WISDOM, JESUS BECOMES OUR WISDOM
THROUGH THE FAITH WE HAVE IN HIS WORD

*"The object of the wisdom which St. Paul preaches to the
Corinthians is the whole of the divine plan concerning humanity, the whole of Revelation; subjectively, it is the same
thing as the virtue of faith, which enlightens the intelligence
about divine mysteries. It is the very Spirit of God Who has
come to pour His secrets into the intelligence of those who
are associated with the life and death of Christ through baptism. He has come down to dwell in their souls and by His
contact has implanted in them the intuition of faith, the
essential subjective wisdom, adherence to transcendental wisdom."* (P. *Allo,* Première Épitre aux Corinthiens, *p.* 113.)

Jesus, light of the world, tells us: "He who follows Me
walketh not in darkness but comes to eternal light." What
must we do, then, to walk in light? We must listen to Christ
in a spirit of faith and accept everything He tells us. Yea,
Lord, I believe it because Thou dost say it; Thou art ever *in*

sinu Patris: Thou seest the Divine secrets in the splendour
of eternal light; we believe what Thou dost reveal to us.
Faith is for us that lamp spoken of by the Apostle who witnessed Thy Transfiguration: that light that shines in the
darkness in order to guide us: *Lucerna lucens in caliginoso
loco.*

> *Christ in His Mysteries,* Part II, chapter
> 12, section 4.

Faith introduces us into that supernatural sphere which is
hidden from the eyes of the world. "Your life is hid with
Christ in God": *Vita vestra est abscondita cum Christo in
Deo.* The only true life, because it does not end, like the
natural life, in death, but has its fruition in the unalloyed
happiness of eternity.

The world sees only, or rather wishes to see and know
only, the natural life both for the individual and for society
at large; it only esteems and admires that which appears,
which shines and obtains temporal success; it judges by outward appearances, according to the eyes of flesh; it relies
only upon human effort, upon the natural virtues: that is its
way of judging and acting. It neglects, it systematically ignores the supernatural life, and smiles at the idea of a perfection that goes beyond reason alone. Human reasoning, in
fact, can only produce human results; purely natural effort
can only be the cause of effects in the purely natural order.
"That which is born of the flesh is flesh," says St. John: *Quot
natum est ex carne, caro est;* [1] that which is the result of
nature, outside the supernatural, "profiteth nothing" in God's
sight: *Caro non prodest quidquam.* [2] A man who has not
faith, who has not grace, may attain by force of energy, of
will and perseverance, to a certain natural perfection; he

[1] Joan. III, 6.
[2] *Ibid.,* VI, 64.

may be good, upright, loyal, just, but this is but a natural morality which, furthermore, ever remains deficient in some particular. Between it and the supernatural life lies an abyss. It is however with this natural perfection and this natural life that the world contents itself.

At a single flight, faith rises higher and uplifts the soul above all the visible universe, bringing it even to God. This faith which causes us to be "born of God," which makes us children of God, through Christ, makes us also conquerors over the world. Such is the wonderful doctrine of St. John in his Epistle: "Whatsoever is born of God overcometh the world. . . ." "Who is he that overcometh the world, but he that believeth that Jesus is the Son of God?" *Omne quod natum est ex Deo vincit mundum. . . . Quis est qui vincit mundum, nisi qui credit quoniam Jesus est Filius Dei?* [3]

> *Christ, the Ideal of the Monk,* Part II,
> chapter 5, section 2.

Hence what have we to do so as to walk in the light? To be guided according to the words of Jesus, according to the maxims of His Gospel, to consider all things in the light of the words of the Incarnate Word. Jesus tells us, for example, that the blessed who possess His Kingdom are the poor in spirit, the meek, those that mourn, those that hunger and thirst after justice, the merciful, the clean of heart, the peace-makers, those that suffer persecution for justice' sake. We must believe Him, unite ourselves to Him by an act of faith, lay down at His feet, in homage, the assent of our intelligence to His Word. We must strive to live in humility, gentleness, mercy, purity, to keep peace with all, to bear contradiction with patience and confidence.

> *Christ in His Mysteries,* Part II, chapter
> 20, section 3.

[3] *Ibid.,* v, 4–5.

To hear Jesus is not only to listen to Him with the ears of the body, He is to be heard too with the ears of the heart. Our faith must be practical, and put into action by works worthy of a true disciple of Jesus, conformed to the spirit of His Gospel. This is what St. Paul calls "to please God," *placere Deo,* a term that the Church herself repeats when she asks for us that we may be worthy children of our Heavenly Father.

And this, despite temptations, trials, sufferings. Do not let us listen to the voice of the Evil One: his suggestions are those of a prince of darkness; do not let us be led away by the prejudices of the world: its maxims are deceptive.

Christ in His Mysteries, Part II, chapter 12, section 4.

If we live thus, in faith, the spirit of Christ will permeate our souls, little by little, guide us in all things, will direct the soul's activity according to the Gospel. The soul, discarding the purely natural light of its own judgment, sees all things through the eyes of the Word: *Erit tibi Dominus in lucem.* Living in truth, it advances continually on the way; united to the truth, it lives with His spirit; the thoughts, feelings, desires of Jesus become its thoughts, feelings and desires; it does nothing which does not coincide fully with the will of Christ. Is this not the very basis of all holiness?

Let us say with ardent faith, like St. Peter: "Lord, to Whom shall we go? Thou hast the words of eternal life": *Verba vitae aeternae habes.* We truly believe that Thou art the Divine Word, come down on our earth in order to teach us; Thou art truly God, speaking to our souls; for God "in these days, hath spoken to us by His Son": *Novissime locutus est nobis in Filio.* We believe in Thee, O Christ, we accept all that Thou dost tell us of the Divine secrets, and because we accept Thy words, we give ourselves to Thee in order to live by Thy Gospel. Thou didst say that if we would be perfect, we must leave all to follow Thee; we believe this and we have come, having left all things to be Thy disciples. Lead us, Thou, Indefectible Light, for in Thee we have the most invincible hope. Thou wilt not reject us; we come to Thee that we may be brought to the Father. Thou hast declared: "Him that cometh to Me, I will not cast out": *Et eum qui venit ad me non ejiciam foras.*

> *Christ, the Ideal of the Monk,* Part I,
> chapter 2, section 1.

3. THE BLESSINGS GOD SHOWERS ON THE SOUL WHICH ABANDONS ITSELF TO HIS WISDOM

We can never repeat often enough how sovereignly God acts in such a soul and how it advances in holiness. He leads it by sure ways to the height of perfection. Sometimes, it is true, these ways appear to go quite in a contrary direction, but God attains His ends, ordering all things with strength and sweetness: *Attingit ergo a fine usque ad finem fortiter, et disponit omnia suaviter.*[4] "All things," said Christ Jesus again to His faithful servant Gertrude, "are ordered by the wisdom of My Providence."[5]

It is thus that God acts. Even when all seems lost, He shows Himself and comes to our aid. God leads the just man through right ways, and shows him His kingdom; and gives him the science of the saints; He makes him glorious in his labours and crowns his works: *Justum deduxit Dominus per vias rectas et ostendit illi regnum Dei; et dedit illi scientiam sanctorum; honestavit illum in laboribus, et complevit labores illius.*[6] These words may be perfectly applied to the soul that gives itself utterly to God.

---

[4] Sap. VIII, 1.
[5] D. Dolan, *St. Gertrude the Great*, p. 218.
[6] Sap. X, 10.

Per vias rectas. God's ways are straight, however winding and crooked they may appear to human eyes. Is not God infinite wisdom and power Whom nothing holds back? "All things are equal in My sight," He said to Catherine of Siena, "for My power equally reaches to them all. It is as easy for Me to create an angel as a worm; it is written of Me that all that I have willed, I have done. . . . Why trouble thyself as to how? Thinkest thou that I know not or cannot find the way of carrying out My plans and My decrees?" [7] Let us then trust God. Our own ways seem to us to be sure and certain, but, says St. Benedict, "there are ways which to men seem right, but the ends thereof lead to the depths of hell." Only souls who let themselves be led by God as children do not go astray.

Ostendit illi regnum Dei. There are many souls in the world who have not understood the Kingdom of God. They have formed a kingdom of their own; but it is God Who is to show us *His* Kingdom: He is the architect of our spiritual edifice. What is this kingdom? The perfect union with God in our heart: *Regnum Dei intra vos est.*[8] In the concrete, the souls wherein God is entirely the master compose His Kingdom. Believe me, if we did but embrace God's will in its entirety, Our Lord would take upon Himself the care of uniting us to Him despite our miseries, despite our absorbing occupations and all that we deem to be distractions and obstacles. While if we do not give ourselves up entirely to God's Will and to His ways, we shall never reach intimate union with Him. Souls who do not give themselves do not understand this; they put obstacles in the way of God's supremacy; while a soul who surrenders itself to Him recognises in all things no other power than His own.

Dedit illi scientiam sanctorum. What is this "science of

---

[7] *Life* by Bl. Raymund of Capua.
[8] Luc. XVII, 21.

the saints" that God gives to the soul whom He leads? It is the knowledge of the truth of things. Every man is a liar, Scripture says.[9] When a man leads himself, by the wisdom of the world, by ways that are merely human, he goes astray because he follows false maxims which are so widespread in this world of darkness. But when he gives himself to God, God enlightens him, because God is the Truth and the Light. The soul comprehends the truth concerning God, itself, and the world; little by little, it sees all things as Eternal Wisdom sees them, it possesses this science which is the only true one, because it leads us to our supernatural end.

Honestavit illum in laboribus suis et complevit labores illius. Wisdom enriches the just man in his labours and crowns his works. The more we come in contact with souls, the more we see that God is *our* holiness. We shall never be holy if we wish to become so in our own way, and not in God's way. We do not altogether know what is good for us; we do not understand the utility of temptations, trials and sufferings. But God is wisdom and He created us. He sees everything in our soul. He beholds with an infinite intensity and in light incomparable. The soul that leads itself by its own sense of what is fitting, easily thinks that all it does must be right, and is very astonished that others do not think the same. This soul builds up its own plan; but what would happen if all succeeded according to its views and desires? It would grow so full of self that it would become insupportable to God and the neighbour. When God sees a soul, He sees its good will, but also its miseries. He allows this soul to be tempted. What is the result of this Divine treatment? That self-love begins to die in the soul in order to give place to the love of God. We may speak in analogous terms of sufferings or of success in our work. Certainly we must do everything as perfectly as possible, for the glory of God,

[9] Ps. cxv, 11.

and, for our part, neglect nothing in order to do so; but we must not wish for success for the sake of success: this is often to meet with a stumbling block. A soul left to itself wishes to succeed, but God permits that it does not succeed, so that it may say to God: "Take me and guide me." Then God replies: "Very well, now that you know how weak and powerless you are, I will lead you." And the more this soul gives itself, the more God acts and blesses its works, doubtless not always according to human foresight, but according to the good of this soul and the interests of His glory. The influence of such a soul in the supernatural world is immeasurable, because its action participates in some way in the very infinity of God's action.

God acts towards us as we act towards Him; God, as it were, measures His Providence according to our attitude in relation to Him: and the more we give ourselves to Him, the more we look upon Him as our Father, as the Spouse of our souls, the more His Providence enters into the least details and circumstances of our life. For a soul totally surrendered to Him, God has ineffable delicacies which show that His gaze is ever fixed upon it; never has mother cared for her child, never has friend gladdened his friend, as God cares for and gladdens this soul.

Christ, the Ideal of the Monk, Part II, chapter 16, section 6.

Feast of St. Joseph, 1900.

The text for the little Chapter for None, *Justum deduxit Dominus per vias rectas,* "[Wisdom] guided the just in right paths," has struck me greatly. These words were spoken first of all of Jacob. In meditating on these words and their application to St. Joseph, I felt a great desire to abandon myself entirely to the direction of this eternal Wisdom. Christ, says St. Paul, has become, in God, our wisdom. Hear ye Him.

Abbot Columba Marmion: A Master of the Spiritual Life, chapter 8.

March 25, 1902.

When Our Lord wishes to unite a soul very closely to Him, He makes her pass through many trials. But if this soul remits herself without reserve into His hands, He arranges *everything* for her greatest good, according to St. Paul's words, "All things work together for good to them that love God." God's glory demands that we hope in Him in difficult circumstances. To hope in God, to rest upon His bosom when things go well is not a lofty virtue and gives little glory to Him Who wishes to be served by faith and *against all human hope.* But always to remain convinced that God will never forsake us, in spite of the difficulties which seem to us to be insurmountable, that His Wisdom, His Love and His Power will know how to find a way, that is true virtue, and the more a soul has passed through such trials, the higher she will attain, once she has definitely entered into God's service.

Union with God, chapter 4, section 3.

16 *Our Justice*

The justice of which St. Paul speaks here is that quality inherent in the soul which renders it "just," or pleasing to God. Christ has "become our justice" because, by His life, Passion and death, He has merited for us the grace which "justifies" us in the Father's eyes.

1. CHRIST HAS RESTORED TO US THE JUSTICE OF WHICH WE WERE DEPRIVED BY THE SIN OF ADAM

As you know, God in creating the first man established him in justice and grace and made him His child and heir. But the divine plan was crossed by sin; Adam, the head of his race, prevaricated. In one moment, he lost for himself and his descendants, all right to the divine life and inheritance. All the children of Adam, having become slaves of the devil,[1] share in his disgrace. That is why St. Paul says they are born "enemies of God," [2] "objects of wrath," [3] and for this reason excluded from eternal beatitude.[4]

Is no one to be found, among the sons of Adam, to redeem his brethren, and take away the curse that weighs upon

---

[1] Acts xxvi, 18; Joan. xii, 31; Col. i, 14.
[2] Rom. v, 10; xi, 28.
[3] I Thess. i, 10; Rom. ii, 5, 8; Ephes. ii, 3.
[4] Rom. ii, 2; v, 15–18.

them all? No—for all have sinned in Adam; none, either for himself or others, can make adequate satisfaction.

Christ, the Life of the Soul, Part I, chapter 3, section 1.

Is man then for ever to be robbed of peace, is all his sighing after this lost possession to be in vain? No. Order is to be re-established, and peace restored; and you know in what an admirable manner. It is in Christ and through Christ that both order and peace are to be found again. "O God," we say in one of the prayers of the Mass, "Who in creating human nature, didst wonderfully dignify it; and hast still more wonderfully renewed it": *Deus, qui humanae substantiae dignitatem mirabiliter condidisti, et mirabilius reformasti.* A wonder that consists in the Word being made Man, in having taken our sin upon Himself in order to offer befitting expiation to His Father, in having restored to us God's friendship and given us His own infinite merits whereby we may retain this friendship.

Christ, the Ideal of the Monk, Part II, chapter 18, section 1.

At the beginning of His public life, Jesus presented Himself to John the Baptist in order to be baptised. The Precursor, who recognized in Him the Son of God, refused to confer the baptism of penance upon Him, but what did Jesus reply to him? "Suffer it to be so now. For so it becometh us to fulfil all justice."

What is this justice? It is the humiliation of the adorable Humanity of Jesus, which, in rendering supreme homage to Infinite Holiness, constitutes the full payment of all our debts towards Divine Justice. Jesus, just and innocent, takes the place of all our sinful race, *Justus pro injustis;* and, by His immolation, He becomes "the Lamb of God Who takes

away the sins of the world," the "propitiation for our sins
and . . . for those of the whole world." It is thus that He
fulfils all justice.

Christ in His Mysteries, Part II, chapter
10, section 1.

That is why St. Paul tells us that if "by the disobedience of
one man [Adam] many were made sinners; so also, by the
obedience of one, many shall be made just." Jesus Christ
then, in His quality of Head, has merited for us all, in the
same way as in substituting Himself for us, He has satisfied
for us. And as He Who has merited for us is God, His merits
have infinite value and an inexhaustible efficacy.

When we say that the works of Christ are meritorious *for
us,* we mean that by them, Christ has won the right that
eternal life and all the graces leading to it or attached to it
should be given to us. It is indeed what St. Paul tells us: We
are "justified freely by His grace, through the Redemption
that is in Christ Jesus." Justified, that is to say, rendered just
in the eyes of God, not by our own works, but by a gratuitous gift of God, namely grace, which comes to us through
the Redemption that is in Christ Jesus. The Apostle makes
us understand, then, that the Passion of Jesus which achieves
and crowns all the works of His earthly life, is the source
from whence eternal life flows for us.

Christ, the Life of the Soul, Part I, chapter 3, section 3.

St. Paul wrote to the Ephesians: "Now in Christ Jesus,
you, who some time were afar off, are made nigh by the
Blood of Christ. For He is our peace." [5] He says again: "God
indeed was in Christ, reconciling the world to Himself, not

[5] Eph. ii, 13–14.

imputing to them their sins." [6] Christ is the holy Victim,
perfectly pleasing to God and in Him God has forgiven us.[7]
As the Psalmist so well says, in Him, justice at length satisfied and peace at length restored have given each other the
kiss of reconciliation: *Justitia et pax osculatae sunt.*[8]

Christ is "the Prince of Peace": *Princeps pacis.*[9] He has
come to fight against the prince of darkness and snatch us
from the power of the devil and to make peace between God
and man. And this Prince of Peace is so magnificent in His
victory that He gives us a share in all His merits in order
that we may for ever keep this peace won by His Blood.
When the Psalmist announces the coming of the Messias, he
says, as characteristic of His visitation: "In His days shall
justice spring up, and abundance of peace, till the moon be
taken away": *Orietur in diebus ejus et justitia abundantia
pacis, donec auferatur luna.*

> *Christ, the Ideal of the Monk,* Part II,
> chapter 18, section 1.

Easter, 1900.

I was much struck by grace while meditating on these
words of Saint Paul: "Who was delivered up for our sins,
and rose again for our justification."

Jesus Christ is infinite and eternal Wisdom, and He
chose, as the means of expiating our sins, His sorrowful
death. Exempt from death *de droit* (since sin, by which
alone death came, *per peccatum mors,* could not touch
Him), He *freely* accepted death for us, in our place. I felt
the great efficacy of this death, and I united myself to Jesus

[6] II Cor. v, 19.
[7] Cf. Eph. iv, 32.
[8] Ps. lxxxiv, 11.
[9] Isa. ix, 6.

in His death, that I may die with Him to sin. I had a great
sense of abandonment, of gratitude, etc.

Resurrexit propter justificationem nostram. The end and
aim of the risen life of Jesus is our justification. I understood
very clearly how much Jesus has our holiness at heart and
how the union of our life with His is efficacious to sanctify
us: "For if, when we were enemies, we were reconciled to
God by the death of His Son; much more, being reconciled,
we shall be saved by His life."

> Abbot Columba Marmion: A Master of
> the Spiritual Life, chapter 8.

2. THE GRACE WHICH JUSTIFIES US IS, IN THE ORDINARY WAY, CONFERRED BY BAPTISM

*It is noteworthy that the doctrine of baptism set out by St.
Paul (Rom. vi) and adopted by Dom Marmion follows upon
Chapters i–v of the same Epistle, where the Apostle speaks at
length of justification.*

St. Paul has said: "God saved us, not by the works of justice we have done, but according to His mercy . . . by the
laver of regeneration, and renovation of the Holy Ghost,
Whom He hath poured forth upon us abundantly, through
Jesus Christ our Saviour; that being justified by His grace,
we may be heirs, according to hope of life everlasting."

The immersion in the waters of the font represents the
death and burial of Christ: we have our part in them by
burying in the sacred waters sin and all affection to sin
which we renounce. The "old man" stained by Adam's
sin, disappears under the waters and is buried (only the
dead are buried) as in a tomb. The coming forth from the
baptismal font is the birth of the new man, purified from
sin, regenerated by the water made fruitful by the Holy
Ghost; the soul of the baptized is adorned with grace, the

principle of Divine life, adorned too, with the infused virtues and gifts of the Holy Ghost. It was a sinner who was plunged into the font, he has there left all his sins, and it is a just man who comes forth from it, imitating Christ come forth from His tomb and living the Divine life.

This double aspect of death and of life characterising the existence of the Incarnate Word amongst men, and realising its maximum of intensity and splendour in His Passion and Resurrection, ought to be reproduced in every Christian, in all those who have been incorporated with Christ in Baptism, for we became disciples of Jesus in the sacred font, by an act symbolising His Death and Resurrection. That is what St. Augustine so well says: "Our way is Christ: therefore look at Christ. He has come to suffer in order to merit glory; to seek to be scorned in order to be exalted. He has come to die but also to rise again." [10] This is the very echo of what St. Paul says: *Ita et vos existimate*. We should regard ourselves as dead to sin,[11] as having renounced sin, so as only to live for God. When we contemplate Christ, what do we find in Him? A mystery of death and of life: *Traditus est propter delicta nostra et resurrexit propter justificationem nostram.*[12] The Christian continues in his life this double element that makes him one with Christ. St. Paul is very explicit on this point; he says: "buried with Him in Baptism, in Whom also you are risen again. . . . And you, when you were dead (to eternal life) in your sins. . . . He hath quickened together with Him, forgiving you all offences." [13] As Christ left the winding-sheet—the image of His state of death and life subject to suffering—behind Him in the tomb, so have we left all our sins in the baptismal waters; in the same way that

[10] *Sermo,* LXII, c. 2.
[11] "To live to sin," "to die to sin," are familiar expressions with St. Paul; they signify "to remain in sin," "to renounce sin."
[12] Rom. IV, 25.
[13] Col. II, 12–13.

Christ came forth free and living from the sepulchre, so we
have come forth from the sacred font, not only purified from
all sin, but with the soul adorned, through the operation of
the Holy Ghost, with grace, the principle of Divine life, and
its train of virtues and gifts. The soul has become a temple
where the Holy Trinity abides, and the object of Divine
complacency.

Listen how St. Paul points out this truth. He tells the Co-
lossians that by Baptism they have stripped themselves of the
old man with his works of death (descended from Adam):
and have put on the new man created in justice and truth
(the soul regenerated in Jesus Christ by the Holy Ghost)
"according to the image of Him that created him." [14] St.
Paul likewise tells the faithful of Ephesus who have been
taught in the school of Christ, "to put off, according to former conversation, the old man who is corrupted according
to the desire of error, and be renewed in the spirit of your
mind. And put on the new man, who according to God is
created in justice and holiness of truth." [15] As long then, as
we are making our earthly pilgrimage here below, we must
pursue this double work of death to sin and life for God:
Ita et vos existimate.

In God's designs, this death to sin is definitive, and this
life is, of itself, immortal: but we can lose this life and fall
again into death by sin. Our work therefore is to guard and
develop this germ until at the last day we arrive at the fulness of the age of Christ. All Christian asceticism proceeds
from baptismal grace. Its aim is to cultivate the divine germ
cast into the soul by the Church on the day of her children's
initiation, so that being free from all obstacle, it may open
out and blossom. *Christian life is nothing else but the pro-
gressive and continuous development, the practical application, throughout our whole life, of this double supernatural*

[14] Col. III, 9-10.
[15] Ephes. IV, 20-24.

result of "death" and of "life" produced by Baptism. There is all the program of Christianity. In the same way too, our final beatitude is nothing else but the total and definitive freedom from sin, death, and suffering, and the glorious unfolding of the divine life sown in us when we received this sacrament.

As you see, the very life and death of Christ are reproduced in our souls from the moment of baptism: but the death is unto life. Oh! if we understood those words of St. Paul: *Quicumque in Christo baptizati estis, Christum induistis.* "As many of you as have been baptised in Christ have put on Christ." Not only have we put on Christ as an outer garment, but we are clad inwardly with Him. We are "engrafted" on Him, in Him, says St. Paul, for Christ is the Vine, we are the branches, and it is this divine sap that flows in us to transform us into Him: *In eamdem imaginem transformamur.* By faith in Him, we have received Him in Baptism: His death has become *our* death to Satan, the works of Satan, and to sin; Christ's life becomes *our* life; that initial act by which we were made children of God, made us the brothers and sisters of Christ, incorporated us with Him, made us members of His Church, animated us with His Spirit. Baptised in Christ, we are born through grace, to divine life in Christ. That is why, says St. Paul, we ought to walk *in novitate vitae.* Let us walk, no longer in the sin we have renounced, but in the light of faith, under the action of the Divine Spirit Who will grant us to bring forth by good works numerous fruits of holiness.

> *Christ, the Life of the Soul,* Part II,
> chapter 2, sections 1–4.

3. JUSTICE AND MERCY

St. Paul writes: "God has saved us not because of works of justice which we have accomplished but because of His mercy—so that no man may glorify himself." True to the thought of the Apostle, Dom Marmion often made divine mercy the theme of his preaching. For him as for St. Paul the idea of mercy is correlated to that of justice in the work of our salvation.

To pour forth on mankind the treasures of mercy, such is the divine plan; the special glory which God wishes to receive is the praise of His merciful goodness by which, inclining over our human misery, He wishes to solace it, elevate and unite it to Him.

In heaven we shall see that, in eternal splendour, God willed to raise a wonderful monument of mercy: *In aeternum misericordia aedificabitur in coelis.* We, humans, whose bodies and souls were formerly laden with so much misery, will form the living stones of this edifice so as to ceaselessly proclaim the infinite goodness of Our God.

And Who is the foundation stone of this edifice?

It is Jesus Christ.

We are all beings full of misery, we may all apply the words of the Psalm to ourselves: "I am poor and indigent"; *Egenus et pauper sum.*

However, let us not fear to state it, the poor one, the man who was laden with misery more than all others, was Our Divine Saviour. How is this? Doubtless, His all holy soul (*Tu solus sanctus, Jesu Christe*) never knew sin nor imperfection and His humanity, hypostatically united to the Word, constantly enjoyed, even in the midst of His sufferings, the infinite delights of the vision of God. However, as He had become our eldest brother and our head, by His Incarnation, He willingly assumed all the miseries, the sufferings of His members; He espoused our human nature with all the attendant weaknesses which went with it; He consented to "take upon Himself the iniquities of all men, His brethren."

This poor one, this Man of Sorrows, Who became such for our sake, asks His Father three times to spare Him. He will obtain humanity's salvation but on the condition that He suffer death, and the death of the Cross.

Since then God is full of mercy for the members of His Son, He has compassion on their misery; He forgives us, opens His paternal Heart to us and lavishes His graces upon us. He thereby repays His Son for all the love which His Son showed Him by His sacrifice.

All God's mercies towards us are responses to the cries of His Son. When Christ's members implore God's mercy, it is His Son Jesus Who asks it through their mouths; it is His cry alone which gives any value to ours.

If we wish then to experience the beneficial effects of this intercession, let us remain closely united to Our Lord; we are the object of God's mercies according to the degree in which He sees us in His Son.

Yes, God is truly wonderful in His works. How right the Psalmist was to cry: *Quam magnificata sunt opera tua, Domine. Omnia in sapientia fecisti.* "O Lord, Thou hast marked all Thy works with the zeal of magnificence and wisdom!" God, in His adorable wisdom and goodness, has known how to combine things so perfectly that He derives His glory from the comforting of our very misery.

This is not only an occasion for Him to exercise His mercy, but, since Jesus Christ has taken upon Himself our faults and our weaknesses and has expiated them in His person, each time that God has mercy on us, He glorifies His Son and utilizes the merits of His precious blood. From the atonements of Christ an incense of adoration and of infinite glory constantly ascends towards "the Father of Mercies."

Mélanges Marmion, pp. 7–10.

June 5, ——.

There are two ways of presenting ourselves before God.

1) Like the Pharisee of the Gospel, leaning on our own works and asking God to reward us for our justice. "I observe all Your law, I fast, I give alms. You ought to be satisfied with me." God detests such self-righteous people, though they be really very correct and irreproachable. 2) Like St. Paul: "I regard all my own righteousness as dung (*ut stercora*); my whole confidence is in Jesus Christ, Who through His merits gives to my works all their value." Hence he glories, not in his works, but in his infirmities. *Libenter gloriabor in infirmitatibus meis.* Such people are dear to God, because they glorify His Son, and this is His sole desire.

December 30, 1904.

Despite our miseries, or rather because of our miseries, we ought to lean fearlessly upon Him. *Libenter gloriabor in infirmitatibus meis.* I see more and more that when we come before the Heavenly Father as the members of His beloved Son—*vos estis corpus Christi et membra de membro*—the sight of our miseries does but draw down His look of mercy. *Abyssus abyssum invocat.* The abyss of our miseries calls upon the abyss of His mercy.

October 5, 1906.

God's glory as derived from us consists principally in the infinite condescensions of His mercy. The more miserable and unworthy we are—provided we have a good will and seek Him sincerely—the more is His mercy exalted in stooping down to our misery. "There is more joy in heaven before God's angels for one sinner who doeth penance, than for the ninety-nine who need not penance."

There is more glory given to God when He condescends to stoop down to a poor, mean, selfish, ordinary creature, than when He communicates Himself to one of those grand, noble, superior natures which, to our eyes, seem to claim His notice. St. Paul understood this so well. "He hath chosen the weak and despicable things of this world to confound the strong, etc., *ut non glorietur in conspectu ejus omnis caro,* that man should not glory in His sight." The triumph of the Passion and of the merits of Jesus Christ is attained when they lift up a poor, weak, miserable creature and unite it with the Divinity.

Union with God, chapter 4, section 2; and chapter 5.

17 *Our Sanctification*

The Church recognises no essential difference between justification and sanctification; sanctification may be considered as the fruit of justification. Through baptism the believer enters into possession of a justice which is a true life; it rests with him to maintain this justice by good works.

Jesus becomes our sanctification in being, by the grace which justifies us, the origin of those good works which make us conformable to Him and pleasing to His Father.

1. CHRIST IS THE SOLE SOURCE OF ALL SANCTIFICATION

The Divine Sonship which is in Christ by nature and makes Him God's own and only Son, *Unigenitus qui est in sinu Patris,* is to be extended to us by grace, so that in the thought of God, Christ is the first-born of many brethren, who are by grace what He is by nature—sons of God: *Praedestinavit nos conformes fieri imaginis Filii sui ut sit ipse primogenitus in multis fratribus.*

We are here at the central point of the Divine Plan: *it is from Jesus Christ, it is through Jesus Christ that we receive the Divine adoption.* "God sent His Son," says St. Paul, "that we might receive the adoption of sons"; *Deus misit Filium suum factum ex muliere, ut . . . adoptionem filiorum reci-*

peremus. The grace of Christ the Son of God is communicated to us so as to become in us the principle of adoption; it is at this fulness of Divine life and grace of Jesus Christ that we must all draw. After having said that the fulness of the Divinity dwells corporally in Christ, St. Paul adds immediately by way of conclusion: *Et estis in illo repleti, qui est caput omnis principatus et potestatis.*[1] Behold! in Him you have all, because He is your Head. And St. John says likewise, after having shown us the Word, full of grace and truth: "And of His fulness we have all received." *Et de plenitudine ejus nos omnes accepimus.*[2]

Thus, not only has the Father chosen us from all eternity in His Christ: *Elegit nos in ipso*—note the expression *In ipso:* all that is apart from Christ does not exist, so to speak, in the Divine thought—but it is also by Jesus Christ that we receive grace, the means of the adoption He destines for us: *Qui praedestinavit nos in adoptionem filiorum* PER JESUM CHRISTUM.[3] We are sons, like Jesus, we by grace, He by nature; He, God's own Son, we His adopted sons: *Et ipse filius et nos filii; ille proprius, nos adoptivi, sed ille salvat et nos salvamur.*[4] It is by Christ that we enter into God's family, it is from Him and by Him that grace and consequently Divine life come to us: *Ego sum vita . . . ego veni ut vitam habeant et abundantius habeant.*[5]

Such is the very source of our holiness. As everything in Jesus Christ can be summed up in His Divine Sonship, thus everything in the Christian can be summed up in his participation of this sonship, by Jesus Christ, and in Jesus Christ. *Our holiness is nothing else but this: the more we participate in the Divine life through the communication Jesus Christ*

---

[1] Col. ii, 10. *Qui est caput Christus.* Ephes. iv, 15.
[2] Joan. i, 16.
[3] Ephes. i, 5.
[4] Migne, P. L. lxviii, 701.
[5] Joan. x, 10.

*makes to us of the grace of which He ever possesses the ful-
ness, the higher is the degree of our holiness.* Christ is not
only holy in Himself, He is *our* holiness. All the holiness
God has destined for our souls, has been placed in the Humanity of Christ, and it is from this source that we must
draw.

"O Jesus Christ," we sing with the Church in the *Gloria*
of the Mass, "Thou only art holy": *Tu solus sanctus, Jesu
Christe.* Only holy, because Thou dost possess the fulness of
the Divine life; only holy, because it is from Thee alone that
we look for our holiness: Thou hast become, as the great
Apostle says, *our* justice, *our* wisdom, *our* redemption, *our*
holiness: *Estis in Christo Jesu qui factus est* NOBIS *sapientia
a Deo et justitia et sanctificatio et redemptio.*[6] In Thee we
find all; in receiving Thee, we receive all; for in giving
Thee to us, Thy Father, Who is our Father, as Thou hast
Thyself said, has given us all: *Quomodo non etiam cum illo
omnia nobis donavit?* All the graces of salvation and forgiveness, all riches, all the supernatural fruitfulness with
which the world of souls abounds, come from Thee alone:
*In Christo habemus redemptionem . . . secundum divitias
gratiae ejus quae superabundavit in nobis.* Let all praise be
given to Thee, O Christ; and by Thee may all praise ascend
to Thy Father for the unspeakable gift He has made us of
Thee!

> *Christ, the Life of the Soul,* Part I, chap-
> ter 1, section 5.

*For a religious who asked him to "sum up in a few points
his teaching on Christ and the spiritual life," Dom Marmion
outlined the following synthesis:*

July 18, 1907.

Here, in two words, is what I try to teach:

[6] I Cor. 1, 30.

Jesus Christ is Infinite Holiness, *Tu solus sanctus, Jesu Christe.*

But He is not only holy in Himself; He has been given to us to be *our* holiness, *Christus factus est* NOBIS *sapientia a Deo et justitia et* SANCTIFICATIO *et redemptio.*

He is our holiness:

1.—*As perfect model: Praedestinavit nos Deus conformes fieri imaginis Filii sui.* God finds in Him all His delights: *Hic est Filius meus dilectus in quo mihi complacui.* He finds them in us according to the degree of our likeness to Jesus.

2.—*As means of union with God.* In Jesus the divine nature and the human nature are united in oneness of Person, and we are united with the Divinity in the measure of our union with the Sacred Humanity [of Jesus]: *Lapis angularis faciens utraque unum.* It is by sanctifying grace that this union with God is brought about, and this grace is the work of the Blessed Trinity in us.

3.—However the effusion of this grace depends on Jesus Christ: *a*) It is He who has merited it; *b*) It is He who applies it through His Sacred Humanity; *c*) This grace tends to reproduce in us the features of Jesus Christ; *d*) The more we lean upon Him, the more abundant is this grace. In fact this grace, poured forth without measure in the Sacred Humanity, is communicated to His members in the measure of their union with Him by faith and love: *Ego sum vitis, vos palmites.*

All the graces that we receive tend to make of us by grace [of adoption] what Jesus is by nature—children of God. That is why this *same* Holy Spirit Who was, in Jesus, the principle of His whole human life, is given to us: *Quoniam estis filii misit Spiritum Filii sui in corda vestra clamantem: Abba, Pater.* It is this Holy Spirit Who achieves in us the image of Jesus and fills us with His life: *Spiritus est qui vivificat.*

There in a few words is all that I know.

Union with God, chapter 2, section 4.

2. THE FUNDAMENTAL CHARACTER OF OUR HOLINESS

God willed to give a train of followers to His Son: that is the unnumbered multitude of the saints. The saints are so many reproductions of the Word, under a less perfect form. The ideal for each one of us is in the Word; each of us ought to be for God a special interpretation of one of the infinite aspects of His Word. This is why we sing of each saint: "There is not found one like to him": *Non est inventus similis illi.*[7] There are not two saints who interpret and manifest Christ with the same perfection.

When we are in heaven, we shall contemplate, in the midst of unspeakable joy, the Blessed Trinity. We shall see the Word, the Son, proceeding from the Father as the archetype of all possible perfection; we shall see that the Sacred Humanity of Jesus interpreted in a universal manner the perfections of the Word to Whom it was united; we shall see that God has associated with Christ so many brethren who reproduce in themselves the divine perfections, manifested and made tangible here below in Christ Jesus. So that Christ is "the Firstborn amongst many brethren" who are to be like unto Him: *Ut ipse primogenitus in multis fratribus.*[8]

Never let us forget that God chose us in His Son Jesus: *Elegit nos in ipso.*[9] In that eternal decree, we find the source of our true greatness. When, by our holiness, we fulfil God's decree concerning us, we become for Him like a part of the glory that His Son Jesus is for Him: *Splendor gloriae.*[10] We

---

[7] Office for Confessor Pontiff. 2nd Ant. of Lauds; cf. Eccli. XLIV, 20.
[8] Rom. VIII, 29.
[9] Ephes. I, 4.
[10] Hebr. I, 3.

are like the prolongation, the rays of this glory, when we strive, each one in his place, to interpret and to realise in ourselves the Divine ideal, of which the Incarnate Word is the unique Exemplar.

Such is the Divine Plan; such is our predestination, that we should be conformed to the Incarnate Word, Son of God by nature, and our model of sanctity: *Praedestinavit* [*nos*] *conformes fieri imaginis Filii sui.*[11]

It is from this eternal decree, from this predestination full of love that for each one of us dates the series of all God's mercies. In order to carry out this plan, in order that His designs for us may be completed, God gives us grace, a mysterious participation in His nature; by grace we become, in His Son Jesus Who has merited it for us, the true adoptive children of God.

We have then not only the simple relation of creatures with God; we have not only to unite ourselves to Him by the homage and the duties of a natural religion based upon our condition of created beings. Without anything pertaining to these relations or duties being destroyed or diminished we enter into more intimate relations with God, those of children, which create in us special duties towards a Father Who loves us: *Estote imitatores Dei sicut filii carissimi.*[12] Relations and duties wholly supernatural, because they exceed the exigencies and rights of our nature, and because the grace of Jesus alone renders them possible.

You now understand what is the fundamental character of holiness for us.

We can only be saints if we are so according to the Divine plan: that is to say, by the grace that we owe to Christ Jesus. That is the primordial condition. Therefore His grace is

11 Rom. VIII, 29.
12 Ephes. V, 1-2.

called sanctifying. This is so true that outside of this grace even salvation is not possible. In the kingdom of the elect there are only souls that resemble Jesus; now the fundamental similitude which we must have with Him is only brought about by grace.

As you see, God has Himself determined the character of our holiness; to wish to give it another character is, as St. Paul says, "to beat the air": *Aerem verberans;* [13] God Himself has traced the way that we must follow; not to take it is to err and finally be lost: *Ego sum via: nemo venit ad Patrem nisi per me;* [14] He Himself has laid the foundation of all perfection, outside of which we only build upon sand: *Fundamentum aliud nemo potest ponere praeter id quod positum est, quod est Christus Jesus.*

This is true of salvation, this is true of holiness: holiness only draws its principle and finds its support in the grace of Christ Jesus.

> *Christ in His Mysteries,* Part II, chapter
> 20, section 2.

3. THE FEELINGS WHICH SHOULD INSPIRE US IN THE WORK OF OUR SALVATION

From this doctrine arise the sentiments that ought to animate us in seeking after holiness: a deep humility on account of our weakness, an absolute confidence in Christ Jesus. Our supernatural life oscillates between two poles: on the one hand we ought to have the intimate conviction of our powerlessness to attain perfection without God's help; on the other hand we ought to be filled with an unshaken hope of finding everything in the grace of Christ Jesus.

Because it is supernatural, because God—sovereignly Master of His designs and gifts—has placed it above the exigen-

[13] I Cor. IX, 26.
[14] Joan. XIV, 6.

cies and rights of our created nature, the holiness to which
we are called is inaccessible without divine grace. Our Lord
has told us: "Without Me you can do nothing," *Sine me*
NIHIL *potestis facere.*[15] St. Augustine [16] remarks that Christ
Jesus did not say: "Without Me you cannot do great things,"
but: "Without Me you can do nothing" which will bring
you to eternal life. St. Paul has explained in detail this doctrine of our Divine Master: we are incapable of having "of
ourselves," *quasi ex nobis,* a single thought that is of any
value for heaven; in this domain all "our sufficiency is from
God": *Sufficientia nostra ex Deo est.*[17] It is He Who gives
us the power to will, and to bring all things to their supernatural end: *Deus est qui operatur in vobis et velle et per-
ficere, pro bona voluntate.* So, then, we cannot do anything
for our holiness without Divine grace.

Ought we therefore to be cast down? Quite the contrary.
The intimate conviction of this powerlessness should neither
lead us to discouragement, nor serve to excuse our idleness.
If we cannot do anything without Christ, with Him we can
do all things. *Omnia possum in eo qui me confortat:* "I can
do all things in Him Who strengtheneth me," St. Paul tells
us again. Whatsoever be our trials, our difficulties, our weakness, we can, through Christ, reach the highest sanctity.

Why is this? Because in Him "are hid all the treasures of
wisdom and knowledge"; because "in Him dwelleth all the
fulness of the Godhead corporally" and being our Head He
has the power of making us partakers of this fulness of life
and holiness, so that nothing is wanting to us in any grace:
Ita ut nihil vobis desit in ulla gratia!

What assurance faith gives to us in these truths! Christ
Jesus is ours, and in Him we find all. *Quomodo non etiam
cum illo omnia nobis donavit?*

[15] Joan. xv, 5.
[16] *Tract. in Joan.,* LXXXI, 3.
[17] II Cor. III, 5.

A soul that lives ever with a like sense of humility and confidence gives great glory to Christ Jesus, because her whole life is the echo of the Saviour's own words: "Without me you can do nothing"; because she declares that He is the source of all salvation and all holiness, and refers all glory to Him.

Christ in His Mysteries, Part II, chapter 20, section 4.

September 1, 1909.

Your last letter almost pained me, for I see that you allow the sight of your miseries—which are very *limited*—to hide the riches which are yours in Jesus Christ, and these are *infinite*. It is a great grace to see our miseries and littleness, which, in reality, are much more extensive than we imagine. But this knowledge is a real poison unless completed by *immense* faith and confidence in the "all-sufficiency" of our dear Lord's merits, riches and virtues which are all ours. *Vos estis corpus Christi et membra de membro.* You are His body and the very members of His members. The members really possess as *their own* all the dignity and merit of the person whose members they are. And this is what glorifies Jesus, namely, to have such a high appreciation of His merits and such a great conviction of *His love in giving them to us* [*Et nos credidimus caritati Dei*] that our misery and unworthiness do not discourage us.

There are two categories of people who give little glory to Jesus Christ:

1.—Those who neither see their misery nor realise their unworthiness, and consequently *don't feel their need of Jesus Christ.*

2.—Those who see their misery, but have not that strong faith in the Divinity of Jesus Christ which makes them, as it were, happy to be thus weak in order that Jesus may be glorified in them. How far you are from glorying in your infirmities!

Strive to have a *very pure intention* in all that you do. Unite your intentions to those of your Divine Spouse and do not trouble about the result. God does not give a premium to success.

Union with God, chapter 4, section 2.

18 *Our Redemption*

The word "redemption" in St. Paul's text signifies deliverance effected by a ransom. If this word is placed last of all, after wisdom, justice and sanctification, it is probably because it includes the preceding; redemption, including deliverance from death by the last resurrection, places the redeemed in a state which will be prolonged for everlasting centuries.

1. CHRIST HAS DELIVERED US FROM SIN AND DEATH BY BECOMING OUR RANSOM

"When," says St. Paul, "the fulness of time was come, God sent His Son made of a woman that He might redeem them who were under the law; that we might receive the adoption of sons": *At ubi venit plenitudo temporis misit Deus Filium suum ut eos qui sub lege erant redimeret, ut adoptionem filiorum reciperemus.* To redeem humanity from sin and restore to it the grace of Divine adoption, such is in fact the fundamental mission of the Incarnate Word, the work which Christ comes to accomplish here below.

His Name, the Name of Jesus, given by God Himself, is not without signification: *Jesus nomen vanum aut inane non*

portat.[1] This Name signifies His special mission of salvation
and denotes His special work: the Redemption of the world.
"Thou shalt call His Name Jesus," says the angel sent to St.
Joseph, "for He shall *save* His people from their sins." [2]

Let us contemplate Him at this solemn moment, unique
in the history of humanity. What does He say? What is it
that He does? *Ingrediens mundum dicit: Hostiam et obla-
tionem noluisti, corpus autem aptasti mihi; holocautomata
pro peccato non tibi placuerunt; tunc dixi: ecce venio. . . .*[3]
"When He cometh into the world He saith [to His Father]:
Sacrifice and oblation Thou wouldst not; but a body Thou
hast fitted to Me. Holocausts for sin did not please Thee.
Then said I: Behold I come." These words taken from St.
Paul reveal to us the very first movement of the Heart of
Christ at the moment of His Incarnation. And having made
this initial act of total oblation, Christ "hath rejoiced as a
giant to run His course": *Exsultavit ut gigas ad currendam
viam.*[4]

For such is the mission He is to fulfil, the course He is to
run. "God has laid on Him," a man like us, of Adam's race,
yet just, innocent and stainless, "the iniquity of us all." *Posuit
in eo iniquitatem omnium nostrum.*[5] Because He has become, as it were, partaker of our nature, and has taken upon
Himself our sin, Christ has merited to make us partakers of
His justice and holiness. "God," according to the energetic
expression of St. Paul, "sending His own Son, in the likeness
of sinful flesh and of sin, hath condemned sin in the flesh."
*Deus Filium suum mittens in similitudinem carnis peccati,
et de peccato damnavit peccatum in carne;*[6] and with yet

[1] S. Bernard, *Serm. I. de Circumcis.*
[2] Matth. i, 21.
[3] Hebr. x, 5–7; cf. Ps. xxxiv, 7–8.
[4] Ps. xviii, 6.
[5] Isa. liii, 6.
[6] Rom. viii, 3.

more astounding energy: "Him, that knew no sin, for us He hath made sin." *Eum qui non noverat peccatum, pro nobis peccatum fecit.*[7] What energy there is in this expression: *peccatum fecit!* The Apostle does not say: *peccator,* "sinner," but even *peccatum,* "sin."

Christ, on His side, accepted to take upon Himself all our sins, to the point of becoming in some manner, upon the Cross, universal sin, living sin; He has voluntarily put Himself in our place, and therefore death will strike Him. He has purchased us "with His own Blood."[8] Humanity is to be redeemed, "not with corruptible things as gold or silver . . . but with the precious Blood of Christ, as of a lamb unspotted and undefiled, foreknown indeed before the foundation of the world."[9]

Let us not forget that we have been "bought with a great price."[10] Jesus Christ shed the last drop of His Blood for us. It is true to say that a single drop of this Divine Blood would have sufficed to redeem us; the least suffering, the slightest humiliation of Christ, even a single desire of His Heart would have been enough to expiate every sin, all the crimes that could be committed; for each of Christ's actions, being the action of a Divine Person, constitutes a satisfaction of infiinite price. But God willed to make the immense love His Son bears towards Him shine forth the more in the eyes of the world: *Ut cognoscat mundus quia diligo Patrem;*[11] He willed to show the ineffable charity of this same Son towards us: *Majorem hac dilectionem nemo habet;*[12] to bring home to us more vividly how infinite is the Divine holiness, and how profound the malice of sin. For these and other reasons

[7] II Cor. v, 21.
[8] Act. xx, 25.
[9] I Petr. i, 18–20.
[10] I Cor. vi, 20.
[11] Joan. xiv, 31.
[12] *Ibid.,* xv, 13.

not revealed to us,[13] the Eternal Father has required all the sufferings and the Passion and Death of His Divine Son in expiation of the crimes of humanity. Indeed, the satisfaction was only complete, when, from the height of the Cross, Jesus, with His dying voice, pronounced the *Consummatum est*. "All is consummated." Then only, the personal mission of the Redeemer here below was fulfilled, and His work of salvation accomplished.

Christ, the Life of the Soul, Part I, chapter 3, section 2.

2. THE BREADTH AND RICHNESS OF OUR REDEMPTION

St. Paul does not weary of enumerating the benefits we gain from the infinite merits acquired by the Man-God in His life and sufferings. When he speaks of them, the great Apostle exults; he can find no other terms to express his thought than those of *abundance,* of *superabundance* of *riches* that he declares *unfathomable.*[14] The death of Christ redeems us, gives us access to the Father, and reconciles us with Him, justifies us and bestows holiness and the new life of Christ upon us. To sum up, the Apostle compares Christ to Adam whose work He has come to repair; Adam brought us sin, condemnation and death; Christ, the second Adam, restores to us justice, grace and life.[15] *Translati de morte ad vitam;*[16] the redemption was abundant: *Copiosa apud eum redemptio.*[17] "But not as the offence, so also the gift [the gratuitous gift of grace] . . . For if by one man's offence

---

[13] The Redemption is a mystery of faith; we can understand in some measure its admirable appropriateness after it has been revealed to us, but in its essence it remains hidden for us. This is what St. Paul calls the *Sacramentum absconditum*. Ephes. i, 9; iii, 3; Col. i, 26.

[14] Rom. v, 17, sq.; I Cor. i, 6–7; Ephes. i, 7–8, 18, 19; ii, 17; iii, 18; Col. i, 27; ii, 2; Philip. iv, 19; I Tim. i, 14; Tit. iii, 6.

[15] I Cor. xv, 22.

[16] I Joan. iii, 14.

[17] Ps. cxxix, 7.

death reigned through one; much more they who receive
abundance of grace, and of the gift, and of justice, shall reign
in life through one, Jesus Christ. . . . And where sin
abounded, grace did more abound." [18]

That is why "There is now no condemnation to them that
are in Christ Jesus." [19]

Our Lord, in offering to His Father in our name, a satisfaction of infinite value, destroyed the obstacle that existed
between man and God: the Eternal Father now regards
with love the human race redeemed by the Blood of His
Son; for His Son's sake He has poured upon it all the grace
it needs to unite itself to Him, to live for God, and of the
very life of God. *Ad serviendum Deo* viventi. [20]

Thus, every supernatural good given to us, all the lights
God lavishes on us, all the helps with which He surrounds
our spiritual life, are bestowed on us in virtue of the life,
Passion, and death of Christ; all the graces of pardon, justification, perseverance God gives and ever will give to souls
in all ages have their one source in the Cross.

> *Christ, the Life of the Soul,* Part I, chap-
> ter 3, section 4.

Hear what St. Paul says on this subject: "Christ is risen
from the dead, the firstfruits of them that sleep"; He represents the firstfruits of a harvest; after Him, the rest of the
harvest is to follow. "By a man came death, and by a man
the resurrection of the dead. And as in Adam all die, so also
in Christ all shall be made alive." God, he says more ener-
getically still, "has raised us up together . . . through Jesus
Christ": con*resuscitavit nos . . . in Christo Jesu.* How is
this? It is that, by faith and grace, we are the living members

[18] Rom. v, 15–20.
[19] *Ibid.,* viii, 1.
[20] Hebr. ix, 14.

of Christ, we share in His states, we are one with Him. And as grace is the principle of our glory, those who are, by grace, already saved in hope, are already also, in principle, risen in Christ.

> *Christ in His Mysteries,* Part II, chapter
> 15, section 6.

Truly, if "God so loved the world as to give His only-begotten Son"; [21] if He "hath delivered us from the powers of darkness, and hath translated us into the kingdom of the Son of His love, in Whom we have redemption through His Blood, the remission of sin"; [22] if, as St. Paul again says: Christ "hath loved us, and hath delivered Himself for us," [23] for each one of us, to testify the love He bears to His brethren; if He has given Himself to redeem us from all iniquity and "cleanse to Himself a people acceptable," [24] why do we still hesitate in our faith and confidence in Jesus Christ? He has expiated all, paid all, merited all, and His merits are ours: we have been "made rich in Him," so that if we will it, "nothing is wanting to us in any grace of holiness." *Divites facti estis in illo, ita ut* NIHIL *vobis desit in* ULLA *gratia.* [25]

Why, then, is it that pusillanimous souls are to be found who say that holiness is not for them, that perfection is something beyond their power, who say, when one speaks to them of perfection: "It is not for me; I could never arrive at sanctity." Do you know what makes them speak thus? It is their lack of faith in the efficacy of Christ's merits. For it is the will of God that all should be holy: *Haec est voluntas*

[21] Joan. III, 16.
[22] Col. I, 13–14.
[23] Ephes. V, 2.
[24] Tit. II, 14.
[25] I Cor. I, 5–7.

Dei, sanctificatio vestra.[26] It is the Lord's precept: "Be ye
therefore perfect, as also your heavenly Father is perfect." [27]
But we too often forget the Divine Plan; we forget that holiness for us is a supernatural holiness, of which the source is
only in Jesus Christ, our Chief and our Head; we do a
wrong to the infinite merits and inexhaustible satisfactions
of Christ. Doubtless, by ourselves, we can do nothing in the
way of grace or perfection; Our Lord expressly tells us so.
Sine me NIHIL *potestis facere,*[28] and St. Augustine, comment-
ing on this text, adds: *Sive parum, sive multum, sine illo
fieri non potest sine quo nihil fieri potest.* That is so true!
Whether it concerns great things or small, we can do nothing without Christ. But by dying for us, Christ has given us
free and confident access to the Father, and through Him
there is no grace for which we cannot hope.

Souls of little faith! Why do we doubt of God, of our
God?

> *Christ, the Life of the Soul,* Part I, chap-
> ter 3, section 4.

3. IT IS ABOVE ALL IN THE SACRAMENTS THAT JESUS CHRIST APPLIES THE FRUITS OF THE REDEMPTION TO OUR SOULS

Christ, being God, is absolute master of His gifts and of
the manner in which He distributes them; we are no more
able to limit His power than we are to determine all His
modes of action. Christ Jesus can, when it seems good to
Him, cause grace to flow directly into the soul without in-
termediary. The lives of the saints are full of these examples
of divine liberty and liberality.

However in the present economy, the normal and official
manner in which Christ's grace comes to us is through the

[26] I Thess. IV, 3.
[27] Matth. V, 48.
[28] Joan. XV, 5.

sacraments He has instituted. He could sanctify us otherwise than He does; but from the moment that, being God, He Himself established these means of salvation—which He alone had the right to determine, since He is the Author of the supernatural order—it is to these authentic means that recourse must first be had. All the practices of asceticism we can invent to maintain and increase the divine life within us, are only of value in so far as they help us to profit more abundantly by these sources of life. They are, indeed, true and pure sources as well as inexhaustible ones where we shall infallibly find the divine life with which Christ Jesus is filled and of which He wills to make us partakers. *Veni ut vitam habeant.*

Let us listen to our Divine Saviour. He teaches us that the water of baptism cleanses us from our sins, that by it we are born to the life of grace, made children of God and heirs of His kingdom: *Nisi quis renatus fuerit ex aqua et Spiritu Sancto, non potest introire in regnum Dei;* He teaches us again that the word of His minister who absolves us, takes away our sins: "Whose sins you shall forgive, they are forgiven them"; He teaches us that under the appearances of bread and wine are really contained His body and blood which we must eat and drink in order to have life; He declares concerning marriage that man cannot put asunder those whom God has joined together; tradition, the echo of the teaching of Jesus, repeats that the imposition of hands confers on those who receive it, the Holy Spirit and His gifts.

For it is He, Christ, the Incarnate Word, Who, inasmuch as He is God, is the efficient, primary and principal cause of the grace produced by the sacraments. Why is this? Because He alone can produce grace Who is the source and author of it. The sacraments, signs charged to transmit this grace to the soul, only act in the capacity of instruments; they are a

cause of grace, a real and efficient cause, but only instru-
mental.

All the efficacy of the Sacraments, in communicating divine life to us, comes then from Christ, Who, by His life, and
His sacrifice on the Cross, has merited every grace for us. He
has instituted these signs to transmit grace to us. If we had
faith, if we understood that these are divine means—doubly
divine; in their first and primordial source, in the ultimate
goal towards which they tend—with what fervour and fre-
quence we would use these means, multiplied on our path
by the goodness of Our Saviour.

Let us then have faith, a lively, practical faith in these
means of sanctification; Christ has willed and merited that
their efficacy should be supreme, their excellence transcendent, their fruitfulness inexhaustible: they are signs charged
with Divine life. Christ has willed to lay up in them all His
merits and satisfactions in order to communicate them to us:
nothing can or ought to take their place. They are, in the
present economy of the Redemption, necessary for salvation.

It must be repeated, because experience shows how in the
long run, even with souls who seek God, the practical esti-
mation of these means of salvation sometimes leaves much
to be desired. The sacraments are, with the doctrine given by
the Church, the official channels authentically created by
Christ to make us attain to His Father. It is to wrong Him
not to appreciate their value, their riches, their fruitfulness,
while He is glorified when we draw from these treasures
acquired by His merits: we thus recognise that we hold all
from Him, and that renders Him very pleasing homage.

God *wills* our sanctification: *Haec est voluntas Dei, sanctificatio vestra.*[29] Christ repeats: "Be you therefore perfect,
as also your heavenly Father is perfect";[30] in these words

[29] I Thess. IV, 3.
[30] Matth. V, 48.

then, it is not simply a question of salvation, but of perfection, of holiness. Now it is not in extraordinary means, in raptures, and ecstasies, that Our Lord has normally placed the life He wills to communicate to us in order to render us perfect, to make us saints, pleasing to His Father: it is first of all in the sacraments. That He should have willed this is sufficient to make our souls, eager for holiness, abandon themselves to this will in all faith, in all confidence. These are the true sources of life and sanctification, all sufficing and abundant sources; in vain shall we go to draw elsewhere; we should forsake, according to the energetic words of Scripture, "the fountain of living water," to dig to ourselves "broken cisterns that can hold no water." All our spiritual activity ought to have no other reason, no other aim, than to make us able to draw always more abundantly, more largely, with more faith and purity, from these Divine fountains and to make the grace proper to each sacrament grow in us with more ease and liberty, more vigour and power.

Oh! let us come with joy to draw at these fountains of salvation: *Haurietis aquas in gaudio de fontibus Salvatoris.* Draw from these salutary waters; enlarge the capacity of your souls by repentance, humility, confidence, and above all, by love, so that the action of the sacrament becomes deeper, vaster, and more lasting. Each time we approach the Sacraments, let us renew our faith in the riches of Christ; this faith prevents routine from finding its way into the soul that frequents these sources; let us draw from them frequently, above all from the Eucharist, pre-eminently the sacrament of life; these are the fountains which Our Saviour, by His infinite merits, caused to spring up at the foot of His Cross, or rather, from the depths of His Sacred Heart.

Christ, the Life of the Soul, Part I, chapter 4, sections 1–3.

4. BY THE SACRIFICE OF THE MASS WE PARTICIPATE IN THE FRUITS OF THE REDEMPTION

As you know, the Council of Trent has defined that the Mass is "a true sacrifice," which "recalls and renews Christ's immolation on Calvary. The Mass is offered as a true sacrifice, properly so called." In "this Divine Sacrifice which is accomplished at the Mass is contained and immolated in an unbloody manner the same Christ Who upon the altar of the Cross was offered in a bloody manner. There is only one victim; and the same Christ Who was offered upon the Cross offers Himself now by the ministry of priests; the difference only exists in the manner of the offering": *Sola offerendi ratione diversa.* Therefore the Sacrifice of the altar renews essentially that of Golgotha; the difference consists merely in the manner of the oblation.

So, then, the Mass is not only a simple representation of the sacrifice of the Cross; it has not only the value of a simple remembrance; but it is a true sacrifice, the very same as that of Calvary which it reproduces and continues and of which it applies the fruits.

The *fruits* of the Mass are inexhaustible because they are the same fruits as of the sacrifice of the Cross.

It is the same Christ Jesus Who offers Himself to the Father for us. Doubtless, since His resurrection, He can no longer merit, but He offers the infinite merits acquired by His Passion. The merits and satisfactions of Jesus always keep their value, just as Christ keeps for ever, with His character of high priest and universal mediator, the divine reality of His priesthood. Now, after the sacraments, there are no means through which Christ's merits are more especially and fully applied to us than through the Holy Mass. The Holy Council of Trent says: *Oblationis cruentae fructus per hanc incruentam* UBERRIME *percipiuntur.* That is why every priest offers each Mass not only for himself but "for all present, as also for all faithful Christians, both living and dead." So extensive and immense are the fruits of this sacrifice, so sublime is the glory it gives to God!

In the following pages of Christ, the Life of the Soul, *Dom Marmion shows how the Mass is a perfect sacrifice of praise, thanksgiving and petition. We only give here the passage where he shows that it is equally a sacrifice of propitiation.*

The Holy Sacrifice is *a source of confidence and pardon.* When we are overwhelmed by the remembrance of our sins and seek wherewith to repair our offences and satisfy Divine justice more fully, so that the penalty of sin may be remitted, we cannot find a more efficacious and reassuring means than the Mass. Hear what the Council of Trent says: "By this oblation of the Mass, God, being appeased, grants grace and the gift of penance; He forgives even enormous crimes and sins": *Hujus quippe oblatione placatus Dominus gratiam et donum paenitentiae concedens, crimina et peccata etiam ingentia dimittit.* Is it that the Mass forgives sins directly? No, that is reserved for the sacrament of penance and perfect contrition; but the Mass contains abundant and powerful graces which enlighten the sinner and cause him to make acts of sorrow for sin that will lead him to penance, and, through penance, restore to him the friendship of God.

If this is true of the sinner not yet absolved by the hand of the priest, it is still more true of souls that are justified but seek to make as full satisfaction as possible for their faults and so to fulfil their desire of reparation. Why is this? Because the Mass is not only a sacrifice of praise, or a simple remembrance of that of the Cross; it is a *true sacrifice of propitiation,* instituted by Christ, "in order to apply to us each day the redeeming virtue of the immolation of the Cross": *Ut illius cruenti sacrificii crucis salutaris virtus in remissi-*

onem eorum, quae a nobis quotidie committuntur, peccatorum, applicaretur. That is why we see the priest, who already possesses God's friendship, offer this sacrifice for his "innumerable sins, offences and negligences." The Divine Victim *appeases God and renders Him propitious to us.*

When therefore the remembrance of our sins troubles us, let us offer this sacrifice: it is Christ Who is offered for us, the "Lamb of God Who takes away the sins of the world," and renews "as often as the commemoration of this victim is celebrated, the work of our redemption": *Quoties hujus hostiae commemoratio celebratur, opus nostrae redemptionis exercetur.*[31] What confidence we ought to have in this sacrifice of expiation! Whatever be our offences and ingratitude, one Mass gives more glory to God than all our wrongs, so to speak, take from Him.

O Eternal Father, look upon this altar, look upon Thy Son Who loved me and gave Himself for me on Calvary; Who now offers His infinite satisfactions for me: *Respice in faciem Christi tui,*[32] and forget those faults I have committed against Thy goodness. I offer Thee this oblation in which Thou art well pleased, in reparation for all the wrongs done to Thy Divine Majesty!

God cannot but hear such a prayer, for it relies on the merits of the Beloved Son Who, by His Passion, expiated all.[33]

> *Christ, the Life of the Soul,* Part II, chapter 7, sections 1–4.

5. OUR CO-OPERATION IN THE REDEMPTIVE WORK OF CHRIST BY OUR UNION WITH HIM IN SUFFERING

Finally, we may further associate ourselves with this mystery by bearing, for love of Christ, the sufferings and adver-

[31] Secret for the ninth Sunday after Pentecost.
[32] Ps. LXXXIII, 10.
[33] Cf. Rom. v, 8, 9.

sities which, in the designs of His providence, He permits us to undergo.

When Jesus was ascending the road to Calvary, bowed down under His heavy Cross, He fell beneath the weight. We see Him humbled, weak, prostrate upon the ground. He Whom Scripture calls "the strength of God," *Virtus Dei,* is incapable of carrying His Cross. It is a homage that His Humanity renders to the power of God. If He so willed, Jesus could, despite His weakness, bear His Cross as far as Calvary: but, at this moment, the Divinity wills, for our salvation, that the Humanity should feel its weakness, in order that it should merit for us the strength to bear our sufferings.

God gives us, too, a cross to carry, and each one thinks that his own is the heaviest. We ought to accept the one given to us without reasoning, without saying: "God might have changed such or such a circumstance in my life." Our Lord tells us: "If any man will come after Me, let him . . . take up *his* cross and follow Me."

There is an essential truth upon which we ought to meditate.

The Word Incarnate, Head of the Church, took His share, the greater share, of sorrows; but He chose to leave to His Church, which is His Mystical Body, a share of suffering. St. Paul demonstrates this by a profound and strange saying. "I . . . fill up those things that are wanting of the sufferings of Christ, in my flesh, for His body, which is the Church." Is something then wanting to the sufferings of Christ? Certainly not. We know that in themselves they were, so to speak, measureless: measureless in their intensity, for they rushed like a mighty torrent upon Christ; measureless above all in their value, a value properly speaking infinite, since they are the sufferings of a God. Moreover, Christ, having died for all, has become by His Passion, the

Propitiation for the sins of the whole world. St. Augustine explains the meaning of this text of the Apostle: to understand the mystery of Christ, we must not separate Him from His Mystical Body. Christ is not the "Whole Christ," according to the expression of the great Doctor, unless He is taken as *united* to the Church. He is the Head of the Church which forms His Mystical Body. Hence since Christ has brought His share of expiation, it remains for the Mystical Body to bring its share: *Adimpletae fuerunt passiones in capite, restabant adhuc passiones in corpore.*

In the same way as God had decreed that, to satisfy justice and crown His work of love, Christ was to undergo a sum of sufferings, so has He determined a share of sufferings for the Church to distribute among her members. Thereby each of them is to co-operate in the expiation of Jesus, whether in expiation of one's own faults, or in the expiation endured, after the example of the Divine Master, for the faults of others. A soul that truly loves our Lord desires to give Him this proof of love for His Mystical Body by means of these mortifications. Here is the secret of the "extravagances" of the saints, of that thirst for mortifications which characterises nearly all of them: "To fill up those things that are wanting" to the Passion of their Divine Master.

> *Christ in His Mysteries,* Part II, chapter 13, section 4; and *Christ, the Ideal of the Monk,* Part II, chapter 9, section 2.

Contemplate Christ Jesus on His way to Calvary, laden with His Cross; He falls under the weight of this burden. If He willed, His Divinity would sustain His Humanity; but He does not will it. Why? Because, in order to expiate sin, He wills to feel in His innocent flesh the burden of sin. But the Jews fear He will not live to reach the place of crucifixion; they therefore constrain Simon the Cyrenean to help to carry His Cross, and Jesus accepts his help.

Simon, in this, represents us all; as members of Christ's Mystical Body, we must help Jesus to bear His Cross. It is a sure sign we belong to Him, if, following Him, we deny ourselves and take up our cross: *Qui vult venire post me, abneget semetipsum, et tollat crucem suam, et sequatur me.*

Here is to be found the secret of the voluntary mortifications of faithful souls, privileged souls, holy souls—those mortifications that afflict and macerate the body as well as those that repress even the lawful desires of the mind. Such souls have doubtless expiated their own sins, but love constrains them to expiate for those members of Christ's body who offend their Chief so that the vigour, beauty and splendour of this Mystical Body may not be diminished. If we truly love Christ, we shall, following the counsel of a prudent director, generously take our share of these voluntary mortifications which will make us less unworthy members of a crucified Head. Was it not this that St. Paul sought? Did he not write that he had suffered the loss of all things so that he might be admitted to the fellowship of Christ's sufferings and be made conformable to His death? *Ad cognoscendum illum et societatem passionum illius, configuratus morti ejus.*

Christ, the Life of the Soul, Part II, chapter 4, section 5.

19 *Our All*

If, by reason of the ineffable solidarity which God the Father Himself has willed to establish between Jesus and us, Christ has become, according to the expression of St. Paul, our wisdom, justice, sanctification, redemption, Dom Marmion may well conclude that Christ has become everything for us. Dom Marmion adopts a practical attitude here. Our all is God, the Trinity, Father, Son and Holy Ghost. But, at present, as long as we are here below, Christ is for us the only way, the infallible truth, the only life. It is only by cleaving to Him and drawing upon the treasures of His Grace, that we attain to the Father, that we are introduced into the bosom of the Father, that we find the Father and are pleasing to Him.

This thought is frequently found in Dom Marmion's writings and he constantly reverts to it. In the text of the manuscript of the Consecration, Dom Marmion, according to his customary procedure when he wished to show the strength of his conviction and share it with his reader, underlined the word "all."

1. THE ETERNAL FATHER WILLS THAT WE SHOULD FIND
EVERYTHING IN HIS SON JESUS

The Eternal Father has appointed Jesus the universal distributor of every gift; "the Father loveth the Son: and He hath given all things into His hand": *Pater diligit Filium et omnia dedit in manu ejus.* Christ communicates to us the grace that He has merited for us.

Many know that our Lord is the only way that leads to the Father: "No man cometh to the Father, but by Me": *Nemo venit ad Patrem nisi per me;* that He has redeemed us by His Blood; but they forget—at least to all practical purposes—another truth of capital importance: it is that Christ is the Cause of every grace and that He acts in us by His Spirit.

Christ Jesus possesses in Himself the plenitude of every grace. Hear what He Himself says: "As the Father hath life in Himself, so He hath given to the Son also to have life in Himself": *Sicut Pater habet vitam in semetipso, sic dedit et Filio habere vitam in semetipso.*[1] And what is this life? It is an eternal life, an ocean of divine life containing all the perfections and beatitude of the Godhead. Now Christ Jesus has this Divine Life "in Himself" *in semetipso*—that is to say, by nature, being fully entitled to it, for Christ is the Incarnate Son of God. When the Father beholds His Christ, He is ravished, for this Infinite God beholds His equal in Christ His Son, and He declares: "This is my beloved Son": *Hic est Filius meus dilectus.*[2] He sees nothing in His Son except what comes from Himself: "Thou art My Son, this day have I begotten Thee": *Filius meus es tu, ego hodie genui te.*[3] Christ is truly "the brightness of His glory, and the figure of His substance;[4] and it gives the Father infinite joy to behold

[1] Joan. v, 26.
[2] Matth. III, 17; XVII, 5.
[3] Ps. II, 7.
[4] Hebr. I, 3.

Him: *In quo mihi bene complacui.*[5] Thus Christ, because He
is the Son of God, is "Life" supereminently: "I am the Life,"
Ego sum vita.[6]

This Divine Life that Jesus possesses personally and in its
plenitude, He wills to communicate and lavish upon us: "I
am come that they may have life, and may have it more
abundantly": *Ego veni ut vitam habeant et abundantius
habeant;*[7] He wills that the life which is His through the
hypostatic union, should be ours by grace, and it is "of His
fulness we all have received": *Vidimus [eum] plenum gratiae et de plenitudine ejus nos omnes accepimus.*[8] Through
the Sacraments, through the action of His Spirit in us, He
infuses grace into us as the principle of our life.

Christ is not one of the means of the spiritual life; He is *all*
our spiritual life. The Father sees everything in His Word,
in His Christ; He finds everything in Him; although His
exigencies for glory and praise are infinite, He finds them
in His Son, in the least actions of His Son; Christ is His
well-beloved Son, in Whom He is well pleased. Why should
Christ not be also our all? Our model, our satisfaction, our
hope, our supplement, our light, our strength, our joy?

Bear this truth well in mind: there is no grace of which a
soul can have need that is not found in Jesus, the Fount of
every grace. For if "without [Him] we can do nothing"
that brings us nearer to Heaven and to the Father, in Him
are laid up "all the treasures of wisdom and knowledge":
In quo sunt omnes thesauri sapientiae et scientiae absconditi.
And they are there laid up that they may be transmitted to
us. Jesus Christ has become not alone "our redemption, but
our justice, wisdom, sanctification"; *Christus factus est
NOBIS sapientia a Deo et justitia et sanctificatio.* If we may

[5] Matth. xvii, 5. Cf. *Ibid.,* iii, 17.
[6] Joan. xiv, 6.
[7] *Ibid.,* x, 10.
[8] *Ibid.,* i, 14 and 16.

sing that He "alone is holy," *Tu solus sanctus,* the reason doubtless is that we are all holy only in and by Him. Everything which He has, we have and it is ours; we are rich with His riches, holy with His holiness.

There is no truth on which St. Paul, herald of the mystery of Jesus, insists more, when he explains the divine plan.

Christ has been established by His Father the Head of the race of the redeemed, of the faithful, with whom He forms one body. His infinite grace is to flow into the members of the mystical organism, "according to the measure of the giving of Christ": *Unicuique nostrum data est gratia secundum mensuram donationis Christi.* And, by this grace which flows from Himself, Christ renders each of the elect like unto Himself, and pleasing, as He is, to the Father. For in the eternal decrees the Father does not separate us from Christ Jesus: the act by which He predestined a human nature to be personally united to His Word is the same act by which He predestined us to become the brethren of Jesus.

We cannot work out our salvation without Christ, without the help of the grace that He gives to us. He is the one, the true Life that saves from death: *Ego sum vita.*

Christ is truly our own, for we are His Mystical Body. His satisfactions, His merits, His joys, His glories are ours. . . . O ineffable condition of the Christian, associated so closely with Jesus and with His states! O surprising greatness of the soul to whom nothing is lacking of the grace merited by Christ in His mysteries! *Ita ut nihil nobis desit in ulla gratia!*

> *Christ in His Mysteries,* Preliminary Conference I, section 4; and *Christ, the Ideal of the Monk,* Part I, chapter 2, section 3.

2. THE GLORY WHICH WE GIVE TO THE FATHER BY LIVING ACCORDING TO THESE TRUTHS

If we could only have a deep conviction that we are pow-

erless without Christ, and that we have all in Him! *Quomodo non etiam cum illo omnia nos donavit?* [9] Of ourselves
we are weak, very weak; in the world of souls there are
weaknesses of all kinds, but that is not a reason for being
discouraged; these miseries, when they are not wilful, rather
entitle us to Christ's mercy. See the unfortunate who wish
to excite the pity of those from whom they ask alms; far
from hiding their poverty, they make a display of their rags,
they show their sores; that is what entitles them to the
charity and compassion of the passers-by. For us also, as for
the sick who were brought to Christ when He lived in Judea,
it is our misery confessed and displayed in His sight that
draws down His mercy. St. Paul tells us that Christ willed
to experience our infirmities—excepting sin—that He might
have compassion on us; and in fact, we read several times in
the Gospel that Jesus was moved with compassion at the
sight of the sufferings He witnessed: *Misericordia motus.*[10]
St. Paul expressly adds that Jesus keeps this sentiment of
compassion in glory, and he immediately concludes: "Let us
go therefore with confidence, *cum fiducia,* to the throne" of
Him Who is the source "of grace"; for if we do so in these
dispositions, we shall "obtain mercy." [11]

Besides, to act thus is to glorify God, it is to render Him
very acceptable homage. Why so? Because the Divine ideal
is that we should find *all* in Christ, and when we humbly
acknowledge our weakness and lean on His strength, the
Father regards us with benevolence, and with joy, because
by this we proclaim that His Son Jesus is the one Mediator
Whom He has willed to give to the world.

See how convinced the great Apostle was of this truth. In
one of his Epistles, after having published his misery, and
what struggles he has to sustain in his soul, he cries out:

9 Rom. VIII, 32.
10 Luc. VII, 13; Marc. VIII, 2; cf. Matth. XV, 32.
11 Hebr. IV, 14–16.

Libenter gloriabor in infirmitatibus meis.[12] Instead of complaining because of his infirmities, his weaknesses and struggles, he "glories" in them. This seems strange, does it not? But he gives a profound reason for it. And what is this reason? *Ut inhabitet in me virtus Christi.*[13] So that it may not be my strength, but the strength of Christ, the grace of Christ that dwells in me and causes me to triumph, and that all glory may be rendered to Him alone.

So we see that of ourselves we can neither will, nor act, nor pray supernaturally: *Sine me* NIHIL *potestis facere.*

Are we to be pitied for this? In no wise. St. Paul, after having detailed our weakness, adds: *Omnia possum in eo qui me confortat.*[14] "I can do all things." *Omnia,* not of myself, but "in Him Who strengtheneth me," so that all glory may be given to Christ, Who has merited all, and in Whom we have all things. There is no obstacle that I cannot surmount, no difficulty I cannot support, no temptation I cannot resist, through the grace Jesus Christ has merited for me. In Him, through Him, I can do all things, because His triumph is to render strong what is weak: *Sufficit tibi gratia mea, nam virtus in infirmitate perficitur.*[15] By this, God wills that all glory should ascend to Him by Christ, Whose grace triumphs in our weakness: *In laudem* GLORIAE *gratiae suae.*[16]

> *Christ, the Life of the Soul,* Part I, chapter 3, section 4.

February 28, 1902.

I am again in great peace, and it is in our Dear Saviour that I find this peace, and more and more all in Him. The feeling is very strong in me that our Lord will be all in all for me: "Wisdom, justice, sanctification," everything, if I

[12] II Cor. XII, 9.
[13] *Ibid.*
[14] *Ibid.,* IV, 13.
[15] *Ibid.,* XII, 9.
[16] Ephes. I, 6.

have constant recourse to Him, and if, without neglecting
the ordinary means [of sanctification], I depend much more
upon Him than upon my own endeavours. Our Lord urges
me more and more to this *simple* self-surrender which includes everything.

> *Abbot Columba Marmion: A Master of*
> *the Spiritual Life,* chapter 8.

May 1, 1906.

For the moment, I will only give you two or three principles which should be the tenor of *your* spiritual life:

1.—God does all things for the glory of His Son Jesus.
Now, Jesus is especially glorified by those who, convinced
of their extreme incapacity, lean upon Him, and look to
Him for light, help, everything.

2.—You should try to realise more vividly that being a
member of Jesus by your baptism and more and more by
each Communion, your needs, your infirmities, your faults
are, in a true sense, the needs, the infirmities, the faults of
Jesus. *Vere languores nostros ipse tulit et dolores nostros ipse
portavit. Posuit in eo Dominus iniquitatem omnium nostrum. Factus est pro nobis peccatum.*

3.—When you feel your weakness and misery, present
yourself fearlessly before the eyes of your Heavenly Father
in the name and in the Person of His Divine Son. *Libenter
gloriabor in infirmitatibus meis ut inhabitet in me virtus
Christi.* The weaker you are, the more our Lord wishes to be
your all.

November 29, 1906.

I have thought of your soul. In spite of your very real
faults and your miseries, which are doubtless much greater
than we see them, God loves you very much and He wishes
to substitute His greatness for your smallness, His wealth

for your baseness, His great wisdom for your insufficiency. He can do all that if you only allow Him to act.

Confiteor tibi, Pater, Domine coeli et terrae, quia abscondisti haec a sapientibus et revelasti ea PARVULIS. "I confess to Thee, O Father, Lord of Heaven and earth, because Thou hast hid these things from the wise and prudent, and hast revealed them to little ones," said Jesus. You are one of these very small people on whom God deigns to look down.

Try to consider God much more than yourself; to *glorify* yourself in your miseries, as being the object and the motive of divine mercies; to love virtue more than you fear vice; to exalt the merits and the infinite power of Jesus by drawing passionately upon them to supply your needs.

There's a programme for a whole year, yes, even for a whole lifetime.

June 5, 1916.

Nothing glorifies the good God so much as a soul who, while *seeing* its nothingness and misery, relies on the merits of Jesus Christ and on the mercy of our Heavenly Father. The souls who do not know their wretchedness believe themselves to be good and pleasing to God on account of their personal goodness. They do not experience an urgent need of Jesus; they give little glory to God. Jesus is our *all*. He is the Complement of our wretchedness, our poverty, and He gives Himself to those who are "poor in spirit."

I wish you to be very expansive, with an open heart: "I have run the way of Thy commandments, when Thou didst enlarge my heart." Sadness is a breath from Hell; joy, the echo of God's life in us.

Union with God, chapter 4, section 2.

3. THAT CHRIST MAY BECOME OUR ALL, WE MUST BE DETACHED FROM SELF AND CREATURES

St. Paul tells us that the tenderness, as well as the authority,

of the fathers of this world has its source in the Heart of
God.[17] And if our Heavenly Father loves us, what will He
not give us? While we were His enemies He reconciled us
to Himself by the death of His Son: He gave Him to us
that He might be our salvation,[18] and, says St. Paul, "how
hath He not also with Him given us all things?" *Quomodo
cum illo non omnia nobis donavit?* [19] All that we can desire
for the perfection and holiness of our souls, we find in Christ
Jesus; in Him are all the treasures of the Godhead: *Omnes
thesauri sapientiae et scientiae.*[20] The indubitable will of the
Eternal Father is that His beloved Son should be *our* redemption, *our* justice, *our* sanctification; [21] that all His
merits, all His satisfactions—and their value is infinite—
should be ours. You are made so rich in Christ, exclaims St.
Paul, "that nothing is wanting to you in any grace": *Ita ut
nihil vobis desit in ulla gratia.*[22]

Oh, if we knew the gift of God! *Si scires donum Dei!* [23]
If we knew what inexhaustible riches we may possess in
Christ Jesus, not only should we not go begging happiness
from creatures nor seeking it from perishable goods but we
should despoil ourselves of them as much as possible in order
to increase our soul's capacity for possessing true treasures.
We should be watchful not to attach ourselves to the least
thing that could keep us back from God.

It is this that gives assurance to our hope and renders it
invincible: when our heart is *truly* loosened from all things,
when we place our beatitude in God alone; when for love
of Him we detach ourselves from every creature, and look

[17] *Ibid.,* III, 15.
[18] Cf. Rom. v, 10.
[19] *Ibid.,* VIII, 32.
[20] Cf. Col. II, 3.
[21] Cf. I Cor. I, 30.
[22] I Cor. I, 7.
[23] Joan. IV, 10.

but to Him for all necessary graces, then God shows Himself magnificent towards us.

What, in fact, is hope? It is a supernatural habit which inclines the soul to look upon God as its unique good and to expect from Him all the graces necessary to attain to the possession of this supreme good: "The Lord is the portion of my inheritance"; *Dominus, pars hereditatis meae.* When the soul has a lively faith, it thus understands that God infinitely surpasses all earthly goods. Faith reveals to us that in the perfect possession of God, is found that priceless pearl of which the Gospel speaks; to acquire it (we detach ourselves from everything), is a homage offered to divine Goodness and Beauty. Faith expands in hope. The soul is so drawn towards God that it desires no other good, and the privation of every other good, except God, does not trouble it.

Deus meus et omnia; My God, Thou art so much everything to me that I have need of nothing but Thee; I wish for nothing but Thee. I could not bear to have anything outside of Thee to which I would attach my heart; Thou alone sufficest me, for "what have I in heaven, and besides Thee what do I desire upon earth?" *Quid mihi est in coelo, et a te quid volui super terram?* "Thou art the God of my heart, and the God that is my portion forever." *Deus cordis mei et pars mea Deus in aeternum.* As St. Paul says, the soul looks upon all the goods (of this earth) *ut stercora,* "and count them but as dung that I may gain Christ"; *ut Christum lucrifaciam.*

> Christ, the Ideal of the Monk, Part II,
> chapter 10, section 3 and *passim.*

The detachment required of us so that Jesus may be really our all, does not exclude, far from it, the love of creatures. This latter is but the extension of our love for Christ to all those who belong to Him or who may belong to Him. Dom

Marmion in his letters has defined in concise terms the essential doctrine on this point.

November 19, 1902.

We may never share our love for God with any other creature; His commandment is formal: "Thou shalt love the Lord God with thy *whole* heart." But in the same way as we love God, we may love others, *because* He loves them, and because He desires that we should love them, and in the order and degree in which He wills that we should love them.

When we love thus, our love for others takes nothing away from God, but it is, on the contrary, another form of our love for Him. To love in this way is a grace which we ought to ask of God and which we ought to try to merit by the intensity of our love for Him. Speaking of St. Teresa an author has written: "The tender affections of her heart passing through the Heart of Jesus drew therefrom a twofold life: they became divine by their principle, they remained human in their expression; like the thrice-holy friendship of Our Lord Himself for the Apostles, His disciples, John and Lazarus . . ."

Place *all* your consolation in God, not in the sense that you should reject all other joy, but that no human consolation should be *necessary* for your peace.

> *Union with God,* chapter 4, section 4;
> and chapter 3, section 2.

20 *Sanctify Us in Truth*

This final invocation summarizes in their most fundamental element, all the preceding petitions. It is by our union with Christ, our all, that we shall realize our sanctity according to the truth of the eternal designs of God for us. Dom Marmion repeats here, and addresses it to Jesus Himself, the petition which Christ in His supreme prayer after the Last Supper addressed to the Father on His disciples' behalf (John xvii, 17): "Sanctify them in the way of truth. Thy word is truth. . . ." We are in the way of truth and we sanctify ourselves therein in so far as we remain in harmony with God's design in our creation and supernatural adoption.

The doctrine is familiar to Dom Marmion, who links it up with that of St. Paul, "doing the truth" (Ephes. iv, 15), and that of St. John, "thou walkest in the truth" (John iii, 4). On March 7, 1907, he wrote from Louvain: "I can say with St. John: 'I have no greater joy than this to hear that my children walk in truth.'" The same thought is found in the letters of May 17, 1915, December 27, 1916, and December 1, 1922.

1. IN THE TRUTH OF OUR CONDITION OF CREATURES

It is through His Word that God has created us: "All things were made by Him," says St. John; "He uttered a word and all things were made." We remain in the truth of the Word, the Creator, and we are sanctified in it, then, by living in conformity with our condition of creature, in that which, according to the designs of God, is essential.

St. Paul tells us that we should "do the truth." What does he mean by this? To speak the truth is to express something that is in accordance with our thoughts. An object is *true* when there is accord between what, by nature, it ought to be and what it is in reality: gold is *true* when it possesses all the properties that we know to belong to the nature of this metal. It is *false* when it has the appearance but not the properties of gold; there is no accord between what it appears to be and what it ought to be considering the elements that we know constitute its nature. A human action is *true* if it really corresponds to our human nature as creatures endowed with reason, will, and liberty. St. Paul says we must do true works, that is, those that accord with our human nature. Every act that is contrary to our nature as reasonable beings, and that does not correspond to it, is a *false* act. We are not statues, or machines; neither are we angels. We are men, and the character that ought, first of all, to be manifested in our actions and that God wishes to find in them, is the character of human works done by a free creature.

By nature, man is a reasonable being. He cannot, like an animal destitute of reason, act only by instinct: what distinguishes him from all other beings of the earthly creation is that he is endowed with reason and liberty. Reason must therefore be sovereign in man; but, as a creature, reason must itself be subject to the Divine Will on which it depends, and that is manifested by the natural law, and by positive laws.

To be "true," which is the first condition necessary in

order to be pleasing to God, each human action must be in conformity with our condition as free and reasonable creatures, subject to the Divine Will; otherwise this action does not correspond to our nature, to the properties belonging to it and the laws that govern it: it is false.

Do not forget that the natural law is something essential in the order of religion. God need not have created me; but since I have been created, I am and remain a creature, and the relations resulting from this fact are unchangeable. One cannot, for example, conceive that a man could be created, for whom it would be lawful to blaspheme his Creator.

It is this character of human action, entirely free, but in accord with our nature and the last end of our creation, and consequently morally good, which must be primarily the distinguishing mark of our works in God's sight: *Qui dicit se nosse Deum et mandata ejus non custodit, mendax est et in hoc veritas non est.*

In order to act as Christians, we must first of all act as men. And this is not without importance. Doubtless, a perfect Christian will necessarily fulfil his duties as man, for the law of the Gospel comprises and perfects the natural law. But one meets with Christians, or rather with some calling themselves Christians, and that not only among the simple faithful, but even among religious and priests, who are exact even to scrupulosity as to their self-chosen practices of piety, and yet hold certain precepts of the natural law very cheaply. These people have it at heart not to miss their exercises of devotion, and this is excellent, but, for example, they do not abstain from attacking a neighbour's reputation, from falsehoods, and from failing to keep their word; from giving a wrong meaning to what an author has written, from not respecting the laws of literary or artistic property, from deferring, sometimes to the detriment of justice, the payment of their debts, and not observing the clauses of a contract exactly.

Such as these "whose religion spoils their morality," to use the expression of the great English statesman, Gladstone, have not understood St. Paul's precept: *Veritatem facientes.* There is a want of logic in their spiritual life, there is "untruth." Many of these souls may be unconscious of this "untruth," but it is not less hurtful, because God does not find in them that order which He wills should reign in all His works.

Christ, the Life of the Soul, Part II, chapter 5, section 1.

2. IN THE TRUTH OF OUR SUPERNATURAL VOCATION

The Father has also called us to the supernatural life in Jesus, His Incarnate Word. "He has chosen us in Him [His Word]—He has predestined us to become His adopted sons through Jesus Christ." Therefore we are sanctified when we live in the truth of our supernatural adoption.

Our natural life, which has its first source in the Word, comes to us from those immediate agents who are our parents.

But, as you know, we are called to a yet higher life, called to share God's own life by becoming "partakers of the Divine nature": *Efficiamini divinae consortes naturae.* This vocation to infinite beatitude is supereminently the work of love which crowns and, in a profound sense, explains all the others. If our natural life comes from God's Hands: *Manus tuae fecerunt me et plasmaverunt me totum in circuitu,* it is from His Heart that the supernatural life springs forth. "Behold," says St. John, "what manner of charity the Father hath bestowed upon us, that we should be called and should be the sons of God": *Videte qualem caritatem dedit nobis Pater, ut filii Dei nominemur et simus.*[1] This Divine life does not destroy the natural life in what it has that is positive

[1] I Joan. III, I.

and good, but, surpassing its possibilities, its exigencies and
rights, it raises and transfigures it.

Now, it is still in the Word that the source of this Divine
life and its outpourings is to be found: God beholds us in
His Word, not only as simple creatures but also in our being
of grace. Each of the predestined represents an eternal
thought of God. "Of His own will hath He begotten us by
the word of truth": *Voluntarie enim genuit nos verbo veritatis;* [2] Christ, the Incarnate Word, is truly the image in conformity with which we must be and remain the children of
God: *Praedestinavit [nos] conformes fieri imaginis Filii
sui;* [3] He is, as I have said, the Son of God by nature, we by
grace; but it is the same Divine life that inundates Christ's
Humanity and our souls with its fulness. This Only-begotten
Son, born of God in the holy splendours of an eternal and
ineffable generation, is the Son of the Living God, for He
possesses Life in Himself; He is very Life, *Ego sum vita,* [4]
and He has become incarnate in order to make us partakers
of this life: *Ego veni ut vitam habeant.* [5]

And how do we participate in this life? By receiving
Christ through faith. "As many as received Him, He gave
them power to be made the sons of God, to them that believe in His name, who are born . . . of God": *Quotquot
autem receperunt eum, dedit eis potestatem filios Dei fieri
his qui credunt in nomine ejus . . . qui ex Deo nati sunt.* [6]
Our access to this new life is a veritable birth; and this birth
is brought about by faith and Baptism, the Sacrament of
adoption: *Renatus ex aqua et Spiritu Sancto.* [7] Thus St. John
writes that "Whosoever believeth that Jesus is the Christ is

[2] Jac. i, 18.
[3] Rom. viii, 29.
[4] Joan. xiv, 6.
[5] *Ibid.,* x, 10.
[6] *Ibid.,* i, 12–13.
[7] *Ibid.,* iii, 3–5.

born of God": *Qui credit quoniam Jesus est Christus, ex Deo natus est.*[8]

Christ, the Ideal of the Monk, Part II, chapter 5, section 2.

Hence, it is no more as simple human creatures that we must be holy, but *as children of God, by acts animated and inspired by grace.*

Grace becomes the principle of the Divine life in us. What is it *to live?* For us, to live is to move in virtue of an interior principle, the source of actions which tend to the perfection of our being. Another life is engrafted, so to speak, upon our natural life, a life of which grace is the principle; grace becomes in us the source of actions and operations which are supernatural, and tend towards a Divine end, namely, one day to possess God, to rejoice in Him, as He knows Himself and rejoices in His perfections.

This point is of capital importance. God might have been content to accept from us the homage of a natural religion; it would have been the source of a human, natural morality, of a union with God conformable to our nature as reasonable beings, founded upon our relations as creatures with our Creator, and our relations with our kind.

But God did not wish to limit Himself to this natural religion. We have all met with men who were not baptised, but who were, however, straightforward, loyal, upright, equitable, just and compassionate, but that can only be a natural goodness. Without rejecting this (on the contrary!), God is not content with it. Because He has decided to make us share in His infinite life, in His own beatitude—which is for us a supernatural end—because He has given us His grace, God demands that our union with Him should be a supernatural union, a holiness which has His grace for principle.

[8] I Joan. v, 1.

Apart from this plan, there is, for us, only eternal loss. God is Master of His gifts, and He has decreed from all eternity that we shall only be *holy* in His sight, *by living through grace as children of God*.

O Heavenly Father, grant that I may preserve within my soul the grace that makes me Thy child! Keep me from all evil that might separate me from Thee! . . .

Christ, the Life of the Soul, Part I, chapter 1, section 4.

3. THE HARMONY WHICH EXISTS BETWEEN NATURE AND GRACE

Although we have received that which is like a new being, by Divine adoption, *nova creatura,* grace (which must become within us the source and principle of new and supernatural operations) presupposes nature and the operations proceeding from it. Far from being opposed to one another, grace and nature, as regards what is good and pure in the latter, are in harmony, each preserving its own character and beauty.

Let us contemplate what took place in Jesus Christ, for we must always regard Him in all things. Is He not the model of holiness? He is God and man. His state of Son of God is the source whence flows the Divine value of all His acts; but He is also man, *Perfectus homo.* Although united in an ineffable manner to the Divine Person of the Word, His human nature in no way lost its own activity, its special manner of acting; this nature was the source of perfectly authentic human actions. Jesus Christ prayed, worked, ate, suffered, slept: those were human actions, which showed that Our Lord was truly man; I dare even say that none has ever been so much as He, for His human nature was incomparably perfect. Only, in Him, the human nature subsisted in the Divinity.

Something analogous is produced in us: grace does not

suppress or reverse nature either in its essence or in its good qualities. Doubtless, it constitutes a new superadded state, infinitely superior to our natural state. A profound modification has been effected in us, both as regards our end which has now become supernatural and the forces which serve to attain it, but our nature is neither troubled nor diminished thereby. It is in exercising our own faculties, intelligence, will, love, sensibility and imagination, that our human nature, even when adorned with grace, must perform its actions: but these acts proceeding from nature, are raised by grace to the point of being worthy of God.

We must, first of all, remain ourselves, live in a manner conformable to our nature as free and reasonable creatures: this is the first element of the "truth" of our actions. I will add: we should live in a way *that corresponds to our individuality.*

We must keep our personality in our supernatural life, as to what is good in it; that is a part of that "truth," that "sincerity," which the life of grace demands. Holiness is not a single mould where the natural qualities that characterise one's personality have to disappear so that only a uniform type may be represented. Far from that. God, in creating us, endowed each of us with gifts, talents, privileges; each soul has its special natural beauty: one shines by depth of intelligence, another is distinguished by strength of will, a third attracts by breadth of charity. Grace respects this beauty as it respects the nature on which it is based; it will but add a supernatural splendour to the natural beauty, raising and transfiguring it. In His sanctifying operation, God respects His work of creation, for He has willed this diversity: each soul, in translating one of the Divine thoughts, has a special place in the Heart of God.

Lastly, we must be "true" by being *in accord with the vo-*

cation to which God has called us. We are not only isolated individuals; we form part of a society which includes different states of life. It is clear that in order "to be in the truth," we must also practise the duties of the special state in which Providence has placed us; grace cannot be in contradiction to this. It would be "untrue" to her state for the mother of a family to pass long hours in church when her presence is required at home for the ruling of her household. It would be "untrue" to his vocation for a religious to employ an hour in private devotions, instead of the work prescribed at that hour by obedience, however commonplace this work might be. Such acts are not entirely "true."

"Sanctify them in truth," was the prayer of Jesus, at the Last Supper, for His disciples.

Such is then, in broad outline, the fundamental law of the practice of our supernatural life. Without changing anything of what is essential to our nature, of what is good in our individuality or requisite for our particular state of life, we must live by the grace of Christ, referring through charity all our activity to the glory of His Father. Grace is grafted on nature and envelops its operations; such is the principal source of that diversity we meet with in the Saints.

Christ, the Life of the Soul, Part II,
chapter 5, sections 1–3.

December 10, 1912.

I am so happy to see that in the midst of *so much* business you keep your eyes fixed on God. RESPICE FINEM; that will keep you in the truth, *et omnia quaecumque facies prosperabuntur.*[9]

December 4, 1917.

I am praying *continually* that God may keep you very

---

[9] "Consider the end, and all that you do shall prosper." Cf. Ps. i, 3.

close to His Heart *in the truth* and that the enemy may not succeed in the midst of the fogs of the moment in detaching you from the Divine will, that is to say, from God Himself.

May 1, 1918.

Be very true with God, and as soon as you let yourself be drawn away to any fault or unfaithfulness (which will happen from time to time) look your Heavenly Father in the face, and show Him your soul in the bare truth.

December 1, 1922.

I can say with St. John that I have no greater joy than to see my children walking in the truth. To be in the truth, we must be in the Word, for He is the Truth. *Ego sum Veritas.*

Now, the truth supposes that we live and act according to the relations which God has established for our nature and our dignity as children of God.

1.—Our nature supposes that the *creature* remain always in most humble adoration before the Creator: that is so essential that *nothing* can change it. Our adoption to the state of child of God raises our nature, but does not destroy it. Hence it comes that when we rebel against God's will, against His permissions, we are no longer in the true attitude of the creature.

2.—Our adoption as *children* supposes that we act always as loving children towards our Heavenly Father, constantly seeking His good pleasure: *Quaerite faciem ejus semper.* This *Facies Dei* is the smile of His loving approbation.

If you always keep the truth of this twofold relation, you will be more and more mixed in truth and in peace.

Union with God, chapter 1.

PART 3. *The Holy Ghost*

In the adorable Trinity, the Third Person, Whose mysterious name Christ Himself has revealed, is the substantial and living Love which unites the Father and Son from Whom He proceeds; this is the "property" of His Divine Personality.

As substantial and infinite Love, we ask of Him firstly to establish His dwelling in us as an ever living spring of charity—Fons vivus, ignis, caritas.

As living Love, vivifying, divinely active, we pray Him ever to carry all our soul's operations on high into the Father's bosom, where all is consummated in Love.

Our daily fidelity to the constant work of this Spirit within us makes our whole life a hymn of praise to the Holy Trinity.

21 *O Holy Ghost, Love of the Father and the Son*

1. HOLINESS IN GOD AND IN THE TRINITY

God alone is holy by essence, or rather, He is holiness itself.

Holiness is the Divine perfection which is the object of the eternal contemplation of the Angels. Open the Scriptures. You will see that twice only, the gates of Heaven were partly opened, in the sight of two great prophets, the one of the Ancient alliance, the other of the New, Isaias and St. John. What did they see? What did they hear? Both saw God in His glory, both saw the angelic choir surrounding His throne, both heard them ceaselessly praising, not the beauty of God, nor His mercy, nor His justice, nor His greatness, but His holiness: *Sanctus, Sanctus, Sanctus, Dominus Deus exercituum; plena est omnis terra gloria ejus.*

Now in what does holiness in God consist?

In God, all is simple; His perfections are, in Him, really identical with Himself; besides, the notion of sanctity can only be applied to Him in an absolutely transcendent manner; we have no term which can adequately render the reality of this Divine perfection. However, it is permitted us to employ a human language. What, then, is holiness in God?

According to our manner of speaking, it seems to us that it is composed of a double element: first, infinite distance from all that is imperfection, from all that is created, from all that is not God Himself.

This is only a "negative" aspect. There is another element which consists in this: that *God adheres, by an immutable and always present act of His will, to the Infinite Good which is Himself,* in order to conform Himself entirely to all that this Infinite Good is. God knows Himself perfectly. His All-Wisdom shows Him His own essence as the supreme norm of all activity. God cannot will, do, or approve anything which is not ruled by His supreme wisdom, according to this ultimate norm of all good, which is the Divine essence.

This immutable adhesion, this supreme conformity of the Divine will to the infinite Essence considered as the ultimate norm of activity could not be more *perfect,* because in God the will is really identical with the essence.

There are, as you know, Three Divine Persons in God, the Father, the Son, and the Holy Ghost, three distinct Persons, but all three having one and the same Nature or Divine Essence. Being infinite Intelligence, the Father perfectly knows His perfections, He expresses this knowledge in one Word, the living, substantial Word, the adequate expression of what the Father is. In uttering this Word, the Father begets the Son, to Whom He communicates all His Essence, His Nature, His Perfections, His Life: *Sicut Pater habet vitam in semetipso, sic dedit et Filio habere vitam in semetipso.* The Son also belongs entirely to His Father, is entirely given up to Him by a total donation which pertains to His nature as Son. And from this mutual donation of one and the same love, proceeds, as from one principle, the Holy Spirit Who seals the union of the Father and the Son by being Their substantial and living Love.

This mutual communication of the three Persons, this infinite loving union between themselves assuredly constitutes a new revelation of holiness in God: it is the ineffable union of God with Himself in the unity of His nature and the Trinity of Persons.

Each of the divine persons is holy by reason of this ineffable union which binds Them infinitely amongst Themselves despite Their distinction.

But the Third Person is specially called holy because He proceeds from the other two by way of love. Love is the principal act by which the will tends towards its end and unites itself with it. It designates the most pre-eminent act of adherence to the norm of all goodness, that is to say, of holiness; that is why the Spirit Who, in God, proceeds from love, bears, *par excellence* the name of "holy."

> *Christ, the Life of the Soul,* Part I, chapter 1, section 1–3.

This Divine Spirit is named Holy, He is the Spirit of Holiness; holy in Himself, He makes holy. In announcing the mystery of the Incarnation, the Angel said to the Virgin: "The Holy Ghost shall come upon thee, . . . and therefore also the Holy which shall be born of thee shall be called the Son of God," *Ideoque et quod nascetur ex te sanctum, vocabitur Filius Dei.* Works of sanctification are especially attributed to the Holy Spirit. He is the divine artist Who by His final touches brings the work to its sovereign perfection. *Dexterae Dei tu digitus.* The work attributed to the Holy Ghost, in the Church as in souls, is that of bringing to its end, to its term, to its ultimate perfection, the ceaseless work of sanctity.

> *Christ, the Life of the Soul,* Part I, chapter 6, section 1.

2. IN JESUS HOLINESS WAS THE FRUIT OF THE SPIRIT'S OPERATION

Let us reverently approach the Divine Person of Jesus Christ that we may contemplate something of the marvels realised in Him, in the Incarnation and since the Incarnation.

As I have said to you when explaining this mystery, the Holy Trinity created a soul which it united to a human body so as to form one human nature, and united this human nature to the Divine Person of the Word. The Three Divine Persons concurred together in this ineffable work, although it is necessary to add immediately that it had for its final term, the Word alone; only the Word, the Son, became Incarnate.[1] This work is then due to the entire Trinity, but it is especially attributed to the Holy Ghost; and this is what we say in the Creed: "I believe . . . in Jesus Christ our Lord who was conceived by the Holy Ghost. . . ." The *Credo* only repeats the words of the Angel to the Virgin: "The Holy Ghost shall come upon thee . . . and therefore also the Holy which shall be born of thee shall be called the Son of God."

You will perhaps ask why this special attribution to the Holy Spirit? Because, among other reasons given by St. Thomas,[2] the Holy Spirit is substantial love, the love of the Father and the Son; now if the Redemption through the Incarnation is a work of which the fulfilment demanded infinite wisdom, it has however its first cause in God's love for us. "God so loved the world," Jesus Himself told us, "as to give His only begotten Son": *Sic Deus dilexit mundum ut Filium suum Unigenitum daret.*[3]

---

[1] To employ an image given by certain Fathers of the Church, a person in putting on his vestments is helped in this action by two other persons; all three concur in the accomplishment of this action, but only one is adorned in these vestments. This image is necessarily only an imperfect comparison.

[2] III, q. XXXII, a. I.

[3] Joan. III, 16.

And think how fruitful and wonderful the virtue of the Holy Spirit is in Christ! Not only does He unite the human nature to the Word but to Him is attributed the effusion of sanctifying grace in the soul of Jesus.

In Jesus Christ there are two distinct natures, both perfect, but united in the Person who embraces them, i.e., the Word. It is the "grace of union" that causes human nature to subsist in the Divine Person of the Word; this grace is of an altogether unique, transcendent and incommunicable order; through it, the humanity of Christ belongs to the Word; it has become the humanity of the true Son of God and the object of the Eternal Father's infinite delight. But the human nature, while being thus united to the Word, is not annihilated and does not remain in immobility: it retains its essence, its integrity, as likewise its energies and capacities; it is capable of action; now, it is "sanctifying grace" that raises this human nature so that it can act supernaturally.

And that is why this sanctifying grace has not been given to the soul of Christ in a limited measure as it is with the elect, but carried to its highest degree: *Et vidimus eum* PLENUM GRATIAE. Now the pouring forth of this sanctifying grace in the soul of Christ is attributed to the Holy Spirit.

At the same time, the Holy Spirit has poured forth on the soul of Jesus the fulness of the virtues and the fulness of His gifts: *Et requiescet super eum Spiritus Domini*.[4] Hear what Isaias sang of the Virgin and of the Christ Who was to be born of her: "There shall come forth a rod out of the root of Jesse [that is, the Virgin] and a flower shall rise up out of his root [Christ]. And the Spirit of the Lord shall rest upon Him, the spirit of wisdom, and of understanding, the spirit of counsel and of fortitude, the spirit of knowledge and of godliness. And He shall be filled with the spirit of the fear of the Lord."

4 Isa. XI, 2.

In a remarkable circumstance related by St. Luke, Our
Lord applied to Himself this text of the prophet. You know
that at the time of Christ, the Jews assembled in the synagogue on the Sabbath day; a doctor of the law chosen from
among those present, took the scroll of the Scriptures to read
the part of the sacred text appointed for that day. St. Luke
relates how, one Sabbath day, Our Divine Lord, then at the
beginning of His public life, entered the synagogue of Nazareth. The book of the Prophet Isaias was given into His
hands and, having unfolded it, He found the place where it
was written: "The Spirit of the Lord is upon Me, wherefore
He hath anointed me to preach the gospel to the poor, He
hath sent Me to heal the contrite of heart, to preach deliverance to the captives . . . to preach the acceptable year of the
Lord." Having folded the book, He restored it and sat down;
and the eyes of all in the synagogue were fixed upon Him.
Then He said to them: "This day is fulfilled this scripture
in your ears." [5] Our Lord made His own the words of Isaias
which compared the action of the Holy Spirit to an unction.[6]
The grace of the Holy Spirit is poured forth upon Jesus, like
an oil of gladness which first anointed Him Son of God and
the Messias, and then filled Him with the plenitude of His
gifts and the abundance of Divine treasures: *Unxit te Deus
oleo laetitiae prae consortibus tuis.*[7] It was at the very moment of the Incarnation that this blessed unction was conferred: and it was to signify this, to manifest it to the Jews,
to proclaim that He is the Messias, the Christ, that is to say,
the Lord's Anointed, that the Holy Spirit visibly descended
upon Jesus under the form of a dove on the day of His baptism when the Incarnate Word was about to begin His pub-

[5] Luc. IV, 16 sq.

[6] In the Liturgy (Hymn *Veni Creator Spiritus*) the Holy Spirit is called *Spirita-
lis unctio.*

[7] Ps. XLIV, 5. Cf. Act. X, 38: Jesum a Nazareth, quomodo unxit eum *Deus
Spiritu Sancto.* See also Matth. XI, 18.

lic life. It was indeed by this sign that Christ was to be
recognised, as was declared by His Precursor, St. John the
Baptist: "He upon Whom thou shalt see the Spirit descend-
ing . . . He it is that baptizeth with the Holy Ghost." [8]

From this moment, the Evangelists show us that in all
things the Soul of Christ is directed by the Holy Spirit and
His activity inspired by Him. It is the Holy Spirit Who leads
Him into the desert to be tempted: *Ductus est in desertum
a Spiritu ut tentaretur a diabolo.*[9] After His sojourn in the
desert, it is "in the power of the Spirit"[10] that He returns
into Galilee; by the action of this same Spirit, He casts out
devils from the bodies of those possessed;[11] it is under the
action of the Holy Spirit that He rejoices when He thanks
His Father for revealing His Divine secrets to little ones: *In
ipsa hora exsultavit Spiritu Sancto.*[12] Finally, St. Paul tells us
that in the chief work of Christ, the one in which His love
for His Father and for us shines out—namely His bloody
sacrifice upon the Cross for the salvation of the world—it was
by the Holy Ghost Christ offered Himself: *Qui per Spiritum
Sanctum semetipsum obtulit immaculatum Deo.*[13]

What do all these revelations show? That in Christ, the
human activity was directed by the Spirit of love. The One
Who acts is Christ, the Incarnate Word. All His actions are
the actions of the one Person of the Word in Whom the
human nature subsists; but it is under the inspiration, by the
promptings of the Holy Spirit, that Christ acted. The human
soul of Jesus had, through the grace of the hypostatic union,
become the soul of the Word; it was filled like to none other

[8] Joan. I, 33.
[9] Matth. IV, I.
[10] Luc. IV, 14.
[11] Matth. XII, 28.
[12] Luc. X, 21.
[13] Hebr. IX, 14.

with sanctifying grace, and lastly, it acted under the guidance of the Holy Spirit.

And this is why all the actions of Christ Jesus were holy.

Let us adore these marvels produced in Christ: the Holy Spirit renders holy the being and activity of Christ; and because, in Christ, this holiness attains the supreme degree, because all human holiness is to be modelled upon it and must be subject to it, the Church sings daily: *Tu solus sanctus, Jesu Christe,* "Thou only art holy, O Christ Jesus." Only Thou art holy because only Thou art by Thy Incarnation the true Son of God; only holy, because Thou possessest sanctifying grace in its fulness that so Thou mayest distribute it to us; only holy because Thy soul was infinitely docile to the promptings of the Spirit of Love Who inspired and ruled all Thy movements, all Thy acts and made them pleasing to Thy Father.

Christ, the Life of the Soul, Part I, chapter 6, sections 1–2.

22 *Set Thyself as a Burning Furnace of Love in the Centre of Our Hearts*

This petition has as its object to secure the fixed abode of the Holy Ghost in our souls, according to the very saying of Jesus: "He will come to you and take up His abode in you."

1. THE PRESENCE OF THE HOLY GHOST IN THE CHURCH

Before ascending into Heaven, Jesus promised His disciples that He would ask the Father to give them the Holy Spirit. He made the gift of this Spirit to our souls the object of a special prayer: *Rogabo Patrem, et alium Paraclitum dabit vobis, Spiritum veritatis.*[1] And you know how the prayer of Jesus was granted and how abundantly the Holy Spirit was given to the Apostles on the day of Pentecost. This marvel marked, as it were, the taking possession of the Church, Christ's Mystical Body, by the Divine Spirit. We may say that if Christ is the Chief, the Head of the Church, the Holy Spirit is the soul of it. It is the Holy Spirit Who guides and inspires the Church, keeping her, as Jesus said, in the truth of Christ and in the light He has brought to us:

[1] Joan. XIV, 16, 17.

*Docebit vos omnem veritatem et suggeret vobis omnia quae-
cumque dixero vobis.*[2]

This action of the Holy Spirit in the Church is varied and
manifold. I have said above that Christ was anointed the
Messias and High Priest by an ineffable unction of the Holy
Spirit; all those whom Christ wills to make participants of
His priestly power that so they may continue here below
His sanctifying mission, are made partakers of it by the
unction of the Holy Spirit: *Accipite Spiritum Sanctum . . .
Spiritus Sanctus posuit episcopos regere Ecclesiam Dei.*[3] It is
the Holy Spirit who speaks by their mouth and gives value
to their testimony.[4] In the same way, the authentic means
that Christ has given to His ministers, whereby they may
transmit life to souls, namely the Sacraments, are never conferred without the Holy Spirit being invoked. It is He Who
fructifies the waters of baptism;[5] it is necessary to "be born
again of water and the Holy Ghost to enter into the Kingdom of God";[6] St. Paul says that God saves us "by the laver
of regeneration" in renewing us by the Holy Ghost.[7] In Confirmation, the Holy Ghost is "given" to be the unction which
is to make the Christian a valiant soldier of Jesus Christ; it
is the Holy Ghost Who, in this Sacrament, gives us the fulness of the state of Christian and clothes us in Christ's own
strength. It is to the Holy Ghost, as is especially shown in
the Eastern liturgy, that the change is attributed whereby
the bread and wine become the Body and Blood of Christ.
Sins are forgiven, in the Sacrament of penance, by the Holy
Ghost.[8] In Extreme Unction, He is besought that His grace

---

[2] *Ibid.,* xiv, 26.
[3] *Ibid.,* xx, 22; Act. xx, 28.
[4] Joan. xv, 26; Act. xv, 28; xx, 22–28.
[5] Joan. iii, 5.
[6] *Ibid.*
[7] Tit. iii, 5.
[8] Joan. xx, 22–23. *Spiritus Sancti proprium est quod sit donum Patris et Filii;
remissio autem peccatorum fit per Spiritum Sanctum tamquam per donum Dei.*

may cure the sick of their languors and sins. In the Sacrament of Matrimony, the Holy Ghost is invoked in order that the Christian bridegroom and bride may, by their lives, imitate the union that exists between Christ and the Church.

Do you not see how full of life, how penetrating and constant, is the action of the Holy Spirit in the Church? Yes, He is indeed, as St. Paul says, "the Spirit of Life," a truth the Church repeats in her *Credo* when she chants her faith in "the Holy Ghost . . . the life-giver": *Credo . . . in Spiritum Sanctum . . .* VIVIFICANTEM; He is truly the soul of the Church, He is the vital principle animating and governing her, uniting all her members one with another and giving them spiritual strength and beauty.

In the first days of the Church's existence, this action was much more visible than in our own days; it entered into the designs of Providence, for it was necessary that the Church should be firmly established by manifesting, in the sight of the pagan world, striking signs of the Divinity of her Founder, of her origin and mission. These signs, the fruits of the out-pouring of the Holy Spirit, were wonderful. We marvel when we read the account of the beginnings of the Church. The Holy Spirit descended upon those who through baptism were made Christ's disciples. He filled them with miraculous gifts as numerous as they were astonishing: graces of miracles, gifts of prophecy, gifts of tongues and many other extraordinary favours granted to the first Christians in order that the Church, adorned with such an abundance of eminent gifts, might be recognised as the true Church of Jesus. Read in St. Paul's first letter to the Corinthians how the great Apostle rejoices in enumerating these marvels of which he was himself a witness; and at almost

S. Thom. III, q. III a. 8, ad 3. The missal likewise says: *Ipse Spiritus Sanctus est remissio omnium peccatorum.* Feria III after Pentecost. See also the post-communion of the prayer *pro petitione lacrymarum. (Orationes diversae.)*

each enumeration of these various gifts, he adds: but it is "the same Spirit" Who is the source of them, because He is Love and love is the principle of all these gifts.

Christ, the Life of the Soul, Part I, chapter 6, section 3.

Since then, the Holy Spirit abides in the Church in permanent, indefectible manner, therein exercising an unceasing action of life and sanctification: *Apud vos manebit, et in vobis erit.* He renders her infallible in the truth: "When He, the Spirit of truth, is come, He will teach you all truth" and will guard you from all error. By His action a wonderful supernatural fruitfulness springs up in the Church; He plants and unfolds in virgins, martyrs and confessors, those heroic virtues which are among the marks of holiness. In a word He is the Spirit Who, by His inspirations, works in souls, rendering the Church which Jesus acquired for Himself by His Precious Blood "holy, and without blemish," worthy of being presented by Christ to His Father on the day of final triumph.

Christ in His Mysteries, Part II, chapter 17, section 4.

2. THE INDWELLING OF THE HOLY GHOST IN EACH JUST SOUL

I have told you that holiness for us is nothing else than the complete unfolding, the full development of that first grace of our divine adoption, that grace given at baptism by which we become children of God and brethren of Christ Jesus. The substance of all holiness is to draw from this initial grace of adoption all the treasures and graces which it contains and that God causes to flow from it. Christ is the Model of our divine filiation. He has moreover merited that it should be given to us, and He Himself has established the means whereby it should come to us.

But the fruition within us of this grace, rendered possible by Jesus, is the work of the Holy Trinity; it is however, and not without motive, especially attributed to the Holy Spirit. Why is this? Always for the same reason. This grace of adoption is purely gratuitous and has its source in love: *Videte qualem caritatem dedit nobis Pater ut Filii Dei nominemur et simus.*[9] Now, in the adorable Trinity, the Holy Spirit is substantial love. St. Paul tells us that "the charity of God" (that is to say, the grace that makes us children of God) "is poured forth in our hearts by the Holy Ghost": *Caritas Dei diffusa est in cordibus nostris per Spiritum Sanctum, qui datus est nobis.*[10]

And from the moment of the infusion of grace in us by baptism, the Holy Ghost abides in us with the Father and the Son. "If anyone love Me, he will keep My word, and My Father will love him, and We will come to him and will make Our abode with him," *Ad eum veniemus et* MANSIO-NEM *apud eum faciemus.*[11] Grace makes our soul the temple of the Holy Trinity. Our soul adorned with grace is truly the abode of God; He dwells within us, not merely as He does in all things, by His essence and His power, by which He sustains and preserves every creature in existence, but in an altogether special and intimate manner as being the object of supernatural knowledge and love. And because grace thus unites us to God, because it is the principle and measure of our charity, it is especially the Holy Spirit who is said "to dwell within us," not in a manner that is personal to Him to the exclusion of the Father and the Son, but because He proceeds through love and it is He who unites the Father and the Son: *Apud vos manebit et in vobis erit,* said Our Lord. Every man, even a sinner, still possesses in himself the vestiges of divine power and wisdom; the just alone, those

[9] I Joan. III, I.
[10] Rom. v, 5.
[11] Joan. XIV, 23.

who are in a state of grace, are partakers of the supernatural charity which is like the exclusive sign of the Holy Spirit. This is why St. Paul, speaking to the faithful, says to them: "Know you not that your members are the temple of the Holy Ghost, Who is in you, Whom you have from God?" *An nescitis quoniam membra vestra templum sunt Spiritus Sancti qui in vobis est, quem habetis a Deo?*

In her liturgy, the Church tells us that the Holy Spirit is Himself the highest Gift: *Donum Dei altissimi;* for He descends into us even from the moment of baptism to give Himself as the object of love. But this Gift is divine and living. He is a Guest Who, full of liberality, wishes to enrich the soul that receives Him. Being Himself the uncreated Gift, He is the source of the created gifts which, with sanctifying grace and the infused virtues, fully enable the soul to live supernaturally in a perfect manner.

Indeed, even supplied with grace and the infused virtues, our soul is not re-established in that original integrity in which Adam was before the Fall. Reason, itself subject to error, sees its power of sovereignty disputed by the inferior appetites and the senses; the will is prone to weakness. What follows from this state? It follows that in the principal work of our sanctification, we are under the necessity of being constantly and directly aided by the Holy Spirit. He provides for this by His inspirations which all go to perfect, to achieve our sanctity. And in order that these inspirations may be well received, He Himself places, in our souls, the dispositions that render us docile and pliable; these are the gifts of the Holy Ghost.

The gifts therefore are not of themselves inspirations of the Holy Ghost, but dispositions which cause us to obey these inspirations promptly and easily.

By these gifts, the soul is made capable of being moved and directed in the path of supernatural perfection and of divine filiation; it possesses, as it were, a supernatural tact, a divine instinct of spiritual things. The soul that, in virtue of these dispositions, lets itself be guided by the Spirit, acts in all security as becomes a child of God. In all its spiritual life, it thinks and acts "supernaturally to the point," if I may thus express myself. You will at once see that the gifts place and dispose the soul to move in an atmosphere where *all* is supernatural, where nothing natural, so to speak, is mingled. By His gifts, the Holy Spirit holds and reserves to Himself the supreme direction of all our supernatural conduct.

As you see, the gifts constitute for the soul a perfection of great value on account of their exclusively supernatural character. They achieve the bringing to perfection of that wonderful supernatural organism by which God calls our souls to live by the Divine life. Granted to every soul in a state of grace, in a greater or lesser measure, the gifts remain in a permanent state as long as we do not drive out, by mortal sin, the Divine Guest Who is their source. As it is always possible for them to increase, they moreover extend to all our supernatural life which they make extremely fruitful because by them our souls are placed under the direct action or immediate influence of the Holy Spirit. Now the Holy Spirit is God with the Father and the Son; He loves us with unspeakable love; He wills our sanctification; His inspirations, all proceeding from His goodness and love, have no other end than to mould us to a greater resemblance to Jesus.

What ineffable goodness is that of our God, Who supplies us so carefully and richly with all that is necessary for us in order to attain to Him! And would it not be doing a wrong to the Divine Guest of our souls if we were to doubt His goodness and love, to fail in confidence in His bounty and liberality or show ourselves heedless about profiting by them?

Christ, the Life of the Soul, Part I, chapter 6, section 4.

3. HUMBLE PRAYER AND GENEROUS DOCILITY ARE THE CONDITIONS NECESSARY TO RENDER THE ACTION OF THE HOLY GHOST STABLE AND FRUITFUL WITHIN US

First of all we must often *invoke* the Holy Spirit. Like the Father and the Son, He is God; He too desires our holiness. Moreover, it enters into the Divine plan that we should pray to the Holy Spirit as we pray to the Father and the Son to Whom He is equal in power and goodness. The Church is our guide in this. She closes the cycle of solemnities celebrating Christ's mysteries with Pentecost, the Feast of the mission of the Holy Spirit; during this time she has wonderful prayers, wherewith to ask grace from the Divine Spirit, aspirations full of love, such as the *Veni Sancte Spiritus*. O Infinite Love, proceeding from the Father and the Son, give me the spirit of adoption; teach me to act always as a true child of God. Abide in me, grant that I may abide in Thee so that I may love as Thou lovest. I am nothing without Thee: *Sine tuo numine nihil est in homine.* . . . I am good for nothing, but keep me united to Thee, fill me with Thy love that so I may remain united through Thee to the Father and the Son! "Come, O Holy Ghost, fill the hearts of Thy faithful and kindle in them the fire of Thy love. Come, Holy Ghost, send down those beams. O Blessed Light, shoot home Thy darts, and pierce the centre of those hearts whose faith aspires to Thee. Living Fountain, burning fire, love, true spiritual unction, come. Pour Thy light into our minds, flood our hearts with charity, strengthen our weakness with Thy constant strength."

Above all, let us beseech the Heavenly Father to send us this Spirit. Through sanctifying grace, we are His children; and, as such, our condition urges the Father to pour down His gifts upon us. It is because He loves us as His children that He gives us His Son; Holy Communion is "the Bread

of children": *Panis filiorum;* [12] again it is because we are His
children that He sends us His Spirit, one of His most perfect
gifts: *Donum Dei altissimi.*[13] Indeed what does St. Paul say?
*Quoniam estis filii, misit Deus Spiritum Filii sui in corda
vestra:* [14] "Because you are sons, God hath sent the Spirit of
His Son within your hearts"; He is the Spirit of the Son,
because He proceeds from the Son as from the Father, and
He is sent by both the Father and the Son. This is why, in
the Preface for Pentecost, the Church sings: "It is truly meet
and just . . . that we always and in all places, give thanks
to Thee, O holy Lord, Father Almighty, eternal God,
through Christ Our Lord, Who, ascending above all the
heavens, and sitting at Thy right hand, did this day send
down upon the children of adoption the Holy Spirit Whom
He had promised": *Promissum Spiritum Sanctum hodierna
die in filios adoptionis effudit.*

So then, it is to all the children of adoption, to all those
who are the brethren of Jesus by sanctifying grace that the
Holy Spirit is given. And because this Gift is Divine and
contains every most precious gift of life and of holiness, His
effusion in us—an effusion which was manifested with such
abundance on the day of Pentecost—"fills the whole world
with overflowing joy": *Quapropter profusis gaudiis, totus in
orbe terrarum mundus exsultat.*

> *Christ in His Mysteries,* Part II, chapter
> 17, section 4; and *Christ, the Life of the
> Soul,* Part I, chapter 6, section 6.

Let us be watchful *not to oppose His action* within us.
Spiritum nolite extinguere, says St. Paul, "Extinguish not
the Spirit"; [15] and again: *Nolite contristare Spiritum,* "Grieve

[12] Sequence *Lauda Sion.*
[13] Hymn *Veni Creator.*
[14] Gal. IV, 6.
[15] Thessal. V, 19.

not the Holy Spirit of God." [16] As I have said, the action of
the Spirit in the soul is delicate because it is an action of
completeness, of perfection; His touches are of infinite delicacy. We must watch in order not to oppose the action of this
Divine Spirit by our levity, our voluntary dissipation, our
carelessness, or wilful deliberate resistances, by an ill-regulated attachment to our own judgment: *Nolite esse pruden-
tes apud vosmetipsos.*[17] In the things of God, do not trust to
human wisdom, for then the Holy Spirit will relinquish you
to this natural prudence which, as you know, St. Paul says
is "foolishness" in God's sight, *Stultitia apud Deum.*[18] This
action of the Holy Spirit is quite compatible with those imperfections which so often overtake us by surprise and which
we regret, compatible too with our infirmities, human limi-
tations, and temptations; our native poverty does not repel
the Holy Spirit: He is the *Pater pauperum,* the "Father of
the poor," as the Church calls Him.[19]

That which is incompatible with His action is calculated
resistance to His inspirations. Why is this? First because the
Spirit proceeds from love, He is Love Itself; and yet although His love for us is incommensurable, and His action
infinitely powerful, the Holy Spirit absolutely respects our
liberty and does not compel our will. We have the sad privilege of being able to resist Him; but nothing thwarts love
like obstinate resistance to its advances. Then, it is above all
by His gifts that the Holy Spirit guides us in the path of
holiness and makes us live as children of God; now, in His
gifts, it is the Holy Spirit Who urges and determines the soul
to act: *In donis Spiritus Sancti mens humana non se habet
ut movens, sed magis ut mota;*[20] the soul's part is certainly

[16] Ephes. IV, 30.
[17] Rom. XII, 16.
[18] I Cor. III, 19.
[19] Sequence *Veni Sancte Spiritus.*
[20] S. Thom. II–II, q. LII, a. 2 ad 1.

not to remain entirely passive, but to be ready to receive Divine inspiration, to listen to it, and be promptly faithful to it. Nothing blunts the action of the Holy Spirit in us like a rigid unbending attitude in regard to those inward movements which bear us Godwards, and urge us to the observance of His commandments, to the accomplishment of His good pleasure, to charity, humility and confidence. To reply "no" voluntarily, deliberately, even in little things, impedes the Holy Spirit's action within us; it becomes less strong and more rare, and the soul remains at an ordinary degree, a mediocre level of holiness; its supernatural life lacks intensity: *Spiritum nolite contristare.*

And if these infidelities are multiplied, and become frequent and habitual, the Holy Spirit is silent; the soul thus given over to itself, without guide and inward support in the path of salvation and perfection, is very near to becoming the prey of the prince of darkness; it is the death of charity: *Spiritum nolite extinguere.* Extinguish not the Holy Spirit, for He is like a fire of love burning within our souls.[21]

Rather let us remain, in the measure of our weakness, but with generosity, faithful to the "Spirit of Truth" Who is also the Spirit of holiness; let us be souls promptly docile to the touches of this Spirit.

When therefore we let ourselves be guided by the promptings of this Spirit of Love; when we are, in the measure of our weakness, constantly faithful to His holy inspirations— those inspirations that lead us towards God and what is pleasing to Him—the result is that we act in the *full* meaning of our Divine adoption; then our souls produce those fruits which are at once the term of the Holy Spirit's action in us and, by their sweetness, are like the anticipated reward of our fidelity to this action. These fruits, as enumerated by

[21] *Ignis,* Hymn *Veni Creator. Et tui amoris ignem accende.* Mass for Whitsunday.

St. Paul, are charity, joy, peace, patience, benignity, goodness, longanimity, mildness, faith, modesty, continence and chastity. These fruits, all worthy of the Spirit of Love and Holiness, are also worthy of our Heavenly Father Who finds His glory in them: *In hoc clarificatus est Pater meus ut fructum plurimum afferatis;* finally they are worthy of Christ Jesus Who merited them for us and to Whom the Holy Spirit unites us: *Qui manet in me et ego in eo hic fert fructum multum.*

At the feast of the Tabernacles, one of the most brilliant Jewish solemnities, Our Lord happened to be in Jerusalem. In the midst of the crowd, He exclaimed: "If any man thirst, let him come to Me and drink. He that believeth in Me as the Scripture sayeth, 'Out of his belly shall flow rivers of living water.'" St. John adds: "Now this He said of the Spirit which they should receive, who believed in Him."

The Holy Spirit Whom Christ, as the Word, sends us, is within us the principle, the source of those rivers of living water, of the grace which springs up within us into life everlasting, that is to say, that makes us bear fruits of everlasting life. . . . Whilst awaiting the supreme beatitude, these waters "make joyful the city" of souls: *Fluminis impetus laetificat civitatem Dei.*

> *Christ, the Life of the Soul,* Part I,
> chapter 6, section 6, *passim.*

23 *Bear Our Thoughts, Affections and Actions, Like Ardent Flames, Continually Heavenward*

The Holy Ghost, being both God and Love, does not remain inactive in the soul where He dwells. His divine operations are powerful and fruitful, and influence the whole activity of the humble and docile soul.

1. OUR THOUGHTS

The Holy Ghost carries our thoughts heavenward *by illuminating us with divine light because, according to the very words of Jesus, He is "the Spirit of Truth Who leads us to the whole truth."*

Let us now contemplate the divine workings of this Spirit in the souls of the Apostles on the day of Pentecost!

He fills them with *truth*. You will at once say: Had not Christ Jesus done this? Certainly He had. Did He not Himself declare: "I am the Truth"? He came into the world to bear testimony to the truth, and you know, also from Himself, that He wholly accomplished His mission: *Opus consummavi.*

Yes, but now that He has left His apostles, it is the Holy

235

Spirit Who is about to become their interior Master. "He shall not speak of Himself," said Jesus, wishing to signify by this that the Holy Spirit—proceeding from the Father and the Son, receiving from Them divine life—will give us the infinite truth that He receives by His ineffable procession. "He will teach you all things and bring all things to your mind, whatsoever I shall have said to you."

Christ in His Mysteries, Part II, chapter 17, section 3.

That promise is ever being fulfilled, for Christ's words do not pass away. Christ, the Incarnate Word, together with His Father, gave us His Spirit on the day of our baptism, which made us children of the heavenly Father and Christ's own brethren. This Spirit abides in us. *Apud vos manebit et in vobis erit.*[1] And what does He do in us, this Divine Spirit, the Spirit of Truth? He brings to our mind the words of Jesus. Our Lord Himself tells us so. What does this mean? It means that when we contemplate the actions and mysteries of Christ Jesus, either in reading the Gospel or a life of Our Lord or when, under the Church's guidance, in the course of the liturgical year, one day it happens that some word, such as we have many times read and re-read without it having particularly struck us, suddenly stands out in supernatural relief in a way we have not hitherto known. It is a flash of light that the Holy Spirit makes all at once to rise from the depth of the soul; it is like the sudden revelation of a source of life hitherto unsuspected, like a new and wider horizon that opens out before the eyes of the soul; it is like a new world that the Spirit discovers to us. He Whom the liturgy names "the finger of God," *Digitus Dei,*[2] engraves this Divine word on the soul, there ever to remain a light

[1] Joan. XIV, 17.
[2] Hymn *Veni Creator.*

and principle of action; if the soul is humble and attentive, this Divine word works therein, silent but fruitful.

When we are every day faithful to consecrate a time, longer or shorter according to our aptitudes and duties of state, in speaking with our Heavenly Father, in gathering up His inspirations and listening to what the Holy Spirit "brings to mind," then the words of Christ, the *Verba Verbi,* as St. Augustine calls them, go on multiplying, inundating the soul with Divine Light and opening out in it fountains of life so that the soul's thirst may be ever assuaged.

Christ, the Life of the Soul, Part II, chapter 10, section 4.

To a greater extent still does the Holy Spirit make us also "know the Son": *Noscamus atque Filium;* He manifests Jesus to us; He is this inward Master Who makes us penetrate into the meaning of His words, and His mysteries; "He shall glorify Me," says Jesus, "because He shall receive of Mine, and shall show it to you": *Ille me clarificabit.* By making divine knowledge abound in us, by keeping us in the presence of Jesus, by inspiring us ever to do what is pleasing to Him, He causes Christ to reign in us. By His infinitely delicate and sovereignly efficacious action, He forms Jesus in us. Is not that the substance of all holiness?

Christ in His Mysteries, Part II, chapter 17, section 5.

By the gift of *knowledge* the Holy Spirit makes us see created things in a supernatural way as only a child of God can see them. There are many ways of considering what lies within us and around us. It is in a different manner that an unbeliever and one who believes in God contemplate creation. The unbeliever has only a purely natural knowledge, however wide and profound it may be; the child of God sees creation in the light of the Holy Spirit, as the work of God wherein His eternal perfections are reflected. This gift makes us know created things, including ourselves, from God's point of view; it makes us know our supernatural end and the means of arriving at it, but with intuitions which preserve us from the false maxims of the world and the suggestions of the spirit of darkness.

Christ, the Life of the Soul, Part I, chapter 6, section 5.

2. OUR AFFECTIONS

We were made to be happy; the human heart has a capacity for the infinite; only God can fully satisfy us. "Thou didst make us for Thyself, O Lord, and our heart is restless until it finds its rest in Thee": *Fecisti nos ad te, et inquietum est cor nostrum, donec requiescat in te.* This is why when we seek anything apart from God or from His will, we do not find stable and perfect happiness.

Different categories of souls are to be met with. You will see some living in continual gladness. Their inward joy radiates outwardly. I am not now speaking of that sensible joy which often depends upon the temperament, the state of health, or of circumstances independent of the will, but of joy abiding in the depth of the soul which is like a foretaste of heavenly bliss. Have these souls then never any trials? Have they no conflicts to sustain, nor contradictions to undergo? Certainly they have, for each disciple of Jesus Christ has to carry his cross; but the fervour of grace and Divine unction make them endure these sufferings joyfully. Other souls do not feel this gladness; inwardly, and often even outwardly, they are troubled, distressed, unhappy. Whence comes this difference?

Because the first seek God in all things, and seeking Him alone they find Him everywhere, and, with Him, supreme good and unchanging bliss: *Bonus est Dominus animae quaerenti illum.* The others are either attached to created things or seek themselves, by egotism, self-love, levity; and it is themselves too that they find—themselves, that is to say, nothingness, and this cannot content them, for the soul, created for God, thirsts after perfect good.

But when the soul seeks God, and seeks Him alone, when it tends towards Him with all its energies, when it clings to no created thing, God fills it with joy, with that overflowing joy of which St. Benedict speaks when he says that in the measure wherein faith, and with it hope and love increase in the soul of the monk, he runs, "with heart enlarged and unspeakable sweetness of love, in the way of God's commandments": *Dilatato corde, inenarrabili dilectionis dulcedine curritur via mandatorum Dei.*

> *Christ, the Ideal of the Monk,* Part I,
> chapter 1, section 4.

It is to this blessed state that the Holy Spirit brings us by His gift of wisdom. What does wisdom here signify? It is a *sapida cognitio rerum spiritualium,* a supernatural gift in order to know or esteem Divine things by the spiritual taste with which the Holy Spirit inspires us. It is an intimate, a deep knowledge that relishes the things of God. We ask for it in the collect for the feast of Pentecost itself: *Da nobis in eodem Spiritu recta sapere. Sapere* is to have not only the knowledge, but the relish for celestial and supernatural things; it is not—far from it—what is called sensible devotion, but a spiritual *experience* of what is Divine, that the Holy Spirit wills to produce within us. It is the response to the *Gustate et videte quoniam suavis est Dominus*: "O taste and see that the Lord is sweet." This gift makes us prefer, without any hesitation, the blessedness of God's service to all earthly joys; it is this gift which causes the soul to say: "How

lovely are Thy tabernacles, O Lord! . . . better is one day
in Thy courts above thousands" of years away from Thee!

> *Christ, the Life of the Soul,* Part I, chap-
> ter 6, section 5.

Having made us ask for wisdom, the Church makes us
beg for God's grace to "always rejoice in the consolation
which comes from the Holy Ghost"—*et de ejus semper con-
solatione gaudere.*

Because He is the Spirit of truth, this Consoler assuages
the needs of our intelligence; because He is the Spirit of
love, He satisfies the desires of our heart; because He is the
Spirit of strength, He sustains us in our toils, trials and tears:
the Holy Spirit is eminently the Consoler. *Consolator optime,
dulcis hospes animae, dulce refrigerium!*

Oh! Come and dwell in us, Father of the poor, Giver of
heavenly gifts, Thou best Consoler, sweet Guest, and Re-
freshment full of sweetness for the soul.

> *Christ in His Mysteries,* Part II, chapter
> 17, section 3.

3. OUR ACTIONS

*The Holy Ghost bears our actions heavenward, by guid-
ing us with His gift of counsel and assisting us with His gift
of strength.*

And what is it this Divine Spirit does in our souls? For
being God, being Love, He does not remain inactive. First
of all, He gives testimony that we are the children of God:
*Ipse Spiritus testimonium reddit spiritui nostro, quod sumus
filii Dei;* He is the Spirit of Love, the Spirit of Holiness,
Whose will it is, because He loves us, to give us a share in
His holiness that we may be true and worthy children of
God.

By the gift of *counsel,* the Holy Spirit responds to this

prayer of the soul: "Lord, what wilt Thou have me to do?"
He keeps us from all precipitation, from all levity, but, above
all, from all presumption, so dangerous in spiritual ways. A
soul that only wishes to be guided by herself, who worships
her own personality, acts without consulting God in prayer.
She practically acts as if God was not for her the heavenly
Father from Whom every light comes: OMNE *donum per-*
fectum desursum est, descendens a Patre luminum.[3] Consider our Divine Saviour. He says the Son, that is to say,
Himself, does nothing "but what He seeth the Father doing": *Non potest Filius a se facere quidquam nisi quod vide-*
rit Patrem facientem.[4] The soul of Jesus contemplated the
Father to behold in Him the model of His works; it was
the Spirit of Counsel that showed Him the desires of the
Father; that is why all that our Lord did was pleasing to His
Father: *Quae placita sunt ei facio semper.*[5] It is a disposition
whereby the child of God is enabled to judge of things according to principles above those of human wisdom. Sometimes, natural prudence, always limited, points out how to
act in such or such a way; then, by the gift of counsel, the
Holy Spirit shows higher principles of conduct which ought
to direct the actions of the child of God.

It is not always enough for us to know God's good pleasure. Owing to our fallen nature, we often need strength to
carry into effect what God requires of us; it is the Holy
Spirit Who, by the gift of *fortitude,* sustains us in particularly difficult moments. There are pusillanimous souls that
fear the trials of the inner life. It is impossible that these
trials should be wanting; they are even so much the deeper
in proportion as God calls us higher. But let us fear nothing:
the Spirit of Fortitude is with us: *Apud vos manebit et in*

[3] Jac. I, 17.
[4] Joan. V, 19.
[5] *Ibid.,* VIII, 29.

vobis erit.[6] Like the Apostles on the Day of Pentecost, we shall be, by the Holy Spirit, endowed with power from on high: *Virtute ex alto,*[7] so as to accomplish the Divine will generously, to obey, like the disciples, God rather than men, if the choice must be made;[8] to support valiantly the adversities we meet with as we come nearer to God. That is why St. Paul prayed so earnestly for the faithful of Ephesus that God would grant them "to be strengthened by His Spirit with might unto the inward man."[9] The Holy Spirit says to such as He fills with fortitude, what God said to Moses when he shrank from the mission given to him of delivering the Hebrew people from the yoke of the Pharaohs: *Ego ero tecum:* Fear nothing, "I will be with thee." Such a one is strong with the very strength of God. It is this strength that makes the martyrs and sustains the virgins. The world wonders to see them so courageous, because it imagines they find their strength in themselves, while in reality they draw it from God alone.

Christ, the Life of the Soul, Part I, chapter 6, section 5.

Ask the Holy Ghost to give you an abundance of His gift of *fortitude,* nothing so honours God as to lean on Him in full confidence, just when we feel weak and incapable.

Union with God, chapter 4, section 3.

The Holy Ghost also bears our actions heavenward, by inspiring us to ever act by the movement of divine charity which He pours into every soul on its baptismal day.

He is personal Love in the life of God. He is, as it were, the breath, the aspiration of the infinite love whence we

[6] *Ibid.,* xvi, 17.
[7] *Ibid.,* xxiv, 49.
[8] Act. iv, 19.
[9] Ephes. iii, 16.

draw life. It is related in Genesis that "the Lord God formed man of the slime of the earth, and breathed into his face the breath of life": *Inspiravit spiraculum vitae.* This vital breath was the symbol of the Spirit to Whom we owe the supernatural life.

Christ in His Mysteries, Part II, chapter 17, section 3.

"In fact," says St. Paul, "the charity of God is poured forth in our hearts, by the Holy Ghost, Who is given to us." This charity, by referring us entirely to God, makes us find in Him the supreme good which we prefer to all other goods. It is the fruit of the grace which renders us pleasing to God so that we become His children. It is true that supernatural charity is not grace, but the two go hand in hand together: *Caritas diffusa est in cordibus nostris per Spiritum Sanctum qui datus est nobis.* Grace elevates our being. Charity transforms our activity. Grace and charity are always united. The degree of one determines the degree of the other.

When we possess Divine grace within us, we fulfil the wish of Our Lord: we "abide in Him," *Manete in me,* and He "abides in us," *Et ego in vobis;* He abides with the Father and the Holy Spirit: *Ad eum veniemus et mansionem apud eum faciemus.* The Holy Trinity, dwelling truly within us as in a temple, does not remain inactive, but unceasingly sustains us so that our soul may exercise its supernatural activity.

Christ, the Life of the Soul, Part II, chapter 5, section 2.

And when this love is ardent, when it is well anchored in the soul, it then governs all the other virtues and every good work; it acts supremely. Because it is powerful, it ever inclines the will towards good, towards God. It manifests itself

by constant fidelity to the Divine good pleasure and to the
inspirations of the Holy Ghost. It is to these souls full of
love, that St. Augustine could say: *Dilige, et quod vis fac:*
"Love, and do what thou wilt," because these souls embrace
only what pleases God; following the example of Christ
Jesus, they can say: *Quae placita sunt ei facio semper,* "I do
always that which pleases My Father in Heaven." That is
perfection.

This life, animated by grace and filled with love, does not
always appear to the eyes of the world; undoubtedly, Our
Lord says, every tree is known by its fruits; the Holy
Spirit Who dwells in the soul makes it produce fruits of
charity and benignity that outwardly manifest the power of
His action; but the principle of this action is altogether hidden, its substantial splendour altogether interior: *Omnis
gloria filiae regis ab intus,* its supernatural beauty is often
veiled beneath the common appearances of everyday life.

With all the energy of our being, by the meritorious practice of the virtues, above all, the theological virtues, and by
the essential disposition of doing all for the glory of the
Heavenly Father, let us aim at leaving the greatest freedom
possible to the development within us of the action of God
and of the Holy Spirit. It is by this "we shall grow up in
Christ Who is our Head"; to this we have been called by
Christ Jesus: *In quo et comprehensus sum a Christo Jesu.*

> *Christ, the Life of the Soul,* Part II,
> chapter 6, sections 3, 7 and 9.

It is principally in our act of prayer that the movement of
the Holy Ghost is felt.

God promised by the prophet Zacharias, that, under the
new covenant, He would pour out upon souls the spirit of
grace and of prayers: *Effundam super habitatores Jerusalem
Spiritum gratiae et precum.* This spirit is the Holy Spirit,

the Spirit of adoption, Whom God sends into the hearts of those He predestines to be His children in Christ Jesus. The gifts which this Divine Spirit confers on our souls on the day of baptism, by the infusion of His grace, help us in our relations with our Father in Heaven. The gift of fear fills us with reverence in presence of the divine majesty; the gift of piety harmonizes, with fear, the tenderness of a child towards a beloved father; the gift of knowledge places the truths of the natural order in a new light; the gift of understanding makes us penetrate into the hidden depths of the mysteries of faith; the gift of wisdom gives us the relish, the affective knowledge of revealed truths. The gifts of the Holy Spirit are very real dispositions which we do not take enough into account. It is by these gifts that the Spirit, Who dwells in the soul of the baptised as in a temple, helps and guides us in our intercourse with the Heavenly Father: *Spiritus adjuvat infirmitatem nostram* . . . IPSE *postulat pro nobis gemitibus inenarrabilibus.*

The essential element of prayer is the supernatural contact of the soul with God whence it imbibes that divine life that is the source of all holiness. This contact is produced when the soul, raised by faith and love, supported by Jesus Christ, yields itself to God, to His will, through the movement of the Holy Spirit: *Sapiens cor suum tradidit ad vigilandum diluculo ad Dominum qui fecit illum, et in conspectu Altissimi deprecabitur.* No reasoning, no purely natural effort, can produce this contact: *Nemo potest dicere: Dominus Jesus, nisi in Spiritu Sancto.* This contact is produced in the darkness of faith, but it fills the soul with light and life.

Prayer is, then, the expression, under the action of the gifts of the Holy Spirit, of the sentiments that result from our divine adoption in Jesus Christ. "We know not what we should pray for as we ought, but the Spirit Himself asketh for us with unspeakable groanings." Now St. Paul says, in the same place, this Spirit Who prays for us and in us, is the Spirit of adoption that "giveth testimony to our spirit, that we are the sons of God, and if sons heirs also, . . . whereby we cry, Abba, Father." This Spirit was given to us when "the fulness of time being come, God sent His Son . . . that we might receive the adoption of sons." Because the grace of Christ makes us the children of God, He has also sent the Spirit of His Son into our hearts so that we may pray to God as to a Father: *Quoniam estis filii, misit Deus Spiritum Filii sui in corda vestra.* Because indeed, we "are no more strangers and foreigners," but members of God's family, built upon the foundation of which Christ Jesus is the chief cornerstone: *Ipso summo angulari lapide Christo Jesu.*

Thus it is the Spirit Whom we have received in baptism, in the sacrament of our divine adoption, Who makes us cry to God: "Thou art Our Father."

> *Christ, the Life of the Soul,* Part II, chapter 10, section 1.

If prayer be the conversation of the child of God with his Heavenly Father, it will bear the impress both of a high degree of piety and of a deep reverence. Indeed for the child of God, for the brother of Christ Jesus, no tenderness, no intimacy is too great, but on the condition that it be always accompanied and sustained by a sense of unutterable reverence before the immense majesty of the Father: *Patrem immensae majestatis.* This is to adore the Father in spirit and in truth.

> *Christ, the Ideal of the Monk,* Part II, chapter 15, section 2.

May 29, 1915.

You see, my child, God has created us for Himself, and we can do nothing greater than to give ourselves up to Him to carry out His wishes. To allow God to act on us in prayer is neither laziness nor inactivity. At such moments, deep down in the imperceptible depths of our soul, there is passing a *Divine* activity more precious than all our human activity. As the soul gets nearer to God, she becomes simpler and no words, no forms can express nor formulate what she would say, but as the Church prays in her liturgy, "O God, to Whom every heart is open and to Whom every *will speaks,* and from Whom there is nothing hidden, purify our hearts by the infusion of the Holy Spirit that we may perfectly love Thee, and worthily praise Thee."

Union with God, chapter 5.

February 24, 1921.

Never forget that prayer is a *state,* and that with souls who seek God prayer becomes continuous, often in an unconscious manner, in the *spiritual depths* of the soul. It is there, in this sanctuary, that the Word espouses the soul *in pure faith, Sponsabo te mihi in fide.* These silent longings, these sighings are the true voice of the Holy Spirit within us which touches the heart of God: *Desiderium pauperum exaudivit auris tua.* "Thy ear, O Lord, hath heard the desire of the poor."

Abbot Columba Marmion: A Master of the Spiritual Life, chapter 18.

24 *Into the Father's Bosom*

The "heights" to which we ask the Holy Ghost to "bear
our thoughts, affections, actions" have as their goal the
bosom of the Father, the sanctuary of the Divinity. Dom Marmion reverts to an idea dear to him and which he has already
expressed in the invocation to the Father. The Son, living
with the same life as the Father, is always in the Father's
bosom and leads us there when we remain united to Him.
Similarly as regards the Holy Ghost; He is the spirit of the
Father and the Son, the ineffable termination of their mutual and unique love. He flows back, if we may thus stam-
meringly speak of these mysteries, towards the Father and
the Son. When we receive the Holy Ghost—Who, according
to the expression of some Doctors of the Church, comes to
us from the Father through the Son—and allow Him to
guide us in all our conduct, He carries us, through the Word,
into the Father's bosom, as to our supreme end. St. Paul ex-
pounds this doctrine when he writes to the Ephesians (ii,
18): "For by Him we have access both in one spirit to the
Father."

For this section we merely quote extracts from the spiritual notes and letters of Dom Marmion during his stay at
Louvain.

March 3, 1900.

When the Word espoused and endowed His Humanity, the Spouse being God, the dowry had to be divine. According to the Fathers and the Doctors of the Church, what the Word truly gave as dowry to His Humanity was the Holy Spirit, Who proceeds from Him as well as from the Father, and is substantially the plenitude of holiness. This was the living and infinite unction with which He consecrated this Human Nature. *Unxit te Deus, Deus tuus, oleo laetitiae prae consortibus tuis*: "God hath anointed thee with the oil of gladness above thy fellows."

For some time I have felt more and more a special attraction towards the Holy Spirit. I have a great desire to be guided, led, moved in all things by the Spirit of Jesus. Our Lord, as Man, did nothing except under the impulsion of the Holy Spirit and under His dependence. Hence it followed that possessing in Himself and Himself alone—as to the hypostatic union—this Holy Humanity, the Word never operated or wrought anything in His Human Nature save through His Holy Spirit.

We, too, have received the same Spirit in baptism, and in the Sacrament of confirmation: *Quoniam estis filii, misit Spiritum Filii sui in corda vestra. Qui adhaeret Domino, unus Spiritus est.* St. Paul speaks constantly of the Spirit of Jesus Who guided Him and enlightened Him in all things.

All that, in our activity, comes from this *Holy* Spirit is holy. *Quod natum est ex Spiritu, spiritus est . . . Spiritus est qui vivificat.* He who yields himself up without reserve or resistance to this Spirit Who is *Pater pauperum . . . Dator munerum* will be infallibly led by the same path as Jesus, and in the manner that Jesus wills for each one. This Spirit led Elizabeth to praise Mary, and Mary is led by the same Spirit of Jesus to magnify the glory of the Lord.

The Holy Spirit leads us to call upon the Father in the

same way as Jesus did: *Spiritus adoptionis in quo clamamus: Abba, Pater;* to glorify Jesus: *Ipse testimonium perhibebit de me;* to pray as is right, in offering the supplications He makes for us in our hearts: *gemitibus inenarrabilibus;* to humility, to compunction, *quia ipse est remissio omnium peccatorum.* It is by Him that we do good to souls (the Apostles did so little before Pentecost). It is He Who fructifies all our activity: *Nemo potest dicere Domine Jesu nisi in Spiritu sancto.*

Oh, I will strive to live in this Holy Spirit!

——, 1904.

Substantial Love of the Father and of the Son, I unite myself to You; I wish to love as You love; I am good for nothing, but deign to permit me to unite myself to You with all my heart and transport me even to the bosom of God.

In January, 1906, he wrote the beautiful synthesis on the Trinity. From this date, as we have said, he enjoyed abundant illuminations which threw light on various aspects of this mystery and particularly on the action of the Holy Ghost in docile and generous souls.

February, 1906.

The words of Our Lord: "This is the work of God, that you believe in Him Whom He hath sent" made it still clearer to me that in Jesus Christ we have everything. He who abandons himself unreservedly to Jesus Christ by faith, fulfils perfectly with Him, in Him and by Him, all his duties towards the Father. Jesus is *one* with His Father: "The Father and I are one." He is "in the bosom of the Father" and he who is united by faith to Jesus does, *in unity,* that which Jesus does for His Father. The member does in its way what the person does: "You are the Body of Christ and members one of another." When we are united by faith to Jesus Christ, and, in the darkness of this faith, we relinquish our intelligence at Christ's feet, and lovingly accept all Jesus does in our name in the full vision of His Father, our prayer is very elevated and said "in spirit and in truth." At such times, the Spirit of Christ sometimes prompts us to remain in silent adoration at the feet of Jesus; at other times, He urges us to unite ourselves to His sacrifice, to His submission to His Father. We should follow these promptings.

October 5, 1906.

God seeks those who adore Him in *Spirit* and in truth. He (the Holy Spirit) is the Spirit of the Father and Son, and those who allow themselves to be led by Him, seek the Father and the Son in truth. He is the *Holy* Spirit, because all His inspirations are infinitely holy. He is the same identical Spirit which inspires Jesus in every act and thought, and it is by union with Him that the interior of Jesus Christ is formed in our hearts. He is the *Pater pauperum,* the Father of the poor, He does not disdain to unite Himself with those who remain in *adoration and spirit of annihilation* in His presence. He is the Spirit of holy charity and being the same in all unites us in holy love.

January 1, 1907.

Our Divine Saviour urges me more and more to live in a total dependence on Him and on the promptings of His Spirit.

Pentecost, 1907.

The Holy Spirit dwells in our hearts. "He shall abide with you, and shall be in you." He proceeds from the Father and the Son, and He bears with Him the whole creation (which

He loves in His "procession") unto the bosom of the Father and the Son.

The more we yield ourselves to this Holy Spirit of love, the more all the tendencies of our being are directed towards the Father. Three spirits tend to take possession of us: the spirit of darkness, the human spirit, and the Holy Spirit. It is very important to distinguish between the action of these spirits, in order that we may give ourselves only to the Spirit of God.

December 2, 1908.

For me Jesus is *everything*. I can neither pray, celebrate Mass nor perform the sacred ministry except in total dependence on His action and His Holy Spirit.

December 15, 1908.

Pray much for me, that Jesus may become the Supreme Master of my spiritual life, and that I may live more and more in great dependence on His Spirit.

> *Abbot Columba Marmion: A Master of the Spiritual Life,* chapters 8, 16 and 18, *passim.*

A few days afterwards, December 25, 1908, Dom Marmion signed the act of consecration which is the subject of these pages.

Let us end with a letter of January 8, 1908, in which Dom Marmion resumes his doctrine on the action of the Holy Ghost in the soul.

In every soul three spirits strive for the mastery. The spirit of falsehood and blasphemy who from the beginning ever suggests the exact contrary of what God whispers. "If you eat of this fruit you shall certainly die," said God. *Nequaquam moriemini:* "You shall not die by any means" was

Satan's reply, and all his suggestions are but the echo of this first lie.

Then there is the spirit of this world, inclining us to judge things according to the maxims of sense and of carnal prudence. *Prudentia hujus mundi stultitia est apud Deum:* "The prudence of this world is folly with God."

Then there is the spirit of God ever whispering in our ears to raise our hearts above nature: *Sursum corda,* to live by faith: *Justus meus ex fide vivit.* This Spirit always inclines us towards simple loving faith, abandon of self into God's hands. It fills us with "peace and joy in believing," and produces the fruits of which St. Paul speaks.

Now, my dear child, in certain persons the action of these several spirits is more tangible and striking than in others. In you the influence of these spirits is very marked. You will always know them by their fruits, even though Satan may try to clothe himself as an angel of light. Our Lord says, *Ex fructibus eorum cognoscetis eos.* You will recognise these spirits by the *fruits* they produce in your soul.

God's Spirit, even when He reproaches us or inclines us to confusion or compunction for our sins, *ever* fills the soul with peace and filial confidence in our Heavenly Father. The other spirits dry up our soul, fill us with naturalistic tendencies, or, if it be the spirit of hell, casts gloom and discouragement into our soul.

I recommend you a great fidelity to the movements of the Holy Spirit. Your baptism and your confirmation have established Him as a living fountain in your soul. Hear His whisperings, and put the other inspirations to flight *at once.* If you are faithful in this, little by little this Divine Spirit will become your guide and bear you with Him into God's bosom.

Union with God, chapter 1.

25 *May Our Whole Life Be a Gloria Patri et Filio et Spiritui Sancto*

Dom Marmion repeats here a phrase from pages written on the Blessed Trinity nearly three years before the Consecration and puts it in the form of an invocation. We can find no better way of illustrating this invocation than to reproduce these pages which were the fruit of the Holy Ghost's inspiration. In re-reading them now, having covered the commentary which we have just made, our readers, by penetrating their profound meaning more deeply, will also appreciate more fully their beauty and their practical and beneficent character.

They contain an epitome of the whole doctrine expounded in this collection.

January 20, 1906.

I have received a strong light upon the manner of honouring the Blessed Trinity and of acting in such a way that our whole life may be a perpetual *Gloria Patri*. These reflections serve me as outline.

The *Father* is the Principle, the Source of all life, *Fons vitae*. The Word and the Holy Spirit proceed from Him, and all creation comes from Him through the Word, in the Holy Spirit.

We honour Him as the First Cause by laying down at His feet our whole being, our plans, our desires, in order that He may take the initiative in everything concerning us.

In this way we imitate Jesus:

(*a*) Who proceeds *entirely* from the Father.

(*b*) Who thought, desired and acted in absolute dependence on Him: "Amen, amen, I say unto you, the Son cannot do anything of Himself, but what He seeth the Father doing." "My doctrine is not Mine, but His that sent me." During His whole life, He did at each instant, "the things that please the Father." He remained in the obscurity of the Nazareth workshop for thirty years, and only began His public mission at the hour fixed by His Father. He limited Himself to preaching to the Jews, because He was sent only to the lost sheep of the house of Israel: "All things must needs be fulfilled which are written in the law of Moses and in the Prophets, and in the Psalms, concerning Me." "One jot, or one tittle shall not pass of the law, till all be fulfilled."

I have understood that without this absolute dependence upon God the most brilliant actions have little value in His eyes, although they may, of themselves, dazzle men. We are in our true place as creatures and children of adoption when we leave to our Creator and our Father the full disposal of our person and of our whole activity. This is particularly true of the religious, and above all of the monk.

The *Son* not only proceeds entirely from the Father, and therefore depends [1] absolutely on Him, but being the perfect Son, He is the perfect image of the Father: "the Image of

---

[1] Not a dependence of time nor of authority but, in the divine "processions," the Father has a priority of nature or origin.

the invisible God." He is the Wisdom of the Father and
perfectly fulfils all the will of the Father, all His designs.

We honour the Son as being like Him—truth and wisdom
—by perfectly fulfilling the Father's every will, His "manifest" will, by a perfect fidelity in accomplishing all the
known will of God. Known by His commandments, His
counsels, His inspirations, and by obedience. And of His
"hidden" will, by leaving all to Him. He accepted for Himself and for His members all the Father's will, and we
honour Him by uniting ourselves to Him in this acceptance,
by asking Him to take away from our heart all desire or
wish to do the least thing that is outside the design of His
will. (We may meditate on the life of Jesus Christ in the
light of this thought, and this meditation will bring much
peace and union with Him.) It is thus we shall perfectly
carry out this precept of Saint Paul: "All whatsoever you do
. . . do all in the name of the Lord Jesus Christ."

For we do only in His name that which He sees to be the
Father's good pleasure for us. Thus are realized these words:
"He must increase, but I must decrease"; then we become
the object of the Father's delight, from Whom comes down
every best gift, every perfect grace. These actions become
great, because they are done in God.

The *Holy Spirit* is the mutual Love of the Father and the
Son. He returns unto the bosom of the Father and of the
Son with an infinite love which is Himself.

We honour the Holy Spirit by uniting ourselves humbly
through Jesus Christ to this love by which we return to God
as our last end. It is this love which gives all the value to our
actions. This love proceeding from the Father and the Son
bears us towards God in dependence and in love. All our
life thus proceeds from the Father in the Son in order to
return to His bosom, in the Holy Spirit.

Thus united to Jesus Christ in His Spirit, our life becomes a sacrifice of love for God and for souls: "Christ, Who by the Holy Ghost offered Himself unspotted unto God." If we turn to the Holy Spirit with love and confidence, He will not fail to fill us with true divine love. For He is the "Father of the poor." "Hope confoundeth not: because the charity of God is poured forth in our hearts, by the Holy Ghost, Who is given to us."

Abbot Columba Marmion: A Master of
the Spiritual Life, chapter 8.

PART. 4 *The Mother of the Incarnate Word*

The pre-eminent dignity of Mother of God places the Virgin Mary in special and immutable relationship with each of the Persons of the Blessed Trinity.

That is why Dom Marmion ends the Consecration with a prayer to the august Mother of Christ. The titles which he accords her, the petition which he makes, summarize in their conciseness the whole essence of his Marian doctrine.

26 *O Mary, Mother of Christ*

1. THROUGH THE INCARNATION OF THE WORD MARY BECAME THE MOTHER OF CHRIST

What has Mary given to Jesus?

While remaining a virgin, she has given Him a human nature. That is a unique privilege that Mary shares with none: *Nec primam similem visa est, nec habere sequentem.*[1] The Word might have appeared here below by taking a human nature created *ex nihilo,* drawn out of nothing, and already formed in the perfection of its organism, as Adam was formed in the earthly paradise. For reasons of infinite wisdom, this was not done. In uniting Himself to humanity, the Word willed to pass through all the stages of human growth in order to sanctify them; He willed to be born of a woman.

But what is so wonderful in this birth is that the Word made it subject, so to speak, to the consent of this woman.

Let us transport ourselves in spirit to Nazareth and contemplate this ineffable scene. The Angel appears to the young virgin. After having saluted her, he delivers his message: "Behold thou shalt conceive in thy womb, and shalt bring forth a son, and thou shalt call His name Jesus. He shall be great, and shall be called the Son of the Most High

[1] Antiphon for the Office of Lauds at Christmas.

. . . and of His kingdom there shall be no end." Mary asks
the angel how this shall be done, since she is a virgin: *Quomodo fiet istud quoniam virum non cognosco?* [2] Gabriel
answers: "The Holy Ghost shall come upon thee, and the
power of the Most High shall overshadow thee. And therefore the Holy which shall be born of thee shall be called the
Son of God." Then, instancing the example of Elizabeth,
who has conceived in spite of her former barrenness, because
it hath thus pleased the Lord, the Angel adds: "No word
shall be impossible with God"; He can, when He so wills,
suspend the laws of nature.

God proposes the mystery of the Incarnation which will
only be fulfilled in the Virgin when she shall have given her
free consent. The accomplishment of the mystery hangs in
suspense until then. At this moment, according to the saying
of St. Thomas, Mary represents us all in her person. It is as
if God awaited the response of the humanity to which He
wills to unite Himself: *Per annuntiationem exspectabatur
consensus virginis loco totius humanae naturae.* [3] What a solemn moment it is! For now the vital mystery of Christianity
is about to be decided. St. Bernard, in one of his most beautiful homilies on the Annunciation, [4] shows us the whole
human race, who for thousands of years have hoped for salvation, the Angelic choirs, and even God Himself, as if in
suspense, awaiting the acceptation of the young Virgin.

And Mary gives her reply: full of faith in the heavenly
word, and entirely submissive to the Divine Will that has
just been manifested to her, she says: "Behold the handmaid
of the Lord, be it done to me according to thy word," *Ecce
ancilla Domini; fiat mihi secundum verbum tuum.* [5] This
Fiat is Mary's consent to the Divine plan of Redemption;

[2] Luc. I, 34.
[3] S. Thom. III, q. xxx, a. I.
[4] *Homil.* IV, *super Missus est*, c. 8.
[5] Luc. I, 38.

this *Fiat* is like the echo of the *Fiat* of the creation; but it is a new world, an infinitely higher world, a world of grace that God Himself creates after this consent: for at this moment the Divine Word, the second Person of the Holy Trinity, becomes incarnate in Mary: *Et Verbum caro factum est.*[6]

It is certain, as we have just heard by the voice of the angel, no human concourse is to intervene, for all must be holy in Christ's conception and birth; but it is from her most pure blood that Mary conceives by the operation of the Holy Ghost, it is from her that the Man-God is to come forth. When Jesus is born at Bethlehem, who is it Who lies there upon the straw? It is the Child-God, it is the Word, Who, while remaining a Divine Person, *Quod erat permansit,*[7] has united to Himself a human nature in the bosom of the Virgin. In this Child there are two quite distinct natures, but only one Person, the Divine Person: the term of this virginal birth is the Man-God: "The Holy which shall be born of thee shall be called the Son of God";[8] this Man-God, this God-made-man, is Mary's Son. This is what Elizabeth, filled with the Holy Ghost, said to her: "Whence is this to me, that the Mother of my Lord should come to me?"[9] Mary is the Mother of Christ, for, as all other mothers do for their children, she formed and nourished with her most pure substance the body of Jesus. This is a dogma of faith. If by His eternal birth *In splendoribus sanctorum,*[10] Christ is truly the Son of God, *Deum verum de Deo vero,* by His temporal birth, He is truly the Son of Mary; the only Son of God is also the only Son of the Virgin.

Such is the ineffable union existing between Jesus and Mary: she is His Mother, He is her Son. This union is indis-

---

[6] Joan. I, 14.
[7] Antiphon for the Office of the Circumcision.
[8] Luc. I, 35.
[9] *Ibid.,* 43.
[10] Ps. CIX, 3.

soluble; and as Jesus is at the same time the Son of God,
come to save the world, Mary is indeed intimately associated
with the vital mystery of all Christianity. All her greatness
is founded on this special privilege of her Divine motherhood.

Christ, the Life of the Soul, Part II,
chapter 12, section 1.

2. FOLLOWING CHRIST'S EXAMPLE, THE CHILD OF GOD SHOULD ALSO BE MARY'S SON

All holiness for us consists in the imitation of Jesus Christ,
in the conformity of our whole being to the Son of God, and
in our participation in His Divine Sonship. To be by grace
what Jesus is by nature is the end of our predestination and
the norm of our sanctity: *Quos praescivit et praedestinavit
conformes fieri imaginis Filii sui.*

Now, in Our Lord some things are essential to Him and
some accidental. Christ was born at Bethlehem, He fled into
Egypt, He passed His childhood and youth at Nazareth, He
died under Pontius Pilate; these diverse circumstances of
place and time are only accidental to Christ's existence.
There are other things so far essential to Him that without
them Christ would no longer be Christ. He is God and Man,
Son of God and Son of man, true God and true Man: these
are constitutive, intangible qualities.

Now, if Jesus Christ is the Son of God by His ineffable
and eternal birth "in the bosom of the Father," *Filius meus
es tu, ego hodie genui te,*[11] He is Son of man by His temporal birth in the bosom of a woman: *Misit Deus Filium
suum, factum ex muliere.*[12]

This woman is Mary, and she is a Virgin. It is from her,
and from her alone, that Christ takes His human nature; it

[11] Act. XIII, 33; cf. Ps. II, 7.
[12] Gal. IV, 4.

is to her He owes it that He is Son of man; she is truly
Mother of God. Mary, therefore, occupies a transcendent,
essential and unique place in Christianity. In the same way
as the quality of "Son of man" cannot be separated in Christ
from that of "Son of God," so is Mary united to Jesus: indeed, the Virgin Mary enters into the mystery of the Incarnation by a title belonging to the very nature of the mystery.

That is why we must contemplate this marvel of a simple
creature being associated, by such close bonds, with the economy of the fundamental mystery of Christianity and, consequently, with our supernatural life, that divine life which
comes to us from Christ, the God-Man, and that Christ gives
to us, inasmuch as He is God, but by means of His Humanity. We must be, like Jesus, *Filius Dei* and *Filius Mariae;* He
is both of these perfectly; if then we wish to reproduce His
likeness within us, we must bear this double quality.

No piety would be truly Christian if it did not include in
its object the Mother of the Incarnate Word. Devotion towards the Virgin Mary is not only important, but necessary,
if we wish to draw abundantly at the source of life. To separate Christ from His Mother in our piety, is to divide
Christ; it is to lose sight of the essential mission of His holy
humanity in the distribution of divine grace. Where the
Mother is left out, the Son is no longer understood. Has not
this befallen Protestant nations? In rejecting devotion to
Mary under pretext of not derogating from the dignity of a
single Mediator, have they not ended in even losing faith in
the Divinity of Christ Himself? If Jesus Christ is our Saviour, our Mediator, our Elder Brother, because He has taken
upon Himself our human nature, how can we love Him
truly, how can we resemble Him perfectly, without having
a special devotion for her from whom He took this human
nature?

Christ, the Life of the Soul, Part II,
chapter 12, introduction.

27 *Mother of Holy Love*

1. BECAUSE OF HER DIVINE MATERNITY OUR LORD LOVED THE VIRGIN MARY WITH A SPECIAL LOVE

A whole crown of graces adorn Christ's Virgin Mother, all due to her Divine maternity. Jesus, as man, depends on Mary; but, as the Eternal Word, He is anterior to her. Consider what He has done for her from whom He was to take a human nature. Being God, that is to say, the Almighty and Infinite Wisdom, He will adorn this His creature with priceless jewels.

First He has, with the Father and the Holy Ghost, *chosen* her in preference to all others. To show the eminence of this choice, the Church, on the feasts of Our Lady, applies to her a passage of Scripture which can only relate in certain points to Eternal Wisdom: "The Lord possessed me in the beginning of His ways, before He made anything from the beginning. I was set up from eternity, and of old before the earth was made. The depths were not as yet, and I was already conceived . . . the mountains had not as yet been established: before the hills I was brought forth": *Ante colles ego parturiebar. . . .*[1] What do these words show? The special predestination of Mary in the Divine plan. The Eternal

[1] Prov. VIII, 23, 25.

Father, in His Divine thoughts, does not separate her from Christ: He comprehends in the same act of love, the Virgin, who is to be the Mother of Christ, and the Humanity of His Son in Whom He is well pleased.[2] This singular predestination is the fountainhead of unique graces for Mary.

The Virgin Mary is *immaculate*. All the children of Adam are born with the stain of original sin, slaves of the devil, enemies to God. This is the law passed by God for all Adam's race. Alone out of all creatures, Mary is to escape this universal law. The Eternal Word will make this one exception—one only—for her in whom He is to be incarnate. Not for a single moment is the soul of Mary to belong to the devil; it will be radiant with purity; and that is why, from the morrow of the Fall of our first parents, God put absolute enmity between the devil and the chosen Virgin; it is she whose heel is to crush the infernal serpent.[3] With the Church, let us often remind Mary of this privilege which she alone possesses, of being without stain; let us love to repeat to her: *Tota pulchra es Maria, et macula originalis non est in te.*[4] "Thy garments are white as snow and thy face like the sun: therefore the King of glory hath ardently desired thee."[5]

Not only is Mary born immaculate, but *grace abounds in her*. When the Angel salutes her, he declares her "full of grace," *Gratia plena;* for the Lord, the source of all grace, is within her: *Dominus tecum.* Then, in the conception and birth of Jesus, *Mary keeps her virginity intact.* She brings forth, while remaining a virgin; as the Church sings, with

[2] *Ipsissima verba quibus divinae scripturae de increata Sapientia loquuntur ejusque sempiternas origines repraesentant, consuevit Ecclesia . . . ad illius virginis primordia transferre quae uno eodemque decreto cum divinae Sapientiae incarnatione fuerant praestituta.* Pius X, Bull *Ineffabilis* for the definition of the Immaculate Conception.

[3] Gen. III, 15.

[4] Antiphon of Vespers for the Feast of the Immaculate Conception.

[5] *Ibid.*

the honour of virginity, Mary has the joy of motherhood:
Gaudia matris habens cum virginitatis honore.[6] There are
the graces that the hidden life with Jesus brings to Mary;
there are those coming from her union with her Son in the
mysteries of His public life and of His Passion; and, to fill
up the measure, there is her *Assumption into Heaven.*
Mary's virginal body, whence Christ took the substance of
His human nature, is not to know corruption; upon her
head is to be placed a crown of inestimable price; she will
reign as queen at her Son's right hand, adorned with the
vestment of glory woven for her by all these privileges: *Adstitit regina a dextris tuis, in vestitu deaurato.*[7]

Now, whence does Mary derive all these signal graces, all
these wonderful privileges, which make her a creature above
every other creature, *Benedicta tu in mulieribus?* From the
eternal choice God made of Mary to be the Mother of His
Son. If she is "blessed among women"; if, for her, God has
set aside so many of the laws He had Himself established, it
is because she is to be the Mother of His Son. If you take
away this dignity from Mary, all these prerogatives would
have no more reason or meaning; for all these privileges
prepare or accompany Mary as Mother of God.

But what is incomprehensible is the love which determined this unique choice that the Word made of this young
Virgin, in order to take from her a human nature.

Christ *loved* His Mother. Never has God so loved a simple
creature; never has son loved his mother as Jesus Christ has
done. He has so loved men, He Himself tells us, as to die
for them, and He could not give them a greater proof of
love: *Majorem hac dilectionem nemo habet, ut animam
suam ponat quis pro amicis suis.*[8] But never forget this truth:
Christ above all died for His Mother, to pay for her privi-

---

[6] Antiphon of Lauds at Christmas.
[7] Ps. xliv, 10.
[8] Joan. xv, 13.

leges. The singular graces Mary received are the first fruits of the Passion of Jesus. The Blessed Virgin would not have enjoyed any prerogative without the merits of her Son; she is the greatest glory of Christ because she has received the most from Him.

The Church gives us to understand this doctrine very clearly when she celebrates the Immaculate Conception, the first, according to time, of the graces received by the Virgin. Read the collect for the feast; you will see that this signal privilege is granted to Our Lady because the death of Jesus, foreseen in the eternal decrees, had paid the price of it in advance: *Deus qui per immaculatam Virginis Conceptionem dignum Filio tuo habitaculum praeparasti, concede, quaesumus, ut qui ex morte ejusdem Filii tui* PRAEVISA, *eam ab omni labe praeservasti.* . . . We may say that Mary was the first object, out of all humanity, of the love of Christ, even of the Suffering Christ: it is above all for her, in order that grace might abound in her in a singular measure, that Jesus Christ shed His Precious Blood.

> *Christ, the Life of the Soul,* Part II,
> chapter 12, section 2.

2. THE PERFECT LOVE WHICH THE MOTHER OF JESUS HAD FOR HER SON

The heart of the Virgin Mary was filled with transports of an immeasurable love for Jesus—of human love at first. God is love. In order that we may have some idea of this love He gives a share in it to mothers. The heart of a mother, with its untiring tenderness, the constancy of its solicitude, the inexhaustible delicacy of its affection, is a truly Divine creation, although God only imparted to it a spark of His love for us. In any case, however imperfectly the heart of a mother reflects the Divine love towards us, God gives us our mothers that they may replace Him for us in some degree. He places them beside us, from the cradle, to guide and protect us, especially during those early years when we need tenderness so much.

Imagine, then, with what predilection the Holy Trinity formed the heart of the Virgin chosen to be the Mother of the Incarnate Word! God took delight in pouring love into her heart, in forming it for the special purpose of loving a Man-God.

The adoration of a creature for its God and the love of a mother for her only son were perfectly and harmoniously blended in Mary's heart.

The supernatural love of the Virgin is not less wonderful. As you know, a soul's love for God is measured by its degree of grace. What prevents grace and love from developing within us? Our sins, our deliberate faults, our wilful unfaithfulness, our attachment to creatures. Each deliberate fault narrows the heart, strengthens egotism. But Mary's soul is perfectly pure. No sin has sullied it, no shadow of fault has ever overcast it. This purity shines in her with a particular brilliance. Mary is a virgin. Her virginity is so precious to her that she remarks on it to the angel when the latter proposes the mystery of the Incarnation to her.

Not only is she a virgin, but her soul is stainless. The liturgy reveals to us that God's special design in granting to Mary the unique privilege of the Immaculate Conception was to prepare for His Word a dwelling place worthy of Him: *Deus qui per immaculatam Virginis conceptionem dignum Filio tuo* HABITACULUM PRAEPARASTI.[9] Mary was to be the Mother of God; and this eminent dignity required not only that she should be a virgin, but that her purity should surpass that of the angels and be a reflection of the holy splendour wherein the Father begets His Son: *In splendoribus sanctorum.*[10] God is holy, thrice holy; the angels, the

[9] Collect for the Feast of the Immaculate Conception.
[10] Ps. CIX, 3.

archangels, the seraphim hymn His infinite purity: *Sanctus,*
Sanctus, Sanctus.[11] The bosom of God, of an infinite purity,
is the dwelling place of the Only-begotten Son of God. The
Word is ever *in sinu Patris;* but, in becoming Incarnate, He
also willed, in ineffable condescension, to be *in sinu Virginis*
Matris. It was necessary that the tabernacle that Our Lady
offered Him should recall, by its incomparable purity, the
indefectible brightness of the light eternal where as God He
ever dwells: *Christi sinus erat in Deo Patre divinitas, in*
Maria Matre virginitas.[12]

Our Lady's soul is of perfect purity; unstained by sin, un-
touched by any shadow of a fault, she is full of grace: *Gratia*
plena. Far from encountering in her any obstacle to the unfolding of grace, the Holy Spirit ever found her heart wonderfully docile to His inspirations, and therefore full of love.

What must have been the joy of the soul of Jesus to feel
Himself loved to such an extent by His Mother! After the
incomprehensible joy arising for Him from the Beatific
Vision and from the look of infinite complacency wherewith
the Heavenly Father contemplated Him, nothing can have
rejoiced Him so much as the love of His Mother. He found
in it a more abundant compensation for the indifference of
those who would not receive Him. He found in the heart
of this young Virgin a fire of undying love that He Himself
further enkindled by His Divine glances and the inward
grace of His Spirit.

Jesus gave Himself to Mary in such an ineffable manner,
and Mary corresponded so fully that after the union of the
Divine Persons in the Trinity, and the hypostatic union of
the Incarnation, we cannot conceive one greater nor deeper.

> *Christ in His Mysteries,* Part II, chapter
> 6, section 4; and chapter 9, section 1.

[11] Isa. VI, 3.
[12] *Sermo* XII, *in Append. Operum S. Ambrosii.*

"I am the Mother of fair love."

In the strict sense, these words are understood of Eternal Wisdom. Holy Church, however, also applies this text to Mary. She being the Mother of Divine Wisdom, what is true of Christ in an absolute sense is true of her also, because the same gifts have been conferred by Him on His Mother.

"I am the Mother of fair love."

Mary is the immaculate form of pure humanity, the masterpiece of all mere created things. Her prerogative of Mother of Divine Wisdom is the only source whence spring all the gifts which she received. Just as in us all the graces and the gifts of the Holy Ghost are the effect of our predestination as children of God, so also for Mary all the magnificent gifts which she possesses of her own derive from her dignity as Mother of God. Mary received from the Father the most perfect of maternal hearts. There was never an atom of egotism in this heart. It is a miracle of love, a treasure house of graces—*gratia plena*. This heart was fashioned not only for Christ Who, when He came unto His own, was not to be received, and Who was to find a compensatory love in His Mother, but was also fashioned for that other Christ, if we may express it thus, Who is the Mystical Body of Jesus. The more we love God, the more we love our neighbour. This was true of Mary also. She enfolds in the same love Christ and His members. She shares her love with His servants. Souls devoted to Mary obtain from her a very pure love. Their whole life is a reflection of her life. There are souls whom the Holy Ghost leads to this high mark of charity, and Mary's desire is to share the love which animates her with those who are hers. Devotion to Mary is a grace which God gives to those who are dear to Him, and the Blessed Virgin will generate a love of Christ in their hearts.

Mélanges Marmion, pp. 79–80.

28 *Fashion Us Thyself According to the Heart of Thy Son*

1. ACCORDING TO THE WILL OF JESUS, HIS MOTHER BECAME OUR MOTHER

The Word not only predestined Mary to be His Mother according to His Humanity, He not only gave her, in filling her with grace, the honour belonging to this dignity, but He *associated her in His mysteries.*

We see in the Gospel that Jesus and Mary are inseparable in Christ's mysteries. When the angels announce the birth of the Saviour in the cave of Bethlehem, the shepherds come and find "Mary . . . and the Infant"; it is Mary who presents Jesus in the Temple as a prelude to the Sacrifice of Calvary; all the life at Nazareth, as I have just said, is lived under Mary's authority; it is at her request that Jesus, at the beginning of His public life, reveals Himself by His first miracle at Cana;[1] the Evangelists tell us that she followed Christ in more than one of His apostolic journeys.

But notice, there is not question here of only a simple material union. It is with her heart and soul that the Virgin Mary enters into the mysteries of her Son. St. Luke tells us that the Mother of Jesus kept all the words of her Son, "pon-

---

[1] Joan. II, 1-11.

dering them in her heart": *Maria autem conservabat omnia verba haec, conferens in corde suo.*[2] The words of Jesus were for her sources of contemplation; can we not say as much of the mysteries of Jesus? When Christ lived these mysteries, He assuredly enlightened the soul of His Mother upon each of them; she understood them, she associated herself with them; all that Our Lord said or did was for her a source of graces. In return for the human life He had received from her, Jesus, so to speak, gave her the Divine life of which He is the source. That is why Christ and the Virgin are so indissolubly united in every mystery; and that is also why Mary has united us all in her heart with her Divine Son.

Now the pre-eminent work of Jesus, the holy of holies of His mysteries, is His Passion; it is by His bloody sacrifice upon the Cross that He achieves the restoration of life to men, that He raises them up again to their dignity as children of God. Christ Jesus willed to make His Mother enter into this mystery by so special a title and Mary united herself so fully to the will of her Son, our Redeemer, that, while keeping her rank of simple creature, she truly shares with Him the glory of having at that moment brought us forth to the life of grace.

Let us go to Calvary at the moment when Christ Jesus is about to consummate the work that His Father has given Him to do here below. Our Lord has reached the end of His apostolic mission: He is about to reconcile all mankind with His Father. Whom do we find at the foot of the Cross at this supreme instant? Mary, the Mother of Jesus, with John, the beloved disciple, the Magdalen and several other women: *Stabat mater ejus.*[3] Mary is standing there; she has just renewed the offering of her Son—that offering she made when she presented Him in the Temple; at this moment she offers

[2] Luc. II, 19.
[3] Joan. XIX, 25.

the "blessed fruit of her womb" to the Eternal Father for the ransom of the world. Jesus has only a few minutes to live; then the sacrifice will be accomplished, and Divine grace restored to men. He wills to give us Mary to be our Mother. This is one of the forms of the truth that the Word is united, in the Incarnation, to all humanity, and that the elect form the Mystical Body of Christ from Whom they cannot be separated. Christ will give us His Mother to be also ours in the spiritual order; Mary will not separate us from Jesus, her Son and our Head.

Then, before expiring and achieving, as St. Paul says, the conquest of the world of souls that He wishes to make His glorious kingdom, Jesus sees, at the foot of the Cross, His Mother, plunged in deep sorrow and the disciple He so much loved, the same who heard and has related to us the Last Words. Jesus says to His Mother: "Woman, behold thy son"; then He says to the disciple: "Behold thy mother." St. John here represents us all; it is to us that Jesus, when dying, bequeathed His Mother. Is He not our "Elder Brother"? Are we not predestined to be like to Him, so that He may be "the Firstborn among many brethren"? Now if Christ has become our Elder Brother in taking from Mary a nature like ours, which makes Him one of our race, is it astonishing that, in dying, He should have given her to be our Mother in the order of grace who was His Mother according to human nature?

And as this word, being that of the Eternal Word, is omnipotent and of Divine efficacy, it creates in the heart of St. John filial sentiments worthy of Mary, as it gives birth in the Blessed Virgin's heart to a special tenderness for those whom grace renders brothers of Jesus Christ. Can we doubt for a moment that, for her part, the Virgin responded as at Nazareth with a *Fiat,* a silent one this time, but equally full of love, humility and obedience, in which the plenitude

of her will lost itself in that of Jesus, so as to bring about her
Son's supreme wish.

Like Jesus, she, at this moment, achieved the act of love of
bringing us forth to the life of grace. Mother of our Head,
according to the thought of St. Augustine, in bearing Him
corporally, she became spiritually the Mother of all the
members of this Divine Head: *Corpore mater capitis nostri,
spiritu mater membrorum ejus.*[4]

St. Gertrude relates that hearing one day, in the chanting
of the Divine Office, those words of the Gospel naming
Christ: *Primogenitus Mariae Virginis,* "the Firstborn Son of
the Virgin Mary," she said to herself: "The title of Only
Son would seem to be more befitting for Jesus than that of
Firstborn." While she was dwelling on this thought, the
Virgin Mary appeared to her: "No," said she to the holy
nun, "it is not 'Only Son' but 'Firstborn Son' which is most
befitting; for, after Jesus, my Sweetest Son, or more truly, in
Him and by Him, I have given birth to you all in my heart
and you have become my children, the brothers and sisters
of Jesus."

Christ, the Life of the Soul, Part II,
chapter 12, sections 2 and 4.

2. THE POWER WHICH THE VIRGIN MARY HAS OF FASHIONING US ACCORDING TO HER SON'S HEART

What shall we ask of the Mother of Jesus, if not that, before and above all, she will form Jesus within us by communicating her faith and love to us?

All Christian life consists in forming Christ within us and
making Him live in us. This is the idea of St. Paul. Now
where was Christ first formed? In the Virgin's bosom, by
the operation of the Holy Ghost. But, say the Holy Fathers,
Mary first bore Jesus by faith and love, when, by her *Fiat,*

[4] S. Aug. *De sancta Virginitate,* n. 6.

she gave the awaited consent: *Prius concepit mente quam corpore.* Let us ask of her to obtain for us this faith that will make Jesus dwell in us: *Christum habitare per fidem in cordibus vestris;* this love which will make us live by the life of Jesus. Let us ask of her that we may become like to her Son; there is no greater favour we could ask her; neither is there any she more wishes to grant us. For she knows, she sees that her Son cannot be separated from His Mystical Body; she remains so united in heart and soul to her Divine Son that, now in glory, she only desires one thing, and this is that the Church, the kingdom of the elect, bought with the blood of Jesus, should appear before Him, as a "glorious" Church "not having spot or wrinkle, but . . . holy and without blemish."

In the Divine plan, *Mary is inseparable from Jesus,* and our holiness consists in entering as far as we can into the Divine economy. In God's eternal thoughts, Mary belongs indeed to the very essence of the mystery of Christ; Mother of Jesus, she is the Mother of Him in whom we find everything. According to the Divine plan, life is only given to mankind through Christ the Man-God: *Nemo venit ad Patrem nisi per me,* but Christ is only given to the world through Mary: *Propter nos homines et propter nostram salutem, descendit de caelis et incarnatus est . . . ex Maria Virgine.* This is the Divine order and it is unchanging. For, notice that this order was not meant only for the day when the Incarnation took place; it still continues as regards the application of the fruits of the Incarnation to souls.

And because here below she is thus associated with all the mysteries of our redemption, Jesus has crowned her not only with glory, but with power. He has placed His Mother at His right hand that she may dispose of the treasures of eternal life by a unique title—that of Mother of God: *Adstitit regina a dextris tuis.* This is what Christian piety means

when it proclaims the Mother of Jesus: *Omnipotentia sup-
plex.*

No one has more influence than the Mother of God *in
obtaining grace for us.* In consequence of the Incarnation,
God is pleased—not so as to derogate from the power of His
Son's mediation but on the contrary to extend and exalt it—
to recognise the credit of those who are united to Jesus, the
Head of the Mystical Body; this credit is so much the more
powerful according as the union of the saints with Christ is
the more intimate.

"The nearer a thing approaches to its principle," says St.
Thomas, "the more it experiences the effects produced by
this principle. The nearer you come to a furnace, the more
you feel the heat which radiates from it." The holy Doctor
adds: "Now, Christ is the principle of grace since, as God,
He is the Author of it, and, as Man, He is the instrument of
it; and the Blessed Virgin being the nearest of any creature
to the Humanity of Christ, Christ having taken this human
nature from her, she has received from Him higher graces
than any creature. But each one receives from God grace
proportionate to his providential destination. As Man, Christ
was predestined and elected in order that, being the Son of
God, He might have power to sanctify all men, *In virtute
sanctificandi;* therefore He, and He alone, was to possess
such plenitude that it might overflow on all souls: *De plenitudine ejus omnes nos accepimus.* The fulness of grace received by the Blessed Virgin had for its end to bring her
nearer than any other creature to the Author of grace; so
near, indeed, that she enclosed in her bosom the One Who
is full of grace, and in giving Him to the world by bringing
Him forth, she, so to speak, gave grace itself to the world,
because she gave Him Who is the source of it": *Ut eum, qui
est plenus omni gratia, pariendo, quodammodo gratiam ad*

omnes derivaret.[5] In giving us Jesus, the Blessed Virgin has given us the very Author of life. The Church sings this in the prayer after the antiphon to the Virgin, during Christmastide, when celebrating Christ's birth: *Per quam merui- mus auctorem vitae suscipere,* "by whom we have been made worthy to receive the Author of life"; and the Church invites the redeemed nations to hymn, in exultation, the Life which this virginal Motherhood has brought to them: *Vitam datam per Virginem Gentes redemptae plaudite.*

If, therefore, you wish to draw largely from the fountain of Divine life, go to Mary; ask her to lead you to this fountain; she it is, indeed, more than any other creature, who will bring you near to Jesus. That is why we so justly name her: *Mater divinae gratiae,* "Mother of Divine grace"; again that is why the Church applies to her this passage of the Scriptures: "He that shall find me, shall find life, and he shall have salvation from the Lord," *Qui me invenerit, inveniet vitam et hauriet salutem a Domino.*[6] Salvation, the life of our souls, only comes from the Lord Jesus, *a Domino,* He alone is the one Mediator; but who more surely than Mary will lead us to Him, who will have more power to render Him propitious to us than His Mother?

> *Christ, the Life of the Soul,* Part II,
> chapter 12, sections 3 and 4.

3. THE FEELINGS OF FILIAL PIETY WHICH WE SHOULD FOSTER FOR THE MOTHER OF CHRIST, WHO HAS BECOME OUR MOTHER ALSO

In order to acknowledge the unique place Jesus has willed to give Mary in His mysteries and the love of the Virgin for us, we should give her the honour, love and confidence due to her as the Mother of Jesus and our Mother.

[5] III, q. xxvii, a. 5.
[6] Prov. viii, 35.

How can we fail to love her if we love Our Lord? If Christ Jesus wishes us, as I have said, to love all the members of His Mystical Body, how can we do otherwise than give the first place in that love to the one who gave Him that human nature by which He became our Head, that Humanity which is the instrument He uses to communicate grace to us? We cannot doubt that the love we show to the Mother of Jesus is extremely pleasing to Christ. If we want to love Christ, if we want Him to be everything to us, we must have a very special love for His Mother.

In what way shall we manifest this love? Jesus, as God, loved His Mother and heaped sublime privileges upon her; we shall show our love by exalting these privileges; if we wish to be greatly pleasing to Our Lord, let us admire the marvellous gifts with which, through love, He has adorned the soul of His Mother. He wills that, with her, we should render unceasing thanksgiving to the Holy Trinity for these graces, and that we should praise the Virgin herself for having been chosen from among all women to give a Saviour to the world. By this, we shall truly enter into the feelings which Jesus had for her to whom He owes it that He is the Son of man. Yes, we shall sing to her: "Thou alone hast ravished the Heart of thy God"—*sola sine exemplo placuisti Domino;* thou art blessed among all creatures, blessed because thou didst believe in the Divine word and in thee are fulfilled the eternal promises.

To be helped in this devotion, we have only to see what the Church does. See how the Bride of Christ has multiplied here below her testimonies in honour of Mary, and how she observes that worship which is called *hyperdulia* since it transcends the worship of all the other saints.

The Church has consecrated numerous feasts to the Mother of God: she celebrates in turns her Immaculate Conception, her Presentation in the Temple, the Annunciation, Visitation, Purification and Assumption.

See, too, how, at each of the principal seasons of the liturgical cycle, she consecrates to the Blessed Virgin a special antiphon, which is to be recited daily at the end of the Canonical Hours by all who are bound to the Divine Office. You will notice how in each of these antiphons, the Church delights in recalling the privilege of the Divine Motherhood, the foundation of all Mary's greatness. Thus, there is not a single day on which the voice of the Church is not uplifted to congratulate Mary on her graces and remind her that we are her children.

Is this all? No. Every day at Vespers, the Church sings the *Magnificat;* she unites with the Virgin herself in praising God for His bountiful goodness to the Mother of His Son. Let us often say after Our Lady and with the Church: "My soul doth magnify the Lord, and my spirit doth rejoice in God my Saviour . . . for He hath regarded the lowliness of His handmaiden. . . . Henceforth, O Mary, all nations shall call thee blessed, for He that is mighty hath done great things in thee."

There is the Rosary, which is so pleasing to Mary because in it we always praise her united with her Divine Son, by ever lovingly repeating the salutation that the heavenly messenger addressed to her on the day of the Incarnation: *Ave Maria, gratia plena.* It is an excellent practice to recite the rosary devoutly every day; thus to contemplate Christ in His mysteries so as to unite ourselves to Him; to congratulate the Virgin on having been so closely associated with these mysteries and return thanks to the Holy Trinity for Mary's privileges. There is the *Angelus,* by which we renew in the heart of the Virgin the ineffable joy she must have felt at the moment of the Incarnation. There are besides many other forms of devotion.

Let us, then, go to her, but let it be with confidence. There are souls who go to her as to a Mother, confiding to her their interests, laying before her their sorrows and difficulties, having recourse to her in all their needs and temptations, for eternal enmity exists between the Virgin and the devil; with her heel, Mary crushes the head of the infernal serpent. On every occasion, such souls as I have spoken of deal with the Blessed Virgin as children with a mother; they will go before one of her statues to tell her what they want. But this is childishness, you may say. Perhaps it is, but has not Christ said: "Unless you become as little children, you shall not enter into the kingdom of heaven"?

Full of confidence, let us then say to her with the Church: "Show thyself our Mother: Mother of Jesus by thy influence with Him; our Mother by mercy towards us. May Christ receive our prayers through thee, this Christ Who, born of thee to bring us life, willed to be thy Son." *Monstra te esse Matrem, sumat per te preces, qui pro nobis natus tulit esse tuus.*

> *Christ, the Life of the Soul,* Part II,
> chapter 12, section 4.

In the morning, after Mass, when I possess Jesus in my heart I consecrate myself to the Blessed Virgin and say to her: *"Ecce filius tuus*—Behold thy son. O Virgin Mary, I am your child; still more I share in the Priesthood of Jesus; accept me for your son as you accepted Jesus. I am unworthy of your gifts, but a member of the Mystical Body of your Divine Son. And He Himself has said: 'All that you do to the least of those who believe in Me, you do it unto Me'; I am one of these *minimis meis;* to refuse me would be to refuse Jesus Himself."

> *Abbot Columba Marmion: A Master of the Spiritual Life,* chapter 18.

Let us ask Our Lady that, from the Humanity of her Jesus Who possesses the fulness of grace, it may be poured forth abundantly upon us, so that by love we may become more and more conformed to this beloved Son of the Father, Who is also her Son. It is the best request we make to her. At the Last Supper, Our Lord said to His disciples: "The Father Himself loveth you, because you have loved Me, and have believed that I came out from God." [7] He could say the same to us of Mary: "My Mother loveth you, because you love Me, and believe that I was born of her." Nothing pleases Mary more than to hear it proclaimed that Jesus is her Son, and to see Him beloved by all creatures.

The Gospel, as you know, has only preserved a very few words of the Blessed Virgin. I have just reminded you of one of these words, that which was said to the servants at the marriage feast of Cana: "Whatsoever my Son shall say to you, do ye," *Quodcumque dixerit vobis, facite.*[8] This word is like an echo of the word of the Eternal Father: "This is My beloved Son, in Whom I am well pleased: hear ye Him": *Ipsum audite.*[9] We can apply to ourselves this word of Mary: "Do all that my Son shall say to you." That will be the best fruit of this conference; it will be, too, the best form our devotion towards the Mother of Jesus can take. The Virgin Mother has no greater wish than to see her Divine Son obeyed, loved, glorified and exalted. Jesus is the Son in whom she, like the Eternal Father, is well pleased.

> *Christ, the Life of the Soul,* Part II,
> chapter 12, section 4.

---

[7] Joan. XVI, 27.
[8] *Ibid.,* II, 5.
[9] Matth. XVII, 5; cf. II Pet. I, 17.

PREFACE OF THE MASS OF THE BLESSED TRINITY

IT IS TRULY MEET AND JUST, RIGHT AND PROFITABLE, FOR US, AT ALL TIMES, AND IN ALL PLACES, TO GIVE THANKS TO THEE, O LORD, THE HOLY ONE, THE FATHER ALMIGHTY, THE EVERLASTING GOD. WHO TOGETHER WITH THINE ONLY-BEGOTTEN SON AND THE HOLY GHOST, ART ONE GOD, NOT IN THE SINGLENESS OF ONE PERSON, BUT IN THE TRINITY OF ONE SUBSTANCE. FOR ALL THAT, BECAUSE REVEALED BY THEE, WE BELIEVE OF THY GLORY, THE SAME WE BELIEVE OF THY SON, THE SAME OF THE HOLY GHOST WITHOUT DIFFERENCE OR DISTINCTION: SO THAT IN THE CONFESSION OF ONE TRUE AND ETERNAL GODHEAD THERE BE ADORED DISTINCTNESS IN PERSONS, ONENESS IN ESSENCE AND EQUALITY IN MAJESTY. WHOM ANGELS AND ARCHANGELS, CHERUBIM LIKEWISE AND SERAPHIM DO PRAISE, NOR CEASE, DAY BY DAY WITH ONE VOICE CRYING OUT, TO REPEAT, HOLY, HOLY, HOLY, LORD GOD OF HOSTS. THE HEAVENS AND THE EARTH ARE FULL OF THY GLORY. HOSANNA IN THE HIGHEST. BLESSED IS HE WHO COMETH IN THE NAME OF THE LORD. HOSANNA IN THE HIGHEST.

PRAYER OF ST. HILARY

Preserve without stain, I entreat Thee, the cult of my faith, and grant that until I sigh my last breath my conscience may bear witness to me, that I, who was baptized in the name of the Father and of the Son and of the Holy Ghost, may forever possess that which I professed in the symbol of my regeneration: Thee, our Father; that I may adore Thy Son with and as Thyself; that I may receive as mine Thy Holy Spirit, Who proceeds from Thee through Thy only Son. Truly, I have a witness worthy of all faith to guarantee my belief, Him Who said: "All things whatsoever the Father hath are Mine," my Lord Jesus Christ, Who dwells in Thee, Who, ever God, is of Thee and beside Thee and Who is blessed forever and forever. Amen.

St. Hilary, *Treatise on the Trinity*

A NOTE ON THE TYPE

IN WHICH THIS BOOK WAS SET

This book has been set in Granjon, a lovely Linotype face, designed by George W. Jones, one of England's great printers, to meet his own exacting requirements for fine book and publication work. Like most useful types, Granjon is neither wholly new nor wholly old. It is not a copy of a classic face nor an original creation, but rather something between the two—drawing its basic design from classic Garamond sources, but never hesitating to deviate from the model where four centuries of type-cutting experience indicate an improvement or where modern methods of punch-cutting make possible a refinement far beyond the skill of the originator. This book was composed and printed by The York Composition Company, Inc., of York, Pa., and bound by Moore and Company of Baltimore. The design and typography are by Howard N. King.